The East End Nobody Knows

THE EAST END NOBODY KNOWS

A History, a Guide, an Exploration

ANDREW DAVIES

MACMILLAN
LONDON

In memory of Margaret Brunel

First published 1990 by
MACMILLAN LONDON LIMITED
4 Little Essex Street London WC2R 3LF
and Basingstoke

Associated companies in Auckland, Delhi, Dublin, Gaborone,
Hamburg, Harare, Hong Kong, Johannesburg, Kuala Lumpur,
Lagos, Manzini, Melbourne, Mexico City, Nairobi, New York,
Singapore and Tokyo

British Library Cataloguing in Publication Data

Davies, Andrew
The East End Nobody Knows.
1. London. East End
I. Title
942.1'50858

ISBN 0–333–47454–6

Typeset by Bookworm Typesetters, Manchester

Printed in Hong Kong

Gateway to the East? An aerial view emphasises the importance of the docks and the number of tower blocks built after 1945.

This street is in the East End. There is no need to say in the East End of what. The East End is a vast city, as famous in its way as any the hand of man has made. But who knows the East End? It is down through Cornhill and out beyond Leadenhall Street and Aldgate Pump, one will say: a shocking place, where he once went with a curate; an evil plexus of slums that hide human creeping things; where filthy men and women live on penn'orths of gin, where collars and clean shirts are decencies unknown, where every citizen wears a black eye, and none ever combs his hair. The East End is a place, says another, which is given over to the Unemployed. And the Unemployed is a race whose token is a clay pipe, and whose enemy is soap: now and again it migrates bodily to Hyde Park with banners, and furnishes adjacent police courts with disorderly drunks. Still another knows the East End only as a place whence begging letters come; there are coal and blanket funds there, all perennially insolvent, and everybody always wants a day in the country. Many and misty are the people's notions of the East End; and each is commonly but the distorted shadow of a minor feature.

ARTHUR MORRISON in his introduction to
Tales of Mean Streets (1901)

ACKNOWLEDGEMENTS

As always, I owe much to my walk groups from Friday Hill House, the Old House at Brentwood, the Town and Around Club and several other organisations and societies who have patiently and enthusiastically followed me on the hundreds of walks which I have conducted over the East End. I am very grateful to Kath Prior, Doreen Ling and Lesley Hooper at Friday Hill House for their cheerful and efficient administration.

My friend Charlie Poulsen, who has been a taxi-driver since 1935 and taking London-history classes for almost as long, has read through several drafts of this book, correcting, arguing and always improving. His knowledge of London, and especially of the East End, is unrivalled, and I am very grateful to him for spending so much time on my book.

A retrospective thank-you to Edward Leeson, Brenda Thomson, Angela Martin and Mary Pachnos for their efforts on my last book, *Literary London*. Ann Rossiter and Fred Martin are a continual and continuing source of intellectual stimulation. Simon van der Borgh, my partner on several other projects, has influenced this book in many beneficial ways.

At Macmillan I am lucky to have as my editor Adam Sisman, and as my agent Andrew Lownie. Both offer unfailing support, guidance and enthusiasm. Thanks to Louise Millar for designing this book and special thanks to the Local History Library at Tower Hamlets for their help and cooperation in finding the illustrations. A general thank-you to the many people in the East End who have over the years taken the time to talk to me about 'life, the universe and everything'; in particular, numbers of East End clergymen have never complained about frequently opening up their churches, often at unsocial hours.

Once again, however, my greatest debt is to my wife, Jean, companion on so many walks, a tireless and ever vigilant editor and critic of my work, and the inspiration for much of what I do.

CONTENTS

Contents

THE ARRANGEMENT AND TITLE OF
The East End Nobody Knows

I have tried to let the story of the East End unfold by means of broadly chronological sections. These are all self-contained, but obviously the reader will get more out of the book if he or she reads it in sequence. The second part of the book comprises ten East End walks which take the reader to the places written about in the main text. I have indexed both sections, which should help the walker who wants further information which is in the main text. There are also notes on sources and suggestions for further reading, together with some useful addresses.

I should also say a few words about the title. Until recently few historians took much interest in the East End and even fewer 'outsiders' explored its hidden delights. One exception was Geoffrey Fletcher, whose off-beat ramblings resulted in many stimulating, intemperate but always lively articles and books. In *The London Nobody Knows* (1965), Fletcher wrote:

> My theme is off-beat London; the unexplored, unknown-to-the-tourist London. There are whole areas of the capital which are never penetrated except by those who, like myself, are driven on by the mania for exploration: Hoxton, Shoreditch, Stepney, for instance, all of which are full of interest for the perceptive eye, the eye of the connoisseur of well-proportioned though seedy terraces, of enamel advertisements, and cast-iron lavatories.

My book is written in a similar spirit, and its title is in part a tribute to Geoffrey Fletcher.

Of course, since Fletcher wrote the above words over twenty years ago, much of the East End has changed. For a start there are rather fewer cast-iron lavatories in existence. In the last few years 'Docklands' has been very much in the public eye, and more people are now aware of the East End's charms. However, I hope that through this book even the most observant resident and the keenest historian will find something which they did not know about before.

THE EAST END
NOBODY KNOWS

A Journey East

When I left university in the late 1970s, I desperately wanted to live in London. Luckily a friend offered me a room in a council flat in Bethnal Green, a part of London about which I knew little. It was a far cry indeed from a world of gowns and mortar-boards, sherry in the Senior Common Room served by suitably deferential servants, and conversation which revolved around the contents of the latest *Times Literary Supplement* or *New York Review of Books*. For the first few weeks I felt quite disorientated and out of place; the couple below me seemed to trade blows and insults at any time of the day or night, the stairs stank of urine, telephone boxes were always vandalised, graffiti covered every inch of wall, and the shops with their metal grilles looked like miniature Fort Knoxes.

Yet as I walked through Victoria Park each day on my way to Bethnal Green station I gradually became aware of certain intriguing sights, such as the isolated stone alcoves on the east side of the park or the bizarre Gothic drinking-fountain which stands near the open-air swimming-pool. At the back of the Bethnal Green Museum of Childhood I could glimpse the irregular gables of an elegant old house. What were they all doing here in a district which never featured in history-books? I went scurrying off to the local library, and after a bit of ferreting around I found that the alcoves, for instance, had been added to 'old' London Bridge in the eighteenth century so that pedestrians could shelter from the oncoming traffic. These alcoves therefore were a part of the bridge which was the subject of the nursery rhyme 'London Bridge Is Falling Down'. The bridge had been taken down in 1832, but the alcoves were saved and ended up here in the greenery of Victoria Park in 1860. The pinnacled fountain was a gift to the people of the East End from the Victorian philanthropist Angela Burdett-Coutts, while Netteswell House by the museum dates back to the late seventeenth century and actually contains traces of Tudor brickwork in its cellar.

To a mind like mine, which had until then assumed that boring old 'history' was made up of dates, plaques and palaces, this was a revelation. I realised that Bethnal Green, too, had its own distinctive and fascinating story to tell, often not superficially apparent yet all the more exciting to explore. I was hooked. Fortunately, being seriously underemployed at the time, I was able to roam the streets of East London at will, delving into alleys and down side-streets, talking to anyone who would talk to me. I wandered around like some 'urban detective', trying to deduce why that road curved as it did, why that house was that shape, what was the origin of that pub's name.

After a couple of years I signed on at the Open University to do a doctorate which dealt with the Victorian East End, and now my 'street-level' knowledge of the district was augmented by sitting in libraries and reading-rooms, wading through piles of books, newspapers and manuscripts. Luckily for both my sanity and my eyesight, I met a girl who lectured at the London College of Furniture in Commercial Road and whose passion was exploring London on foot. A kindred spirit! I was fortunate enough to encounter someone whose idea of a good time was a walk along Poplar High Street looking for the remains of the old workhouse! And so I returned to the 'living history' of the East End, meandering down stinking alleys in Spitalfields and clambering over bleak wastes in Limehouse. Always our walks were worthwhile. One morning we stumbled across the charming early nineteenth-century York Square with its little garden hidden away behind Commercial Road; later that day we found the octagonal hydraulic tower beside Limehouse Basin which had been built in 1852 and once worked the dockside cranes. It turned out to be the oldest hydraulic station in the world.

A further stroke of good fortune came my way when I was asked to take courses on London history at various adult education centres, which meant that I was now actually being paid for walking around London and doing what I would have done anyway. What is more, I could take groups wherever I wanted: this week Mayfair, next week Whitechapel; today Bond Street, tomorrow Shadwell Park. As I passed other London guides on their fifth 'Jack the Ripper Walk' that week, I blessed this country's wonderful adult education system which gave me the chance to talk about and show people parts of London never reached by commercial tourist organisations.

After a while members of the classes began to ask me to suggest suitable books about the East End or to write down my walk routes. Although it was easy to recommend a number of excellent autobiographies and books on aspects of the area's past, there was nothing which provided both a readable general history together with a series of walks. *The East End Nobody Knows* will, I hope, be enjoyed as much by those reading it at home as by those who wish to know the East End at first hand. Both the main part of the book and the walks stand independently of each other, but it will certainly help walkers to have read the main part of the book first. I have tried to convey the unfolding history of the East End, emphasising the people, places and events which have shaped the area. I have tried, too, to put over the enthusiasm which I feel about the East End – not, I think, an uncritical enthusiasm but the sense of excitement which I always feel when strolling around its streets and that I find missing from many history-books. Above all, *The East End Nobody Knows* is a tribute to the many supremely fascinating hours which I have spent here, watching this extraordinarily varied part of London changing from day to day.

'Beyond Here Be Dragons': From Village to Building Site

In the Victorian period maps of London often simply omitted the East End, considering that the area was 'beyond the pale' and of no interest to anyone – anyone who mattered, that is. It was almost a reversion to the Middle Ages when map-makers confronted by the limits of their geographical knowledge used to warn travellers that 'Beyond Here Be Dragons'. Today London's cartographers are once again faced with the problem of the East End, but this time the difficulty arises because the area is changing so rapidly that they are unable to keep up with the pace of development. A map of the East End is now out of date before the surveying has been completed.

The phrase 'the East End' was first used by

journalists and commentators a hundred years ago as a convenient and perhaps ironic contrast to the affluent 'West End' of department stores, smart squares and royal parks.[1] The East End might have been a city within a city, yet it was largely ignored by historians, tourists – the area has always lacked hotels, and when the American writer Jack London wished to go there in 1902 the manager at Thomas Cook's Cheapside branch told him: 'We are not accustomed to taking travellers to the East End; we receive no call to take them there, and we know nothing whatsoever about the place at all' – and cab-drivers. When Jack London did eventually set off, his cab-driver could not believe that anyone should voluntarily want to be taken to such a place.[2]

In the 1980s, of course, all this has changed. Television producers fall over themselves in their eagerness to take the cameras eastwards, and a soap opera set in the East End attracts a weekly television audience of millions. Almost every glossy magazine and newspaper has run features on 'Docklands', this 'new' part of London which has magically arisen from the ashes of the old and distinctly unfashionable East End. The year 1987 alone saw the opening of both a new airport that carries passengers to and from Europe and a new railway which opens up hitherto inaccessible parts of the East End. A trip on the Docklands Light Railway takes the passenger past brightly coloured new buildings full of suited young executives hunched over computer terminals and with car-parks full of BMWs. Wine-bars are springing up all over Wapping and the Isle of Dogs, up to thirteen museums are planned for the area,[3] the windows of recently opened estate agents are crammed with astronomically priced apartments and penthouses – the word 'flat' is much too prosaic to convey adequately the splendours on offer. The Tobacco Dock development with its new shops and places to lounge and stare is being touted as 'the East End's Covent Garden', while both *The Times*

and the *Daily Telegraph* are now based in the East End. All this would have been impossible to imagine even ten years ago when, in the aftermath of the closure of the upstream docks, the area seemed doomed to exist for ever under a pall of defeat, decay and desolation. The 'new' Docklands is now championed by the Government as an important success in its planned regeneration of Britain's inner cities and considered a model of its kind.

The last five years have witnessed an unprecedented reversal of the usual trend in London's history whereby west is best and east doesn't bear thinking about. For centuries East London was a place through which the traveller passed as quickly as possible but in which only a few unfortunates lived, huddled together amongst the bleak marshes. The Romans left no significant settlements but laid down a number of routes which are still much in use today, clogged with traffic and fumes. Their width and straightness remain as a testimony to the ingenuity of these imperial engineers of nearly 2,000 years ago who knew full well that good communications were essential if they were to control the country. Kingsland Road was once part of Ermine Street leading to York. The narrower Old Ford Road and Bethnal Green Road were the exit to the ford over the River Lea. Whitechapel Road provided access to and from Essex and Colchester, while the Highway was the riverside track. Otherwise the Romans used East London only as a conveniently isolated spot in which to bury their dead, complying with the strict laws prohibiting burial within the walls of a city. A census of the district during Roman times would have come up with a population figure of 0.

After the departure of the Romans in AD 410, East London did not become any more popular. By the time of the Domesday Book at the end of the eleventh century Stepney's population had slowly climbed to about 700, but the low-lying land was still often flooded by the Thames.[4] Later the 'stink' industries

Wren's Trinity Almshouses on Mile End Road. They still look very similar despite war damage.
Mile End Road is rather busier.

were located here in order to isolate them from the crowded City. The slaughterhouses of Aldgate, sugar-making in Shadwell, lime-burning in Limehouse, and the breweries of Spitalfields and Mile End all date from the sixteenth and seventeenth centuries. The pre-vailing south-westerly wind carried the domestic pollution from the streets of West-minster and the City away towards the east, and if one stands by General Wolfe's statue high up in Greenwich Park the muck and grime of London can still be seen drifting eastwards, confirming what the economist Sir William Petty wrote of as long ago as 1662 as 'the fumes, steams, and stinks of the whole Easterly Pyle'.[5] The creation of the stink industries fixed the eastern side of London as an industrial area to which the poor would come seeking work. The wealthy went west, the poor came east – a process of segregation apparent in virtually all of the world's major cities. For centuries the East End was doomed to be London's poor relation.

At least during the Middle Ages the stinks were set among fields, pastures and commons. City worthies built fine country houses in these villages just to the east of London, and some of these mansions remain, such as those in Stepney Green Gardens, whose elegant proportions and fine doorways have miracu-lously survived along with the little green in front of them. There were also traditional manor-houses belonging to each village. Most of these have long since been destroyed, but a fragment of Bromley Hall remains, an Eliz-abethan house remodelled in 1700 and now clinging forlornly to the edge of the northern approach to the Blackwall Tunnel, its ancient windows splattered with the mud churned up by lorries which pass within inches of it. Much of the 'Poor's Ground' or old village green of Bethnal Green has survived, too, where in

June 1663 Samuel Pepys remarked in his diary that he had found 'the greatest quantity of strawberries I ever saw, and good'.

There were many almshouses in the East End, well positioned so that their occupants might have the benefits of rural surroundings. They often had the benefit of some fine architecture. The Trinity Almshouses in Mile End Road were built by Sir Christopher Wren in 1695, while the almshouses for the iron-mongers opened in 1715 and paid for out of the will of Sir Robert Geffrye, a former Lord Mayor of London, now house the Geffrye Museum of Furniture. This collection of period rooms, dating from the sixteenth century to the 1930s, is one of the treats of East London and deserves to be more widely known. Surrounded by an attractive garden, the outside of the museum remains as it did over 250 years ago, with a statue of Geffrye himself standing over the entrance to what was once the chapel.

Yet, however charming the almshouses or the fields of East London, nothing could stop the onward rush of the capital's inexorable expansion. The less attractive side of this growth was to be seen here in the east and not in the elegant stuccoed terraces of Belgravia and Kensington. During the Victorian age the East End lost most of its rural charms beneath an avalanche of industrialisation together with the overcrowding and poverty which accompanied it. One by one villages like Bethnal Green, Bow and Hackney which had

for so long been on the fringes of the metropolis were sucked into this sprawling mass, their fields and gardens filled rapidly with cheap housing. Those inhabitants who could afford to retain a rural lifestyle fled further north or east. This century has brought the ravages of German bombing, the building of unpopular tower-blocks and then the closure of the docks – a series of changes which has exacerbated an already dismal economic picture and led to Tower Hamlets, Hackney and Newham being ranked amongst the very poorest boroughs in the country.

Now, however, with the introduction of the London Docklands Development Corporation in 1981 by Margaret Thatcher's Conservative government, the City has started to shift east and the 'old' East End will never be the same again. Some have argued that this is simply the complaint voiced down the ages of people fearful of widespread change. Perhaps what is new this time is the blatant contrast of rich and poor living side by side. Prince Charles was shocked by what he saw in Spitalfields in July 1987, remarking of the Bengali people whose workshops he visited that 'They are working and living in conditions almost as bad as those on the Indian subcontinent. It really is not acceptable.'[6] Yet the Prince was back a few weeks later to see another side of the borough: the luxury apartments surrounding Shadwell Basin, which now contains not slime and deadwood but windsurfers and canoeists.

So Where Is the East End?

So far I have not tried to define the boundaries of 'the East End'. Much ink has been spilt in the past on this very question. The *Encyclopaedia Britannica* thought that it started east of Aldgate Pump, the stone fountain beside

the well which has now been covered up. A fountain remains at the junction of Leadenhall Street and Fenchurch Street, sporting the brass head of a very fierce-looking dog. Others have reckoned it as beginning a few hundred yards further to the east, by what was known as Gardiner's Corner at the junction of Whitechapel Road and Commercial Road. Gardiner's was a prominent department store which had begun as marine outfitters but soon branched out. Gardiner's is no longer the gateway to the east: it has been demolished. Thomas Burke in the 1930s considered the East End to be the then Metropolitan Borough of Stepney: very roughly today's Borough of Tower Hamlets.[1] Geoffrey Fletcher thought that Bermondsey and Rotherhithe on the south side of the Thames were a part of the East End because their inhabitants regarded themselves as such.[2] Ashley Smith defined the East End as being the riverside districts on the north of the Thames, while Robert Sinclair included West Ham and East Ham on the Essex side of the River Lea.[3]

I have used the term 'East End' to refer to the area stretching from Shoreditch and the City in the west to the River Lea in the east, and from Hackney in the north to the Thames in the south. But definitions are only there to be helpful and not to act as straitjackets, so I have not been constrained by my own boundaries and have felt free to discuss 'Docklands', which includes the old Surrey Docks on the south of the river as well as 'the Royals' to the east of the Lea. 'East London' pushes out to incorporate Newham across the Lea and parts of the boroughs of Islington and Waltham Forest to the north.

The term 'East End' was first used in the 1880s when sweeping changes were transforming London. The Victorians, or at least some of them, made strenuous efforts to get rid of the poor from central London on the principle of 'out of sight, out of mind'. Shaftesbury Avenue, Charing Cross Road, Victoria Street, Farringdon Road and Farringdon Street, Kingsway and Aldwych were just some of the major thoroughfares driven through the capital's more slummy areas in the nineteenth and early twentieth century, causing mass eviction of poor tenants who had no alternative but to head towards the cheaper housing of the east. It was a 'tale of two cities', one of which had decided that the other should be poor.

The East End in Myth and Legend

From the second half of the nineteenth century the 'East End' began to enter the popular imagination. Suddenly there were books written about this mysterious place east of Aldgate, usually revealing as much about the writer as about the subject. The Victorians enjoyed stories of daring exploration, and here was uncharted territory full of people whose poverty made them fitting recipients of a little missionary work.[1] *In Darkest London, In Darkest England, The Bitter Cry of Outcast London* and *The People of the Abyss* might refer to a distant continent, peopled by savages. Professor Huxley made this connection quite explicit: 'I have seen the Polynesian savage in his primitive condition, before the missionary or the blackbirder or the beach-comber got at him. With all his savagery, he was not half so savage, so unclean, so irreclaimable, as the tenant of a tenement in an East London slum.'[2] At least Huxley had once been a doctor in the East End and knew from firsthand experience about conditions there. Others who drew upon the East End as a background for garish and fictional goings-on boasted of their ignorance. Thomas Burke, for example, published a collection of stories in 1916 under the title *Limehouse Nights*, the majority of which focus on relationships between young and relatively innocent English girls and the inhabitants of Chinatown in Limehouse who are invariably represented as dope-filled, sexually obsessed deviants. Burke's stories sold well, and one of them was filmed by the great American film director D. W. Griffith as *Broken Blossoms*, with Lillian Gish as the forlorn waif Lucy. In fact Burke's knowing style was a sham. In his autobiography, *Son of London*, the author admitted he had no knowledge whatever of the Chinese people: 'I had thus been able to write those stories with the peculiar assurance a man has who knows nothing of what he is writing or talking about.'[3]

A similarly cavalier attitude was adopted by Arthur Henry Ward, better-known under his pseudonym 'Sax Rohmer'. Apparently Rohmer once consulted a ouija board as to how best he could earn a living, receiving the answer 'C-H-I-N-A-M-A-N', whereupon Rohmer published *The Mystery of Doctor Fu Manchu* in 1913.[4] Its subsequent popularity prompted Rohmer to turn out a long sequence of novels about Fu Manchu, the evil genius who was supposedly based in Limehouse and threatened to unleash the 'Yellow Peril' on an unsuspecting outside world. Rohmer's description of the Chinaman is clearly intended to send shudders of horror and revulsion through his right-thinking reader:

> Imagine a person, tall, lean and feline, high-shouldered, with a brow like Shakespeare and a face like Satan, a close-shaven skull, and long, magnetic eyes of the true cat-green. Invest him with all the cruel cunning of an entire Eastern race, accumulated in one giant intellect, with all the resources of science past and present .... Imagine that awful being, and you have a mental picture of Dr Fu Manchu, the yellow peril incarnate in one man.

English and Chinese mingle in Limehouse.

No matter that Rohmer had never been to Limehouse in his life, nor that the Chinese community there was numbered in hundreds, let alone the fact that they were generally regarded as being amongst the East End's most law-abiding inhabitants. The novelist Arnold Bennett went visiting Limehouse in April 1925: 'On the whole a rather flat night. Still we saw the facts. We saw no vice whatever. Inspector [of Police] gave the Chinese an exceedingly good character.'[5] As Burke and Rohmer realised, anything to do with the East End was fair game.

This 'poetic licence' is especially obvious when it comes to crime. Take the many films made about Jack the Ripper, all of which invariably show the murderer luring his victims down dark fog-filled alleys. Never mind the fact that the murders took place during the late summer of 1888, or that the Metropolitan Commissioner in charge of the case remarked on that autumn's long clear nights –

the ever present fog fits more neatly into the stereotype of what the Victorian East End should 'really' look like. There seems to be something about Jack the Ripper that makes even the most respected academics lose their senses. Professor Bill Fishman, discussing the theory that the murderer was thought by some to wear a deerstalker hat, commented: 'It was Scotland Yard's failure to catch the Ripper that prompted Dr Arthur Conan Doyle to conjure up a super-sleuth who could: ironically building the physical image of Sherlock Holmes on that of society's elusive quarry – cloak, cane, deerstalker hat and all.'[6] Too bad that Conan Doyle wrote the first Sherlock Holmes novel a year *before* the first Jack the Ripper victim, let alone that the deerstalker hat was an invention not of Doyle but of Sidney Paget, the artist who illustrated the stories in *the Strand Magazine*. No matter: another Jack the Ripper myth is now out and about, and it will take more than this book to kill off the Holmes story.

The East End and 'crime' are often thought to go together. Yet in his book *East of Aldgate* (1935) the journalist Horace Thorogood recalled how newspaper editors propagated the standard myths about the East End: 'When I first came to London as a cub reporter, if news was dull everywhere else we could always rely on giving the front page the necessary lurid touch by "hitting up" the East End police-court reports, or sending a man down there to discover a "den" or a "gang" or a "thieves' kitchen".'[7] Even today excitable journalists simply cannot resist letting their imagination run riot; a reporter in the *Evening Standard* of 22 May 1987 wrote of the East End as if it had been Britain's answer to Al Capone's Chicago: ' ... the memory of blue-chinned men cradling shotguns in the back of their chauffeur-driven limos hangs over the muddy site of Canary Warf like a pall of smoke.' As is so often the case with the East End, journalists and historians can always be sure to find evidence to fit in with their preconceived ideas.

Although the 'mysterious' East End has proved a gift to the writer of fiction, the world of finance has until recently seen little there to interest it. *The Economist,* for instance, in its issue of 28 April 1984 attacked the London Tourist Board for wasting some of its resources in 'sponsoring tourism in urban wildernesses like Tower Hamlets', quite overlooking the fact that the Borough of Tower Hamlets contains within its boundaries one of the country's foremost tourist attractions, namely the Tower of London which is visited by over 2 million paying customers each year. Other buildings in this 'wilderness' testify to a history not regal but just as interesting. The mosque at the corner of Fournier Street and Brick Lane was originally founded in 1743 as a Huguenot chapel and has since been a Methodist chapel, a missionary hall and a synagogue – a series of changes which demonstrates more tellingly than most history-books the rôle of migration in London's history. I hope, too, that the ten walks recommended in this book will show the sceptic that the East End has much to offer.

By contrast there is another attitude to the East End which seeks to wrap it up in a cosy haze of well-being and neighbourliness. It is nostalgic for a land of 'cheeky cockney chappies' talking in rhyming slang, where racism and domestic violence are unknown and everyone's idea of a good time consists of a jolly 'knees-up' in the local pub. Much of the power behind this image derives from its usual description as 'cockney', a name worn as a badge of pride and somehow thought to symbolise the irrepressible and chirpy spirit of the East End. The term 'cockney' was first used in the Middle Ages by countrymen when abusing the 'townees', a 'cokenay' being a cock's egg and therefore some kind of misfit or deformity. By the seventeenth century the word was used to describe Londoners in general, or more particularly those born within the sound of the 'Bow Bells' of St

Mary-le-Bow church, Cheapside. Then, virtually all Londoners were; nowadays, only a handful are.

During the nineteenth century the term 'cockney' was taken eastwards along with the working classes as they migrated towards work. A stereotype developed which was reinforced both by music-hall performers, many of whom came from the East End, and by the cartoonist Phil May (born in Leeds) whose 'cockney types' fixed the image firmly for the middle-class readership of *Punch* and other magazines. May's neckerchiefed and capped costermongers embodied a kind of 'street-wise' intelligence quite unknown in the drawing-rooms of Victorian and Edwardian England. Shaw's Alfred Doolittle – note the surname – in his play *Pygmalion* was May's theatrical parallel.

This century the cockney has been associated with comedians like Max Miller, the 'Cheeky Chappie' (born in Brighton), but the image received its most powerful confirmation during the Second World War when East London's docks drew upon the area the full might of the Luftwaffe. As a means of propaganda the legendary cockney resilience and cheerfulness were a vital ingredient in the image of 'London Can Take It' purveyed both at home and abroad. In war films of the time there was always an irrepressible and chirpy cockney. One of the most vivid books written about London during the Blitz was by a former Lord Mayor of Stepney, F. R. Lewey, and focuses on the East End: it was entitled simply *Cockney Campaign*.

The cockney image is complicated by confusion as to where today's cockneys actually live. In *The London Encyclopaedia* the term still refers to all Londoners, although I have yet to meet someone from Chelsea or Hampstead who appreciates this point.[8] For others 'Cockneyland' is the East End centred on Poplar; while a recent guide, *Where to Live in London*, describes Walthamstow as a 'Cockney stronghold'.[9] Further confusion arises from popular association of cockneys with 'Pearlies' and also with cockney dialect and rhyming slang, much of which is the creation of scriptwriters. This sense of a foreign language has been evident in the BBC's 'EastEnders'. Recent attempts to establish the series on American television led the BBC to issue potential American viewers with an eight-page glossary to help them 'decipher' what is being said.[10]

At least this image of the 'knees-up' East End is preferable to that of Jack the Ripper and Fu Manchu – it is positive and sympathetic, rather than negative and denigratory – but it is an image for all that, and the reality of East End life and its people is much too varied and fascinating to deserve being summed up in a generalised image.

The Thames and London's Poor Relation

A stroll eastwards through Wapping takes the pedestrian along a road called Wapping Wall. Today it is a thoroughfare lined with wharfs and warehouses which are being speedily transformed into rooms with a view, offices and studios. (There are confident assertions that Wapping has more artists than Chelsea.)

At one end is to be found the famous Prospect of Whitby, a riverside pub which dates back to 1520. When the Prospect first opened its doors to customers the pub's landlord must have been continually worried that the building might at any moment be flooded by the Thames. The river then was not the embanked and – we smugly believe – tamed waterway of today but a much wider and wilder channel which flowed wherever the mood took it. Wapping Wall formed one of the barriers erected in the twelfth century in an attempt to make East London less swampy and more inhabitable.

The one basic fact underlying the very existence of London is simple: no Thames, no London. London is a chapter in the history of the Thames and not vice versa; the river is primarily responsible for the shape of the capital. Before the coming of the Romans in AD 43, there was no such place as London. Dense forest and the intimidating width of the Thames meant few settlers built camps here. The Romans, however, thought the site ideal, mainly because the presence of the Thames offered them opportunities for trading with the Continent. They founded their city where they did because the river upstream was too shallow for their ships. The tide provided free power for their craft to enter and leave. The two hills of Ludgate Hill and Cornhill on the north bank meant that they had a commanding view over the Thames, while the Fleet and Walbrook rivers offered extra transport facilities as well as two convenient harbours. The city of the Romans was also far enough inland to be free from sudden attack by marauders, and the land upon which the city was sited was high and relatively dry on either bank so that secure foundations could be laid.[1]

All these factors guaranteed that London with the essential assistance of the Thames would establish itself as the capital of Roman England. As James Bird has summed up, Verulamium (St Albans) on the Ver and Camulodunum (Colchester) on the Colne were no match for London on the Thames.[2] Although the Roman roads were excellent,

their wheeled traffic was rudimentary and hence the Thames was vital in offering cheap and efficient water-transport. The Roman historian Tacitus wrote in AD 60 that London 'was filled with traders and a celebrated centre of commerce'. Vessels coming up the Thames brought imports of olive oil, wine, bronze, marble and millstones; ships going the other way included the 800 grain-ships which supplied the Roman legions in Germany. Even after the Romans left Britain in AD 410 it was the Thames which kept London alive during the Dark Ages. The Venerable Bede wrote of London in AD 604 that it was 'a trading centre for many nations who visit it by land and sea'.[3]

So far all this seems like one big success story: the Thames and London each helping the other. Downstream it was a different story. Here, east of London, it was bleak and inhospitable. The meandering Thames flooded the marshes, bringing in its wake damp and disease; not until the late nineteenth century was malaria finally eradicated from the estuary. A series of walls, such as that at Wapping, were built in an effort to beat back the Thames, and they formed a significant landmark which gave rise to such place-names as 'Blackwall', where the wall was covered with dark moss and vegetation, and 'Millwall' from the windmills nearby. Poplar trees had been planted, too, in order to form a natural windbreak, hence 'Poplar'. The Isle of Dogs was also drained in the early fourteenth century. Despite these measures, however, the Thames, unruly and self-willed, condemned East London to a role on the sidelines, observing the surging development of the capital but taking no part in it. Not until the time of Henry VIII did East London begin to benefit from the existence of the Thames.

Monasteries and Lucky Horseshoes:
St Dunstan (924–88) and the Medieval Church

The departure of the Romans in AD 410 made little difference to East London. The fields and farms continued as before, the tiny villages lived on undisturbed. Little of East London life between the Romans and the Normans has come down to us. The scattered population, numbered in hundreds rather than in thousands, has left no records for the history-books, except for one important legacy: the villages took their names from the Anglo-Saxon chieftains who owned them, and thus we know that a thousand years ago three of these chiefs were called Waeppa (Waeppa's people became Wapping), Stebba (Stebba's people became Stepney) and Haecka (hence Hackney). But the first person significant in the history of the East End, and who is more than a shadow on the page, is Dunstan, the former monk who was appointed Bishop of London in 959.

Born into a noble family in 924, Dunstan had been educated at Glastonbury Abbey where he later became abbot. Although internal domestic politics had once forced him into a two-year exile in France, Dunstan moved swiftly up the ecclesiastical ladder on his return, becoming successively Bishop of Worcester, then Bishop of London and finally, in 961, Archbishop of Canterbury. He crowned Edgar as King of England in 973, devising a coronation service which is still the basis of the one used a thousand years later.

Though he was only briefly Bishop of London, Dunstan has strong connections with the East End. He replaced the little wooden church of All Saints which stood on Stepney Green with a larger stone building. The green itself is smaller now, and much of the St Dunstan's we see today was rebuilt in the fifteenth century. However, a stroll around the warm and intimate interior of one of England's most charming churches reveals a

R.Cooper sculpt.

ST DUNSTAN.

From an ancient Painting in Lambeth Palace.

St Dunstan, Bishop of London and then Archbishop of Canterbury, who rebuilt the church on Stepney Green which still stands at the heart of the East End.

thousand-year-old stone rood showing Christ on the Cross which comes from Dunstan's day. After his canonisation in 1029, the name of the church was changed to St Dunstan and All Saints.

Apart from his church duties, Dunstan was also a keen metalworker, and his hobby gave rise to two stories. The first relates how one day the Devil came to tempt the saint by conjuring up alluring images of sin and

11

wickedness. Dunstan responded to these overtures by picking up a pair of hot tongs and tweaking the Devil's nose! The tongs became Dunstan's symbol and are still to be seen not only over the main entrance to St Dunstan's church but also in the arms of the Borough of Tower Hamlets. The second story tells how the Devil once asked Dunstan to shoe his horse. Instead the crafty Dunstan fixed the shoe to the hoof of the Devil himself. Howling with pain, the Devil promised that if Dunstan would only take off the shoe he would never enter a house with a horseshoe outside. This is why we still hang 'lucky horseshoes' outside houses, always with the open end towards the sky to 'hold the luck'.[1]

Dunstan seems to have been an endearingly practical man. For example, he ordered every priest to master a handicraft so that he could in turn pass on his skills to others. He discouraged the massive drinking bouts then common, as well as the practice of polygamy. After Dunstan's death in May 988 the religious institutions founded in the East End tried to emulate his example.[2]

Not only did they give a focus for local people, but their significance is underlined by the way in which their names have lived on. For instance, Queen Matilda in 1147 founded the priory of St Katherine's by the Tower on a thirteen-acre piece of land. It stood where our marina of St Katharine's does today with its complex of hotels, conference centres, shops and restaurants. A grubby plaque in what remains of Spital Square records that here in 1197 Walter Brune and his wife Rosa set up a priory whose facilities later incorporated a 'spital house', or hospital for lepers – hence 'Spitalfields'. The priory of Holywell was founded in Shoreditch in the twelfth century, as was the convent of St Leonard's in Bromley – famous for its link with Geoffrey Chaucer's Prioress 'Madame Eglentyne' who was proud of her elegance and fine table manners. In his delightful portrait Chaucer smiles affectionately at her limited horizons:

. . . Frenssh she spak ful faire and fetisly,
After the scole of Stratford atte Bowe,
For Frenssh of Parys was to hire un-knowe.

To the north-east of the Tower of London lay a Cistercian abbey. Many of Stepney's peasants were buried here during the Black Death of 1348–9 which wiped out nearly 50,000 people, half of London's population. A recent archaeological dig has revealed more than a thousand of these corpses, at first buried neatly in rows but then, as the bubonic plague tightened its grip, hastily thrown into a gravel pit. A legacy of this abbey's presence today is the small Grace's Alley which leads into Wellclose Square.[3]

Another prominent landmark was the great Tower of London itself, built at the command of William the Conqueror in order to intimidate native Londoners and emphasise to them that the Normans were here to stay. The Domesday Book of 1086 showed that the population of East London numbered no more than 700, but the Constable of the Tower still exercised certain rights over the eleven hamlets to the east as regards recruitment and pressing of labour – which gave rise to the name of 'Tower Hamlets'.

When Dunstan rebuilt his Stepney church in the tenth century it was, and remained for several centuries, the church nearest to the River Thames. It therefore became known as 'the church of the high seas', and traditionally any child born at sea is reckoned to be a parishioner of Stepney. Indeed, until recently all births, marriages and deaths at sea were registered at St Dunstan's. Over the west door is a carving of a ship, and the churchyard contains the impressive table-top graves of several mariners, although the body of Stepney's most famous sailor, Captain James Cook, lies several thousand miles away in New Zealand. However, a plaque on 88 Mile End Road marks the site of the house where he lived in the 1760s and 1770s before his departure in 1776 on his third and last voyage to Australasia, where he was murdered in February 1779.

Many of London's most ancient churches were substantially rebuilt during the eighteenth century, but fortunately St Dunstan's escaped this fate. Today only a visitor with the meanest historical imagination could fail to appreciate both the church and the shade of the great tenth-century churchman St Dunstan which permeates every brick and stone of the building – even though a stone in the wall of the tower, inserted in the 1660s and supposedly a remnant of the walls of Carthage, reminds us: 'Time consumes all; it spares none.' Thus St Dunstan and All Saints remains, a medieval country church surrounded by a great city. Across the road stands the 'city farm' called Stepping Stones, and the sounds of animals carry to the churchyard as they must have done a thousand years ago.

The bridge over the river Lea which was shaped like a bow.

When the Queen Got a Ducking: The Origin of Bow Bridge

The River Lea winds southwards through East London and joins the Thames by Bow Creek. It presented a formidable obstacle to the Romans when they wished to march between London and what was originally their capital, Colchester. They built a straight road through

13

Bethnal Green, today's Old Ford Road, and crossed the Lea at the little ford which served travellers for over a thousand years.

In the early twelfth century, however, Queen Matilda seems to have fallen in; the antiquarian John Leland described her as 'well washed in the water'.[1] Matilda was determined that this would never happen again and she commanded a new stone bridge to be built over the Lea. It had three narrow arches shaped like bows, and thus the neighbouring village gained its name. Although subsequently repaired then widened in 1741, this original Bow Bridge stood until 1835, catering for the thousands of people journeying between London and the prosperous region of East Anglia.

The Lea itself was a vital channel for bringing food downstream to the growing London market, particularly huge quantities of grain. The water-supply attracted millers, printers and dyers, and in the eighteenth century the Bow porcelain industry started here. Unfortunately, as London spread ever eastwards in Victorian times the 'stink industries' began to use the Lea as a convenient drain. Even today a walk along Leamouth Road and Orchard Place confronts the pedestrian with a bewildering array of noxious smells. There is one unique industrial building on the Lea which is of great historic importance and hopefully is to be preserved as a museum, namely the tide-mill of 1776 at Three Mills in Bow whose giant watermills operated the millstones which milled the grain. Two tide-mills allowed the tidal water upstream to flow freely but held back the water further down by means of flood-gates. When this water-level had dropped sufficiently the flood-gates were opened and the rushing water turned the mill wheels.

The Blind Beggar of Bethnal Green

The story of the blind beggar is one of the East End's most enduring legends, although different books give different versions and even different names to the characters involved. The most commonly accepted story runs as follows.[1] In 1265, Simon de Montfort's army was defeated by Prince Edward's men at the battle of Evesham. His son Henry was wounded and left for dead on the battlefield. Fortunately for him, a baron's daughter sought him out, patched up his wounds and enabled Henry to escape in disguise. They subsequently married, but for safety's sake spent the next few years living as beggars near Bethnal Green. At some point Henry de Montfort acquired a dog.

He and his wife had a beautiful daughter called Bessy who was courted as a young girl

An idealised representation of the Blind Beggar of Bethnal Green, his daughter Bessy and his dog.

14

by four suitors. All but one of them rejected her when they learnt of her parents and their vagabond lives. However at the wedding feast the existence of the de Montfort family name and fortune was revealed to the bridegroom, and no doubt they all lived happily ever after. It seems such a nice cheerful story that it is almost a shame to mention that A. J. Robinson and D. H. B. Chesshyre have suggested that Bessy was likely to have been a fifteenth-century prostitute, working as a barmaid at the Queen's Head inn in Romford.[2]

Whatever Bessy's status or the identity of the Blind Beggar himself, the legend has left its mark locally in several ways. There is a statue of the Blind Beggar and his dog by Elizabeth Frink on the north side of Roman Road opposite Smart Street. The churchwardens' staves at St Matthew's, Bethnal Green, carry the emblem, which is also present inside the local library on Bethnal Green. A drawing of the Blind Beggar and his daughter was the official crest of the old borough council of Bethnal Green until it was subsumed into the new borough of Tower Hamlets in 1965. There is the Blind Beggar pub along the north side of Whitechapel Road whose sign sports a painting of father and daughter. Finally, Bethnal Green can boast a Montfort House, an Evesham House – and even a Bessy Street, although her charms must surely have been more alluring than this rather squalid little thoroughfare!

The 'White Chapel'

For hundreds of years St Dunstan's was adequate to accommodate the small congregation of little-populated East London. By the thirteenth century, however, it had become too small, and so a new church was built on the outskirts of London. This building was a prominent landmark for travellers passing to and from the city through Aldgate. It was covered in limewash in an attempt to preserve it from the elements, and this 'white chapel' subsequently gave its name to the district. Officially known as St Mary Matfelon (the derivation of 'Matfelon' is uncertain), it was often rebuilt and has two particularly interesting associations.

In the seventeenth century Richard Brandon was buried here. Brandon is certainly not a well-known name in the history-books, and in fact he worked for most of his life as a ragman in Rosemary Lane (now Royal Mint Street). But he does have one enduring claim to fame, for it was Brandon who cut off the

The altar-piece in St Mary's Matfelon which caused a scandal in 1710 after the Rector insisted that his hated rival, the Dean of Peterborough, should be depicted as Judas Iscariot.

The old hay market held in Whitechapel High Street for three hundred years until 1928. St Mary's Matfelon, once the 'white chapel', is on the right.

head of Charles I on 30 January 1649, receiving £30 for his labours. Apparently Brandon died of remorse soon afterwards, and at his funeral the crowd shouted: 'Bury him in the dunghill!'[1]

In 1710, St Mary Matfelon became the focus of ecclesiastical controversy. People came flocking to St Mary's when the then rector commissioned a new altarpiece, depicting his hated theological opponent the Dean of Peterborough as Judas Iscariot. The Bishop of London finally ordered the removal of the painting.[2]

In the nineteenth century St Mary's possessed a dominating open-air pulpit from which preachers could harangue pedestrians, and its clock jutting out over Whitechapel Road was a familiar sight. During the Second World War the church was badly bombed and it was pulled down. Its site is now a public garden called St Mary's, but the outline of the church can still be seen on the grass together with a marooned but impressive table-top tomb and a clutch of graves in one corner.

The third medieval East End church was St Mary, Bow. It was once situated on the village green and surrounded by fields and farms. Today it perches precariously on a traffic island, sadly incongruous. Bow Road is always swarming with motorists, who doubtless curse this obstruction in the middle of the highway as they thunder past its delicate Gothic windows. The chapel was built in 1311 and expanded into a church in about 1490 for those parishioners who were finding that the muddy tracks made it difficult to reach St Dunstan's. Parts of the lower tower still date from that time, but over the years it has been altered and also suffered extensive bomb damage during the last war.

It is well worth braving the traffic to cross the road and look inside the little church, where it is surprisingly quiet thanks to merciful double glazing. The sense of having stepped into the heart of some rural community is amazing. Sadly there are no owls in this churchyard, which is perhaps best appreciated at three o'clock in the morning when the traffic occasionally diminishes.

Who Is the Gentleman?
Wat Tyler and the Peasants' Revolt of 1381

For most of the Middle Ages the East End was just fields, farms and the eleven 'tower hamlets'. Nevertheless the East End played a part in several significant political events. In May 1299, for instance, after Westminster Hall had been badly damaged by fire, a meeting of Parliament was held at the mansion of Henry le Waleis which stood on the west side of St Dunstan's, Stepney Green. It was an important meeting: Edward I was forced to confirm the granting of the Magna Carta, originally obtained from King John, which conceded that taxes should not be imposed without parliamentary consent – a principle that had to be fought for yet again in the seventeenth century during the Civil War.[1]

Less than a hundred years later the East End was the scene of an episode in the Peasants' Revolt of 1381 led by Wat Tyler and the 'hedge priest' John Ball. The authorities were faced by the continual problem of paying for the Hundred Years' War in France and they decided to impose a poll tax over and above ordinary taxation. Initially levied in 1377 at 4*d* (2p) per head, by November 1380 it had risen to 1*s* (5p) a head, a large sum in those days. Sporadic outbreaks of violence preceded a general uprising in the summer of 1381. The extraordinary pungency with which these supposedly uneducated peasants expressed their political philosophy puts the modern labour movement to shame. Wat Tyler, for example, noted that 'We are men formed in Christ's likeness and we are kept like beasts', while one of the slogans simply asked:

> When Adam delved and Eve span,
> Who then was the gentleman?

Wat Tyler and 40,000 peasants marched to London to see Richard II, who was just a fourteen-year-old boy. On 14 June the King agreed to meet Tyler and his followers. The place chosen? A contemporary chronicler described it as 'a fine open space which is called the Mile End, situated in the midst of a pleasant meadow'. Today that meadow has shrunk to the strip of grass called Stepney Green Gardens, hard pressed now to accommodate 400 people let alone 40,000. Here it was that king met commoner. Tyler, a hardened veteran of the French wars, spoke for the peasants and demanded an end to the poll tax, the division of church land and a termination of the feudal system whereby a few were lords and the many were serfs usually treated as little more than chattels.[2]

It seems almost like a pantomime or a fairy-story with the brave young king agreeing to meet his people and deal with them justly. In fact, despite his youth, Richard showed that he was already well versed in the art of political deviousness. He agreed to the peasants' demands, ordering that thirty clerks should draw up charters dissolving the old order; he was of course playing for time. The next meeting took place in Smithfield, and by then Richard knew that many of the fickle peasants were already drifting home and that his own army was approaching London. A mêlée was engineered, Tyler was stabbed and later murdered by William Walworth, and Richard assured the peasants that all was well and that they should quietly disperse. They did so, confident in the King's promises.

They were wrong. The reprisals instigated by Richard and his men were bloody and widespread. When reminded of his previous promises, Richard replied in words which still chill the blood in their callousness: 'Oh, you wretched men, detestable by land and sea, you who seek equality with lords are not worthy to live .... You will remain in bondage, not as before, but incomparably harsher.

17

For as long as we live and, by God's grace, rule over this realm, we will strive with mind, strength and wealth to suppress you so that the rigour of your servitude will be an example to posterity.' But Richard was no prophet. Although the events which took place on Stepney Green might seem on the face of it to have ended in defeat and death, the jolt given to the English rulers by the Peasants' Revolt ensured that the feudal system was not comprehensively reimposed. Serfdom in England was dead, centuries be-fore its extinction in France and Russia.[3] Instead there arose the sturdy independent yeoman who was nobody's chattel. John Bull was created here in the fields of the East End. A walk around the vicinity of Stepney Green today brings the walker to the mural by the junction of Bow Common Lane and Canal Road which depicts the revolt, but surprisingly there is no Wat Tyler Street or John Ball Road, although local and justly forgotten worthies are commemorated (Vallance, Brushfield).

Tower Hill

One of the most remarkable aspects of the Peasants' Revolt of 1381 was the self-control and discipline shown by Wat Tyler and his followers. Lawyers' records were burnt, as was the Savoy Palace of the hated John of Gaunt, but only four people in authority were killed. As A. L. Rowse observes, this was 'a small number for such an upheaval: the mob was more merciful than the governing class, when it recovered its nerve'.[1]

These four individuals were taken from the Tower of London and beheaded on Tower Hill, the patch of land which is now called in part Trinity Square Gardens. One victim was the Lord Chancellor, Sir Robert Hales, responsible for levying the poll tax and nick-named 'Hob the Robber'. Another was the Archbishop of Canterbury, Simon Sudbury, whose grisly despatch was recorded by the chronicler Seymour; seeing that death was at hand, Sudbury

with comfortable words (as he was an eloquent man and wise beyond all the wise men of the realm) spoke fairly to them. Lastly, after forgiveness granted to the executioner that should behead him, kneeling down, he offered his neck to him that should smite off his head. Being stricken in the neck but not deadly, he putting his hand to his neck said, 'Aha, it is the Hand of God.' He had not removed his hand from the place where the pain was, but that being suddenly stricken again, his finger ends being cut off and part of the arteries, he fell down, but yet he died not, till being mangled with eight several strokes in the neck and head, he fulfilled most worthy martyrdom.[2]

Like Tyburn, Tower Hill was a place of execution from the Middle Ages until the eighteenth century. But whereas Tyburn in the west catered for 'common people', Tower Hill was reserved for the nobility – a reversal of the usual social pattern in London. Henry VIII's wives were executed inside the Tower of London away from the gaze of the populace – a small but important concession.

Those who lost their lives on Tower Hill included 2 archbishops, 6 dukes, 10 earls, 1 marquis, 1 viscount, 15 barons, 33 knights, 1 bishop and 1 prior.[3] Just as at Tyburn, the executions attracted huge crowds drawn by the barbaric spectacle. Several inns profited from being able to offer their customers a good view of the proceedings. Lord Lovat, the last person beheaded in England, died on Tower Hill in April 1747. He at least enjoyed the perverse pleasure of seeing a stand containing a thousand spectators collapse under their own weight. About twenty people died in this accident, including the man who had built the stand in the first place. The last three executions on Tower Hill took place in 1780 after the Gordon Riots when two women and a man were found guilty of attacking the pub of a Roman Catholic and hanged; one of the women was coloured.[4]

Today the site of the scaffold is clearly marked in Trinity Square Gardens, north of the Tower. It is overshadowed by the two massive memorials to members of the merchant navy killed in both world wars. That of the Second World War contains 24,000 names and seems to go on for ever. There are few more moving sights in London than to visit it after Remembrance Day and see the poppies which, even after forty years, relatives and friends place beside the names of loved ones.

Ratcliff Cross Stairs and the Tudor Sea-Dogs

One of the most pleasant ways in which to spend a sunny afternoon in the East End is to linger in Shadwell Park, simply watching the Thames go by. Once the site of an unsuccessful fish-market, the park was opened in 1922 and called the King Edward VII Memorial Park. It sports excellently kept flowerbeds and gardens, a bowling-green, a café and many benches. Even the ventilating shaft of the Rotherhithe Tunnel which stands close to the river is more aesthetically pleasing than functional.

Shadwell Park was the scene of many famous comings and goings. Just beside the ventilating shaft can be found a stone commemorating several sixteenth-century seamen who departed from nearby Ratcliff Cross Stairs, which lay on the eastern part of the park at the bottom of Butcher Row, on their way to unknown destinations. Some never returned. Sir Hugh Willoughby took three ships to search for the north-west passage to India in May 1553. The crew of 115 men included one parson and was under explicit instructions 'that no blaspheming of God or detestable swearing be used in any ship, nor communication of ribaldry, filthy tales, or ungodly talk'.[1] These precautions to ensure heavenly approval did not seem to work. Willoughby's ship and one other were blown off course, and he was forced to winter in Lapland where their food ran out and everyone died of starvation. Ships and corpses were found several years later. Richard Chancellor, the captain of the other vessel, managed to reach northern Russia and then travelled overland to Moscow where he stayed with Ivan the Terrible. However, on a return journey in November 1556, Chancellor was shipwrecked off Scotland and drowned.

Of the other names on the memorial, Stephen Burrough and his son William explored the northern edges of Russia, while Sir Martin Frobisher undertook three voyages from Ratcliff Cross Stairs. Frobisher seems to have been a typical sixteenth-century 'sea-dog', not averse to a little piracy on the side in order to pay the bills. When Frobisher and his company embarked on their first voyage in June 1576 he left with Elizabeth I's farewell message ringing in his ears that she had 'good liking to their doings'. He returned with an

19

Eskimo captured through trickery – he soon died in England, apparently of heartbreak, one of the earliest victims of imperialism – and also lumps of rock which the alchemists, hoping to curry favour with Elizabeth I, pronounced to be gold.[2] Not surprisingly, Frobisher was twice sent back to gather more of this 'precious ore', amassing some 800 tons in all. In fact it turned out to be worthless and ended up as paving material for the London streets.[3] Temporarily out of favour because of this disappointment, Frobisher regained his position through his part in the defeat of the Spanish Armada in 1588. He eventually died of wounds sustained during the capture of Brest in 1594 and was buried at St Giles, Cripplegate, the ancient church hidden within the Barbican complex.

Another memorial in the East End marks the departure of intrepid adventurers, the Virginia settlers. A plaque attached to Brunswick Wharf power station records that from here on 19 December 1606 three ships, *Susan Constant*, *Godspeed* and *Discovery*, set sail for North America. The ships' company consisted of 105 emigrants, 12 labourers, 4 carpenters and 48 'gentlemen'. Under the leadership of Captain Newport, supported by Captain John Smith, they landed in Virginia on 26 April 1607. On 24 May the 105 survivors of this perilous journey founded a settlement on the James river in Virginia which proved to be the first English plantation in America that survived and eventually prospered.

The Port of London

The vessels leaving Ratcliff Cross Stairs for foreign lands would have been fitted out nearby, because there was a growing relationship between this part of London and the Thames. For the first time in the history of the capital, the fact that the river passed through the East End was to benefit its inhabitants and villages. The Port of London was gradually expanding eastwards, offering work to any who were prepared to move there.

The Thames had been commercially important since the Normans established a dock at Queenhithe in the City during the twelfth century. This dock suffered from the major inconvenience of being located above the stone London Bridge erected between 1176 and 1209. Goods had to be unloaded in 'the Pool' and then be transported upstream by barge. Not surprisingly, it was only a matter of time before another dock, founded at Billingsgate, ousted Queenhithe as it was on the 'right' or eastern side of the bridge.

During the sixteenth century East London began to acquire an independence and a value in its own right because of its maritime links; the contemporary historian John Stow paid a generous tribute to the riverside districts of Stepney: 'It is to be further remarked of this Parish of Stepney, on the Southern parts of it especially, that it is one of the greatest Nurseries of Navigation and Breeders of Seamen in England, the most serviceable Men in the Nation; without which England could not be England; for they are its Strength and Wealth.'[1]

In the early sixteenth century Henry VIII located the nascent shipbuilding industry at Woolwich, Deptford and Blackwall rather than in the already overcrowded City. The noise from the yards did not matter in what was then a sparsely populated neighbourhood. Some of the maritime industries which sprang up in the riverside hamlets are remembered in local street-names such as Cable

Street where the ships' cables were made.

During the sixteenth century naval power in Europe was shifting to the west away from the Mediterranean, and London's only trading rival, Antwerp, was sacked by the Spanish in 1576 and again in 1585. An ever increasing number of ships came sailing up the Thames in order to unload, bringing goods of rather more value than poor Frobisher's 'gold'. In fact there were so many vessels that Billingsgate quay was unable to cope with the demands made of it and Elizabeth was forced in 1558 to set up a number of 'legal quays' where commodities could be unloaded and then stored. Shrewd observers, such as the members of the newly formed East India Company which had been granted its royal charter in 1600, could see that commerical logic demanded that the Port of London should continue to grow eastwards away from the City.

Thus in 1614 the East India Company opened its own repairing-dock and building-yard at Ratcliff. This establishment occupied more than ten acres. Within four years the Company was employing over 200 workmen at this site and even built its own private chapel which is still there, much altered and hidden away between the trees and undergrowth in the recreation-ground off Poplar High Street. After years of neglect and vandalism, this church, now known as St Matthias, has been closed. Anyone who cares to peer through the cracks in the door or the broken windows can glimpse inside the wooden columns which support the building and that are supposed to have come from the masts of old 'East Indiamen'.[2]

The Great Plague of 1665 was particularly virulent in Stepney, resulting in problems when it came to obtaining fresh recruits for the Royal Navy. Clarendon wrote of the plague striking down so many sailors that 'Stepney and the places adjacent, which were their common habitations, were almost depopulated'.[3] Nevertheless the population of East London continued to increase because of its riverside importance. A community of about 21,000 people in 1600 had become over 91,000 by 1700 and then 125,000 in 1780.[4] The vast majority of East Londoners were employed on the riverside, either sharing in the growth of Britain's overseas empire or else working as Thames watermen – the London taxi-drivers of their day who would row their fares to and fro across 'London's High Street'. The East End banks were riddled with their landing-spots, namely the 'stairs' which are still marked on London maps to this day. These are probably the most ancient ways in London, indicating the whereabouts of the dry paths which led to coracles and, later, ships.[5] Some still afford a glimpse of the river between high walls, but few allow access to the Thames; many are now being built over.

By the end of the eighteenth century nearly 14,000 ships were using the Port of London each year, which meant that sometimes there were 1,400 vessels moored simultaneously. Delays of up to three months before the cargo could be unloaded were commonplace.[6]

The Rise and Fall of Bishop Bonner and the Manor of Stepney

Throughout the Middle Ages the Manor of Stepney was owned by the Bishops of London. They also owned a country residence in Bethnal Green, and the Bishops' route to it can still be traced through some of the road-names which survive. Leaving the City through the Bishop's Gate, they would have followed the road which now bears that name, turning into Bethnal Green Road and then taking Bishop's Way to their mansion which stood on the site of today's London Chest Hospital. Of all the Bishops of London, only Dunstan and Edmund Bonner have left their mark on the East End.

Bonner was the last Bishop to own the Manor of Stepney. Following the tradition of churchmen such as Becket and More who were also active in politics, Bonner worked as Cardinal Wolsey's chaplain, surviving his master's subsequent disgrace. Bonner was often used by Henry VIII as a high-powered emissary to the Pope, and in 1539 he received his reward when the King appointed him Bishop of London. Unfortunately for Bonner, the turmoil affecting both Church and State led him to be deprived of his position under Edward VI, but he was reinstated in 1553 when Mary ascended the throne. It was now that Bonner made a hated name for himself, being foremost in the persecution and execution of supposed heretics.

Yet with the death of Mary and the accession of Elizabeth the wheel of fortune went full circle once more and Bonner was deprived of his bishopric and then thrown into the Marshalsea prison in the summer of 1559. There he stayed for the remaining ten years of his life. Although much hated – he was buried secretly late at night after his death in 1569 in case the crowd tried to tear his corpse apart – Bonner's name lives on in the East End in Bonner Street, Bonner Road and even Bonner

Bishop Bonner, the hated sixteenth-century churchman who was reputed to burn heretics in his garden.

School. His ghost is supposed to haunt Bonner's Fields, land which became Victoria Park in the middle of the nineteenth century. He is said to ride around in a black coach, and to see him is fatal![1]

During Bonner's first setback the Manor of Stepney was appropriated from the Bishops of London. In 1550 it was granted by Edward VI to Thomas Wentworth, the head of the family which owned it until the early eighteenth century and which is commemorated in the name of Wentworth Street. At first glance it might seem to be of little importance who owned the Manor. In fact both the Bishops and the Wentworths were extremely short-sighted in their handling of their property, granting only twenty-one-year leases to developers.[2] Naturally no wealthy individual planning a residence would contemplate building in the East End under such terms, preferring instead to go west towards Bloomsbury, Soho and Mayfair where the leases were longer. Once again, it was a case of 'west is best'.

22

The Theatre and the Curtain: London's First Playhouses

Not only does the East End as a whole have many strong links with the story of London entertainment, but also Shoreditch was the site of the country's first ever permanent playhouse, the Theatre, which was built in the vicinity of Curtain Road in 1576. Then the area was largely made up of fields where, in the Middle Ages, the City's young men came to practise their archery. Bowling Green Walk, the narrow path which joins Pitfield Street to Hoxton Square, reminds us of another local recreation, now vanished.

The Theatre was built because of a statute of 1572 which threatened the many troupes of strolling players wandering the roads of Elizabethan England. Describing them as 'rogues and vagabonds', this Act promised dire punishments ranging from ear-lopping to hanging for those caught without a licence signed by two Justices of the Peace.[1] It was because of such hostility against those whom the authorities considered to be spreaders of sedition and unrest that the most prestigious company, the Earl of Leicester's Men led by James Burbage, decided to come 'off the road'.

Having borrowed capital of £600 from his brother-in-law, a wealthy grocer, Burbage built the Theatre on to the back of a tavern called the George. Nothing of this remains, only the name of New Inn Yard, but a visit to the galleried inn of the same name in Southwark gives some hint of the atmosphere, even though this pub dates from 1676. Why did Burbage put the playhouse in semi-rural Shoreditch rather than in the crowded City which supplied his audiences? He knew that the City Fathers, already influenced by ideas of thrift, hard work and industry which were later to be dubbed 'Puritanism', would never allow a place of entertainment to be built within their jurisdiction. Burbage therefore selected Shoreditch and the site of a former priory called Holywell because it was outside the City boundaries. A plaque on the side of 86–88 Curtain Road commemorates where the Theatre once stood.

The Theatre was soon imitated by the Curtain nearby, and both playhouses offered a cheap open-air entertainment in which a robust fare of plays was punctuated by jigs, swordfights and much crude knockabout humour.[2] As expected, the disapproving City Fathers were soon writing to the Privy Council in 1597, complaining that such playhouses 'are a special cause of corrupting their youth, containing nothing but unchaste matters, lascivious devices, shifts of cozenage, and other lewd and ungodly practices'.[3] An actors' colony grew up in Shoreditch, amongst whom was a certain William Shakespeare who is thought to have lived in Holywell Street. His fellow-playwright Ben Jonson killed an actor called Gabriel Spencer in a duel in Hoxton Fields – the land between today's City Road and Kingsland Road – and only escaped hanging because of a legal technicality. The parish church of St Leonard's became known as 'the actor's church' (a name used today for St Paul's, Covent Garden), and buried here are Will Somers, once Henry VIII's clown and James Burbage. In 1913 the London Shakespeare League, presided over by the East End councillor the Reverend Stewart Headlam, installed a plaque inside the church to honour the district's links with Elizabethan drama, remembering 'the players, musicians, and other men of the theatre who are buried within the precincts of this Church'.

Burbage had taken a twenty-one-year lease on the plot of land at the back of the George, and at its expiry friction arose with the ground landlord over the increased terms he was asking. Neither side would back down, and the deadlock was finally broken by Richard

Burbage, James's son. Late on Boxing Day night, 1598, Burbage, Shakespeare and a few trusted members of the company met outside the Theatre and proceeded, with the help of some carpenters, to dismantle the wooden building. They loaded the wood on to carts that were then trundled down Bishopsgate and over London Bridge to Bankside in Southwark where they started to erect a new playhouse which they called the Globe. In a nice touch of continuity, the timber from the Theatre was used to form the seating of the Globe.[4] The Curtain continued in Shoreditch until the 1620s when it was pulled down, as was the nearby Fortune theatre, whose site is marked by a plaque in Fortune Street.

Jolly Jack Tar in the East End: Some Riverside Pubs

> Bold Jack, the sailor, here I come,
>   Pray how d'ye like my nib,
> My trowsers wide, my trampers rum,
>   My nab, and flowing jib?
> I sails the seas from end to end
>   And leads a joyous life;
> In ev'ry mess I finds a friend,
>   In ev'ry port a wife.

So wrote Charles Dibdin, the eighteenth-century composer who claimed that his songs with their characterisation of 'Jolly Jack Tar' had made more recruits for the King's navy than all the press-gangs which scoured London's streets.[1]

The growth of London as a port meant that the riverside villages were the haunts of off-duty sailors eager to enjoy onland what they missed out on at sea. Women and drink were the two principal requirements, and Wapping in particular became a kind of shanty town made up largely of brothels, drinking-places and cheap lodgings. Ratcliff Highway's exploitation of sailors was almost a local industry (the Highway is still notorious, but for the speed of its traffic rather than for its women). In Nelson's day Wapping High Street could boast 140 ale-houses. The few which remain are no longer the haunt of rowdy and violent sailors but of well-heeled tourists clutching cameras and guidebooks.[2]

The Prospect of Whitby, London's oldest riverside pub, frequented in the past by Samuel Pepys, J. M. W. Turner and Charles Dickens.

The oldest of these remaining taverns is the Prospect of Whitby in Wapping, founded back on the riverside in 1520 in the days of Henry VIII. Once infamous for its connection with smuggling, it was known as the Devil's Tavern until the name was changed in honour of the *Prospect* collier from Whitby which regularly moored nearby in the Thames. Samuel Pepys was a regular visitor, as later were the artist J. M. W. Turner and Charles Dickens. It should be dear to the hearts of gardeners, because in 1780 a sailor called John Westcombe, recently returned from a journey to Japan, sold some fuchsias and chrysanthemums here to a market-gardener, the first time that those flowers had been seen in this country. [3]

Also in Wapping is the seventeenth-century Town of Ramsgate, once known as the Red Cow after a popular barmaid with flaming-red hair! Its new name came from the Kent fishermen who sold their catches just beside the pub on Wapping Old Stairs. Two other pubs well worth a visit are the Grapes in Narrow Street, Limehouse, an eighteenth-century building whose veranda offers a fine view over the river, and the Gun on the Isle of Dogs. Not so well known, though it also has a good view over the Thames, the Gun took its name from the royal salute of twenty-one guns fired to greet *Henry Addington*, the first vessel to enter the West India Dock when it was opened in 1802. The Gun has an especially cosy and intimate atmosphere, and legend has it that Emma Hamilton and Lord Nelson often met here for private conversation. The house at 3 Coldharbour, just up the road from the pub, is known as 'Nelson's House' and does in fact date from the Admiral's time.

Not all the East End's finest pubs are on the river. One with a fascinating history is the Widow's Son in Devons Road, Bow. Hanging from the ceiling is a collection of currant buns which are a reminder of the widow whose only son went to sea, consoling her that on his

It's Good Friday and a sailor strings up another bun at the Widow's Son pub in Bromley.

return by next Easter they would eat hot cross buns together. Every Good Friday the widow laid a table, setting aside a bun for her son, even though he never came back. After her death the buns were hung from the ceiling of the cottage, which became known as the 'Bun House'. Eventually it was pulled down and a pub put up on the site called the Widow's Son. Every Good Friday, in a custom which now goes back 200 years, another hot cross bun is attached to the bundle.

'Till Three Tides Had Overflowed Them': Execution Dock, Wapping Old Stairs

At the end of the alley leading to the Town of Ramsgate pub in Wapping is a gibbet, a disturbing reminder of Execution Dock which once stood by Wapping Old Stairs. Here, convicted pirates would be hanged and their corpses displayed in chains 'till three tides had overflowed them', a visible deterrent to every sailor as he passed up and down the Thames. The bodies tended to bloat, leading to the expression 'What a wapper!'

The best-known of all the pirates hanged at Execution Dock was Captain William Kidd. Having distinguished himself in the wars against the French, Kidd was sent to America in 1696 in order to clear its coast of pirates. Kidd soon decided that it was more lucrative to become one himself. He was finally captured in 1699 and charged with seizing French ships. Kidd claimed that he had in fact been acting under Admiralty orders, a defence which was never followed up at his Old Bailey trial. Indeed, the whole trial seems to have been a mockery; Kidd had no legal representation, and the only witnesses against him were two members of his own crew, who testified that Kidd had killed one of their colleagues with a bucket. The proceedings were rushed, possibly to prevent the defendant naming certain influential statesmen and politicians who had shared the profits from his exploits.

On 23 May 1701, Kidd was taken to Execution Dock to be hanged. His friends had hatched an escape plot and rushed the soldiers on guard. Unfortunately for them, Kidd, like all condemned men, had got himself drunk and therefore was quite unable to take advantage of the confused situation. He was recaptured and despatched. One of Kidd's ships, supposedly with a fortune of £70,000 on board, has never to this day been found.[1]

The last executions at Execution Dock took place in December 1830.

Truman's and the East End Breweries

Towards the end of the twelfth century the Norman clerk William Fitzstephen wrote a glowing description of London:

Amongst the noble and celebrated cities of the world, that of London, the capital of the kingdom of England, is one of the most renowned, possessing above all others abundant wealth, extensive commerce, great grandeur and magnificence. It is happy in the salubrity of its climate, in the profession of the Christian religion, in the strength of its fortresses, the nature of its situation, the honour of its citizens, and the chastity of its matrons; in its sports too it is most pleasant, and in the production of illustrious men most fortunate.[1]

Fitzstephen did not, however, find London quite perfect: 'The only inconveniences of London are, the immoderate drinking of foolish persons, and the frequent fires.'

The staple drink consumed in the Middle Ages was sweet-tasting ale, downed in huge quantities because of the unhealthy water-supply. Then it was discovered that the addition

Truman's Brewery in Brick Lane, a home of brewing for over three hundred years.

of hops created a new brew which was not only more satisfying but also kept longer. It was called beer. At first there was much hostility to this new drink; one writer in 1542 condemned beer as 'a natural drink for a Dutchman. And now of late days it is much used in England to the detriment of many Englishmen ... for the drink is a cold drink: yet it doth make a man fat and doth inflate the belly ....'[2]

By the late seventeenth century several brewers had begun to transform the industry from its small-scale domestic beginnings into a substantial commercial enterprise, usually located in East London where the smells inevit-

ably caused by brewing could float away into open fields. There was also a good supply of clean fresh water. Joseph Truman entered the industry in 1666 and quickly began to develop the Black Eagle Brewery situated at the north-west end of Brick Lane, Spitalfields. His son Benjamin was born at 4 Princelet Street and had greatly expanded the family firm by the time of his death in 1780. Truman's fortunes are supposed to have been made in 1737 when the then Prince of Wales celebrated the birth of his daughter the Duchess of Brunswick by dispensing free beer to the crowds. However, they did not think much of the brew and began to throw it into each

27

other's faces. The next day the Prince tried again, but this time he handed out Truman's and the crowd was rather more appreciative.[3] The fact that Benjamin Truman was knighted in 1760 shows how important the large breweries had become in terms of political influence. Other partners joined the business, notably Messrs Hanbury and Buxton, both of whom have streets in the vicinity named after them. During the nineteenth century Truman's claimed that they manufactured enough beer 'to float a seventy-four-gun ship'. It was indeed the largest brewing company in the world.

The directors of Truman's were always careful to maintain their local connections.[4]

They played a part in the preservation of Epping Forest, they heavily endowed the London Hospital, and they paid the salary of the curate at Christ Church, Spitalfields. Their buildings in Brick Lane were radically redesigned in 1977, and a modern gleaming office stands opposite the Vat House and the stables. The older buildings are beautifully reflected in the shining surface of the new, giving anyone interested in architecture the best of both worlds. Two other East End breweries date from the eighteenth century and remain on their old sites: the Albion Brewery in Whitechapel Road and Charrington's in Mile End Road.

Big Ben and Bow Bells:
The Whitechapel Bell Foundry

In the eighteenth century, Whitechapel Road was lined with the attractive houses of the wealthy who wanted to live in what was then countryside and enjoy the view over the neighbouring fields. Bulldozer and bomb have done their best between them to wipe out these buildings, but they have not been totally successful. On the south side of Whitechapel Road between St Mary's Gardens and the East London Mosque stands an attractive Georgian terraced building which is now – as it has been for the last 250 years – the home of the Whitechapel Bell Foundry. It is one of only two such businesses in the country, the other being in Loughborough.

Originally started in 1570, the foundry first stood on the north side of Whitechapel High Street – roughly where Woolworth is now. It moved in 1738, and over the centuries it has become the country's foremost producer of bells, especially for cathedrals such as St Paul's and Southwark. 'Great Peter' of York Minster came from the foundry as well as 'Great Tom'

The Whitechapel Bell Foundry, established in 1420 and housed in this building since 1738.

Some of the bells cast at the Whitechapel Bell Foundry.

of Lincoln Cathedral and the 'Bow Bells' of St Mary-le-Bow in Cheapside whose sound makes one a cockney. The 13½-ton 'Big Ben' of the Houses of Parliament was made here, too.[1] Everything to do with the bells is carried out on this site, from the moulding and casting to the frame construction, and a visit to the foundry is a privilege. Sometimes they leave the workshop doors open, and one can see bells dating back to the sixteenth century (they are always named and dated very carefully) waiting for attention. The sense of history and pride is very strong here, and one feels that the men (and recent woman) are very much in touch with those who have gone before them in the mysteries of their craft.[2]

Also worth investigating is the old street-sign on the east side of the foundry in Plumber's Row. Faded and difficult to read, the pedestrian can just make out the inscription 'This is Baynes Street 1746', which immediately takes the passer-by back to the days before houses were numbered and streets properly signposted.

Judge Jeffreys and the Red Cow

One visitor who is supposed to have enjoyed seeing the pirates hanged at Execution Dock was Judge Jeffreys, who reputedly visited the Angel pub in Bermondsey on the south side of the river, sitting there with his drink and gazing over contentedly at the poor wretches opposite. Some of the stories told about Jeffreys are fictional, but the true stories are so vivid as to require no embellishment.

Born in Wrexham in 1648, Jeffreys trained as a lawyer and, although notorious for his drinking habits and bad manners, hitched his star to the Stuart régime and rose quickly through the legal hierarchy. In September 1685, at the age of only thirty-seven, he was appointed Lord Chancellor and sent down to the West Country by James II to punish those involved in the Duke of Monmouth's failed rebellion. Jeffreys went to work with a will, inflicting such punishments at the 'Bloody Assizes' that his name is still a byword for ferocity. One woman was sentenced to be whipped through all the market-towns of Dorset; a man called John Tutchin was to be flogged every fortnight for seven years; up to 300 people were hanged and another 800 transported into what was effectively slavery. Moreover Jeffreys made a personal fortune out of trading pardons, so that his hypocrisy matched his cruelty.

Yet Jeffreys' misdeeds were eventually to catch up with him. In 1688, James fled the throne, forcing his favourites and placemen to try to do likewise. Jeffreys disguised himself as a sailor, shaved off his eyebrows and hired a collier to take him to Holland. But, while the vessel was being loaded with the 35,000 guineas and the silver which he had amassed, Jeffreys went ashore for a drink at the Red Cow (now the Town of Ramsgate) in Wapping. This foolhardy and incomprehensible behaviour is explained by the fact that Jeffreys was suffering from a cancerous growth whose pain was only relieved by copious draughts of alcohol.

It was Jeffreys' bad luck to be recognised by another customer at the Red Cow that day. This man, a local moneylender, had once appeared before the judge and left the court shaken and murmuring 'While I live, I shall never forget that terrible countenance'. He didn't. Jeffreys was seized by a mob, and only the swift intervention of the militia saved him from being lynched. There then arose the cruel irony of Jeffreys begging to be incarcerated for his own safety in the Tower of London, the very place where several of his own victims had ended their days.

From this point Jeffreys' decline was sad. Deserted by his friends and associates, knowing that the crowd outside was only too eager to get their hands on him, and with his health deteriorating swiftly, Jeffreys' demise was rapid. One day a barrel of Colchester oysters arrived for Jeffreys, his favourite food. 'Thank God, I still have some friends left,' he said. He opened the barrel to find only shells and a hangman's halter. Jeffreys died in the Tower of London on 18 April 1689, aged forty.[1]

The Huguenots:
The East End's First Wave of Immigrants

In 1701 the writer, journalist, businessman and spy Daniel Defoe published a poem called *The True-Born Englishman* in which he poured ironic scorn on those who claimed that English racial purity was being irretrievably tainted by alien immigrants. He argued that we are 'a mongrel race':

> Thus from a mixture of all kinds began
> That heterogeneous thing, an English-
>   man . . . .
> We have been Europe's sink, the jakes
>   where she
> Voids all her outcast progeny . . . .
> A Turkish horse can show more ancestry
> To prove his well-descended family . . . .
> These are the heroes that despise the
>   Dutch,
> And rail at new-come foreigners so
>   much,
> Great families of yesterday we show,
> And lords whose parents were the Lord
>   knows who.

Defoe's poem is of particular relevance today in the light of a recent upsurge of racial attacks on Asian people in Tower Hamlets and Newham. By and large, however, with certain dishonourable exceptions, the capital's treatment of immigrants has been to its credit — certainly when compared with the record of other countries. And nowhere else is London's cosmopolitanism more evident than in the East End where different cultures mix and sometimes clash. Walk along Fieldgate Street which runs south of Whitechapel Road. There, within fifty yards of each other, are a tiny synagogue and a massive new mosque sporting bulbous domes like giant gilded onions. From here the tape-recorded muezzin's call to prayer booms out over a district which contains Irish Catholic churches, German Catholic churches and German Protestant churches.

Three Jewish burial-grounds are still to be found within half a mile of each other on the north side of Mile End Road, together with the East End's five working synagogues which administer to the 7,000 Jews still living in the area. Stand by the main entrance to Southwark Park on the south side of the river and note the Norwegian church, the Finnish church and the Swedish church. Or there is the plaque outside the doctors' surgery in Brick Lane which carries its information in Bengali and almost as an afterthought in English. The conglomeration of these peoples and their cultures explain in part the curious vibrancy of the East End in the face of persistent economic deprivation. Certainly there are pockets of migrants elsewhere in London — the Chinese in Soho, the Italians in Clerkenwell, West Indians in Brixton — but it is only in the East End and Docklands that so many diverse groups are to be found together.

Yet why should it be the East End which has attracted successive waves of newcomers? Once again the answer lies partly in the pattern of development of the City of London where the trades functioned as guilds which acted as a combination of employers' association and closed shop. It was impossible to set up in business as, say, a butcher, a fishmonger or a mercer until one had undergone a seven-year apprenticeship and had been received into the appropriate guild — unless of course one worked outside the City where the writ of the guilds did not run. For newcomers to London with no chance of being accepted into a guild, residence in the suburbs was a necessity. However, this does not answer the question why the East End should have been so attractive and not South London, which after all was also outside the City's jurisdiction and offered space for building and development.

A photograph taken in the 1930s of two of the East End's last surviving weavers.

One short answer is that new arrivals in London usually landed on the north bank of the river near the Tower of London. A hundred years ago, for example, the thousands of Jewish refugees coming here from Poland and Russia disembarked at Irongate Stairs close to St Katharine's Dock. This meant that Aldgate and Whitechapel were close at hand. Few of these immigrants would have had anywhere else to go, and thus they settled where no extra expense was required in moving. The headquarters of the Jews' Temporary Shelter was set up in 1885 at 82 Leman Street and then moved to Mansell Street nearby. In any case, accommodation and food in the East End were relatively cheap – as indeed they should have been for the poor quality on offer. Arthur Morrison in his documentary novel *A Child of the Jago* (1896)

was just one of the many observers who pointed out that if rents charged for all the one-room slum lodgings in the East End were added together they would equal, space for space, that obtainable from houses in Kensington.

The first wave of immigrants to colonise the East End were the French Huguenots who fled religious persecution in France.[1] The Edict of Nantes (1595) had guaranteed freedom of worship to the Huguenots, or Protestant followers of John Calvin, but in 1685 Louis XIV revoked the Edict and launched a campaign against all French people who were not Catholics. Over 200,000 Huguenots left France in the years immediately after 1685; of whom about 60,000 went to Holland and slightly fewer to England. Most settled in three quarters of London: in Soho, in

A fine example of the craftmanship used in many East End Georgian houses.

Wandsworth, but mainly in Spitalfields where the Huguenots quickly established a silk-weaving industry. Like Soho, the street-pattern of Spitalfields is still today very much as it was when the district was laid out in the late seventeenth century, as is clear when John Rocque's map of Spitalfields in the 1740s is compared with the *A-Z* map of the same district.[2] As for the Huguenot presence today, a stroll around Spitalfields takes the walker along Fleur-de-Lis Street, Nantes Passage, Calvin Street and, in Bethnal Green, to Weavers' Fields and Shuttle Street. Often, too, a glance up at the attics of many Spitalfields houses, especially in Fournier Street, reveals the long-windowed lofts in which the weavers tried to make the most of every scrap of daylight. Also still visible outside a number of houses are the handsticks which hang down over the pavement, used by the weavers as their trade signs. A house in Fournier Street bears a painted fleur-de-lis above its fine eighteenth-century doorway.

Some Huguenot weavers accumulated substantial fortunes, as is demonstrated by a few surviving houses in Spital Square, Elder Street and Fournier Street with their splendid carved doorcases and decorative drainpipes.[3] Sometimes a front door is left open and it is possible to catch a glimpse of fine panelling and original staircases made of mahogany and walnut. The Huguenots set up their own hospital in the neighbourhood in 1708, founded by de Gastigny, William III's master of Buckhounds, and they also stamped their religion on the area. By 1700 nine French nonconformist churches had been established in Spitalfields.

There seems to have been little hostility towards the newcomers. For one thing they brought with them much valued skills, for they were not only weavers but also jewellers, engravers, printers, watchmakers and goldsmiths. There was no native silk-weaving industry with a guild to protect it and, paradoxically, the Huguenots were able to profit from the English aristocracy's desire to imitate French fashions. In any case the Huguenots were, as might be expected, vehemently antagonistic towards the Englishman's traditional enemy, the French. In 1694, when the Bank of England was incorporated in order to raise money to fight the French, it was the Huguenot community which put up a considerable amount of the finance. Seven of the Bank's twenty-four founder-directors were Huguenots, including the first governor Sir John Houblon.[4] The Huguenots were rapidly integrated into London life; by the second half of the eighteenth century, for instance, their use of the French language had died away. Their churches, too, closed down, leaving behind only the French Protestant Church which remains in Soho Square.

As for the Spitalfields silk-weaving industry, it was handicapped from the start by the appalling English climate which prevented the growth of the mulberry trees on which the silkworms fed. Of the hundreds of trees planted, only one can still be seen today, hidden away in the little garden of the House of St Barnabas in Soho Square where it stands gnarled but defiant. Until recently another tree stood in the courtyard of Mulberry House in Victoria Park Square and there is also a Mulberry Street in Whitechapel. The lack of home-grown trees meant that the weavers were dangerously dependent on supplies from abroad. The trade was reasonably secure when foreign silks were prohibited as imports, as they were from 1766. However, it was disastrous when in 1860 the Government's free-trade policy permitted the duty-free import of French material, although by then competition from the North of England and the introduction of the power loom had already seriously weakened the Spitalfields industry. In 1824, 50,000 people in East London were employed in the silk industry; by 1880 the figure had shrunk to just 3,300.[5] The best way to get an impression of the fine quality of the weavers' work is to visit the exhibits upstairs at the Bethnal Green Museum of Childhood. Even though the Huguenots' culture may have been assimilated, it is estimated that two out of every three English people today have Huguenot blood in their veins.[6]

Almshouses in the East End

The rural charms of East London in the eighteenth century and its relatively cheap land prices meant that it was an ideal spot for the City companies to build almshouses for their elderly members. Fresh air, open fields, companionship – these almshouses must have provided a haven of peace for their inmates, even if daily attendance at the prominently sited chapel was obligatory.

There were dozens of almshouses in the East End – Shoreditch alone had nineteen by the early eighteenth century – but as the tide of building flowed further eastwards during the Victorian period most of these early almshouses were demolished and their inhabitants moved further out into the countryside. One of the East End's greatest pleasures, however, is provided by the handful of original almshouses which survive, and they are well worth a visit. They offer a thoroughly rewarding experience for anyone interested in domestic architecture who would appreciate their cottage charm. They often have beautifully tended gardens, too.[1]

Pride of place must go to the Trinity Almshouses along the Mile End Road which were built by Sir Christopher Wren in 1695. The chapel stands proudly at the end of the path with two lines of intimate redbrick terraced houses facing each other. They are a perfect combination of classical architectural features and common sense. The land for them was provided by a Captain Henry Mudd of Ratcliff, who played a major part in the running of Trinity House during the seventeenth century. This organisation was granted

The Trinity Almshouses on Mile End Road, paid for by Captain Mudd and built by Sir Christopher Wren.

its charter by Henry VIII in 1514 and supervises Britain's lighthouses and river pilots. Its first master, Sir Thomas Spert, was buried at St Dunstan's on Stepney Green where his memorial can be seen. The inscriptions on the Trinity Almshouses still proclaim Mudd's intention that they should house 'twenty eight decayed masters and commanders of ships, or the widows of such'. The gable ends exhibit perfectly detailed model ships complete with the rigging. It is touching to think that the architect of St Paul's was happy to design tiny

35

though beautiful homes for impoverished individuals. The almshouses were almost pulled down at the end of the nineteenth century, but a campaign to save them was led by William Morris. This gave rise to the publication *The Survey of London* which still continues. Though the buildings were damaged during the Second World War, they have been well restored.

The Ironmongers' Almshouses built in 1714 under the will of Sir Robert Geffrye are now the home of the Geffrye Museum of Furniture, a treasure of the East End whose future is uncertain because of the imminent abolition of the Inner London Education Authority which runs it. It is a gallery of period rooms carefully furnished and decorated according to the taste of a particular age, and one can walk from the oak furniture and rush lights of the sixteenth century through the restrained elegance of the eighteenth century and the opulence of a room furnished in 1851 to a perfect 1930s lounge. This period-room approach was introduced by Marjorie Quennell, co-author of the pioneering *History of Everyday Things in England*. It is one of the nicest places in London, and its staff are charming. It is surely inconceivable that the Geffrye Museum should do anything else but flourish and prosper.

Other almshouses which have been recently renovated are the Drapers' Almshouses in Rainhill Way (formerly Priscilla Road) in Bow. They take a bit of finding, but the effort is worth it. Once occupying three sides of a quadrangle, like the Trinity Almshouses, with six houses on each side, all that remains is the chapel and four houses on the south side. An inscription records that the almshouses were provided for in the will of John Edmunson, 'Saylemaker'.

Also worth a visit are the Dame Jane Mico Almshouses of 1856 which stand on the south side facing St Dunstan's Stepney Green, and the almshouses of 1860 tucked away in Puma Court off Norton Folgate. No longer in existence, but worth a mention because of their founder's name, are the Bancroft Almshouses of 1735 which once stood on the site of the present Queen Mary College, Mile End Road. Bancroft seems to have been a repellent man who amassed his fortune through the extortions he practised as a City officer. He was obviously concerned about his resurrection on Judgement Day and specified in his will that for his coffin 'the top or lid thereof be hung with strong hinges, neither to be nailed, screwed, locked down, or fastened any other way, but to open freely, and without any trouble, like to the top of a trunk'.[2]

Three East End Masterpieces: Nicholas Hawksmoor's Churches

In 1710 a High Church Tory government took office, worried amongst many other things by what it saw as the heretical tendencies of London's growing population. In particular it was concerned that the capital's new suburbs springing up outside the boundaries of the City were without suitable churches. In 1711 this administration passed the Fifty New

Churches Act, proposing to erect additional churches for the villages of London such as Bermondsey, Shadwell and Limehouse. Funds were provided by a tax on coal entering London. In fact the ambitions of the Government drastically exceeded its resources. By March 1726 the commissioners entrusted with carrying out the work were admitting

One of the finest views in London: Nicholas Hawksmoor's Christ Church at the end of Brushfield Street, Spitalfields

that 'ye Expence of building with stone, purchasing Scites for Churches, church yards and ministers houses is so very great and does so far exceed the Calculations formerly made that ye Committee Conceive it will be utterly impracticable to build one Half of the Churches at first proposed'.[1] In all, twelve churches were built together with some repairs and improvements to existing buildings. It was the greatest good fortune for the East End that three of the twelve were erected here, and all by one of Britain's finest architects, Nicholas Hawksmoor.

Born in Nottinghamshire in 1661, the son of a farmer, the young Hawksmoor was lucky enough to begin his career at eighteen as 'Scholar and Domestic Clerk' to Sir Christopher Wren, working with him on Chelsea Hospital, Greenwich Hospital, the City churches and Westminster Abbey. He was a strong enough character, however, to develop an unmistakable style of his own. His buildings are powerful and passionate. In his private life, a contemporary obituary noted, 'he was a tender Husband, a loving Father and a most agreeable companion'.[2] His only failing seems to have been that he suffered from gout. (The character portrayed in Peter Ackroyd's *Hawksmoor* bears no relation whatsoever to the eighteenth-century architect.)[3]

Hawksmoor's St Anne's, Limehouse. The mysterious stone pyramid is just visible in front of the church.

Hawksmoor's three East End churches were and, miraculously, still are Christ Church, Spitalfields, St Anne's, Limehouse, and St George's in the East. Their soaring majesty ensured that they stamped themselves indelibly on the landscape; their lofty towers and spires still dominate the horizon. With their mastery of form and space they could have been built by no one else. For centuries St Anne's was an international landmark, being the first major building seen by ships from all countries as they journeyed up the Thames to the Port of London. Christ Church has a tower and steeple of 225 feet that looks down on Spitalfields, while St George's in the East possesses the most extraordinary pepper-pot turrets. The exteriors are of fine Portland stone which gleams at pedestrians when recently cleaned, as is the case with St Anne's, and inside giant columns support massive ceilings and give the visitor the impression that he has wandered into a cathedral. The only way to appreciate the three churches is to visit them; for anyone interested in London, let alone the East End, they are a 'must'.

The building of the churches was fraught with difficulties owing to financial problems. In November 1723, for example, Hawksmoor is to be found recommending the employment of a workman to prevent pilfering, 'he having bin very Useful in Preserving the said Buildings from Mischife daily done by the Mobb'.[4] Similarly the actual consecration of all three churches was delayed by the slowness in raising money to pay the rectors. This was a sign of things to come. The character of Spitalfields, Shadwell and Limehouse deteriorated over the next two centuries, and their churches were dragged down with them. For instance, the churchyard of Christ Church was commonly known as 'Itchy Park' because of the tramps and beggars who slept in it at night and who rubbed themselves against the railings. Jack London came here in the winter of 1902–3: 'It was a welter of rags and filth, of all manner of loathsome skin diseases, open

Nicholas Hawksmoor's St George's in the East, scene of the famous religious riots in 1859 and 1860.

sores, bruises, grossness, indecency, leering monstrosities and bestial faces. A chill raw wind was blowing, and these creatures huddled there in their rags, sleeping for the most part, or trying to sleep.'[5]

Lightning damaged Christ Church in 1841, although this disaster was nothing when compared with the Victorian 'improvements' in 1866 when the interior was mutilated by ripping out the galleries and box pews. By 1958 the church was in such a sorry state that it was actually closed on safety grounds, but it is now being restored to some of its former magnificence by the removal of the nineteenth-century alterations. The crypt functions as a rehabilitation centre, and each summer an ambitious and successful music festival is held in the church. St Anne's, Limehouse, was badly damaged by a fire in 1850, and it took six years to raise the money to restore the building. It still contains the highest church clock in London; until Big Ben took over in 1857 it was London's main timekeeper.[6] As for St George's in the East, its interior was blown out during the Blitz in 1941, leaving behind Hawksmoor's exterior. A modern church has been constructed inside the shell of the old, meaning that this is the only church in London which is really two

churches. The crypt has been cleared of its 764 lead coffins, and it is hoped to turn it into a local arts centre.

One last Hawksmoor mystery remains. In the churchyard of St Anne's lies a stone pyramid. Why? Nobody knows for certain. Some historians claim that several sea-captains are buried underneath, others that it was an embellishment to the church that Hawksmoor was unable to include. The more imaginative hint at extra-terrestial involvement. But, whatever the explanation, it is just part of the endless fascination of Hawksmoor's three East End masterpieces.[7]

Dick Turpin and Jack Sheppard

One form of crime not peculiar to East London but perhaps especially frequent here during the eighteenth century was highway robbery. Each week hundreds of travellers would make their way to and from Essex and East Anglia along Whitechapel High Street and Whitechapel Road, which were lined with travellers' inns. Most of these have now been converted into pubs, although the Queen's Head in Fieldgate Street still retains its covered archway under which the coaches loaded and unloaded their passengers. Whitechapel Road, Mile End Road and Bow Road offered many opportunities to the intrepid highwaymen. For one thing there was no lighting (anyone who can remember the blackout during the Blitz will have a fair idea of what that meant), and for another the width of these roads enabled thieves to lurk in the nearby alleys and still get a good view of the passing travellers. One reason for Whitechapel Road's width was because the Statute of Westminster passed in 1283 stipulated that major roads should be 'enlarged so that there be neither dyke, tree nor bush whereby a man may lurk

to do hurt' up to within 200 feet of either verge.[1] In that case why aren't all London roads wider? As the centuries passed developers began to encroach on the verges. Whitechapel Road and the others mentioned above were also, however, drove-roads, and the cattle, no respecters of orderly traffic-signs or regulations, kept the thoroughfare wide by brute force. Mile End Waste was where the cattle grazed.

The most famous highwayman of the eighteenth century was surely Dick Turpin. He is thought to have preyed on travellers passing through East London, but it is difficult to distinguish ugly fact from the fictions preferred by subsequent hack writers, playwrights and novelists. For a start he was not the dashing and glamorous figure of popular legend; a 'Wanted' poster once described him as 'very much marked with small pox, about five feet nine inches tall, a butcher, about twenty six years of age'.

Turpin was born in Hempstead, Essex, in 1705 and was initially apprenticed to a butcher in Whitechapel until he was discharged 'for the brutality of his manners'. Undaunted, he set up his own butcher's shop on the fringes of Epping Forest during which business he became involved in the receiving and selling of stolen deer. Turpin decided to join some thieves called 'the Gregory Gang', notorious for torturing their victims during robberies. This gang's activities came to an abrupt end in February 1735 when one of its members was captured and promptly informed on his former associates, most of whom were eventually caught and executed. Turpin, however managed to escape to Holland where he lay low for several months before returning to Essex and carrying out further robberies together with another outlaw called Matthew King. The area around the East End seems to have been a particularly rewarding hunting-ground for Turpin and King, especially the fields between Hackney and London which survive today, much reduced, as London Fields. Still attractive to criminals, this rather threadbare space is regarded as 'a mugger's paradise'.

On 30 April 1737, Turpin and King were ambushed by law officers while having a drink in the Old Red Lion pub just off Whitechapel High Street. King was fatally wounded, possibly shot in the back by Turpin as a diversion. Turpin escaped to Epping Forest where he continued to plunder unsuspecting travellers despite the £200 reward on his head. After a while Turpin thought it prudent to move northwards to Yorkshire where he was less well known. He assumed a new identity as John Palmer, horse dealer. Needless to say, few of the horses with which he dealt had been obtained legally.

In October 1738 the hot-headed Turpin got himself foolishly caught up in a street-brawl and was detained in the local house of correction at Beverley, where the investigating magistrates soon realised that Palmer was in fact the infamous Dick Turpin. On 7 April 1739 he was hanged outside York Castle, so friendless that he had to pay for mourners to watch his exit. Inevitably perhaps, there arose several legends with which his name is indelibly linked, no matter what historians may write to the contrary. He never owned a horse called 'Black Bess', nor does the double grave at St George's churchyard, York, contain the remains of Turpin and Black Bess; instead Turpin's companion is a common felon.[2] Neither did Turpin ever ride fifteen hours non-stop from London to York in order to give himself an alibi – a feat which had in fact been accomplished in 1676 by an earlier highwayman called John 'Swift Nicks' Nevison. But who today remembers Nevison? No one wrote a story about him. Yet, thanks to Harrison Ainsworth's exciting novel *Rookwood* (1824) and other publications which glamorise him, everyone 'remembers' Turpin. The Old Red Lion, where Turpin was nearly captured, was rebuilt at the end of the nineteenth century and still stands close to the south exit of Aldgate East station, although it is now empty and tatty. A hollow in Epping Forest is traditionally pointed out as 'Turpin's Cave' which he used as a hideaway.[3]

A near-contemporary of Turpin was another famous highwayman with East End links, Jack Sheppard. He was born in March 1702 in White's Row, Spitalfields, where his father was a carpenter. He was baptised at St Dunstan's, Stepney Green. Sheppard began work as a linen draper's apprentice in Drury Lane but after a few years decided that lawful activity did not earn him enough to buy presents for his girlfriend, Elizabeth Lyon, otherwise known by her friends as 'Edgworth Bess'. Sheppard later had another girlfriend with the even more wonderful name of 'Poll Maggot'. After a short-lived criminal career which included two escapes from Newgate Prison, Sheppard was 'shopped' by the double-crossing Jonathan Wild, who in fact invented the 'double-cross': when he put two crosses against a man's name, it showed that Wild was going to turn him over to the authorities. Sheppard was executed at Tyburn in November

1724. Wild himself was hanged there in the following year. The profession of highwayman was gradually curtailed by the introduction of banks and cheques as well as by the more stringent licensing of taverns and inns which prevented them from being criminal haunts. The enclosure movement eliminated many tracts of forest and wood, while the Bow Street Horse Patrol at work from 1763 made the pursuit of their particular livelihood ever more difficult for the few remaining highwaymen.

'The London': The London Hospital, Whitechapel Road

Wedged between Whitechapel Road and Commercial Road is the London Hospital, the largest general hospital in the country. A stroll through its sprawling buildings reveals both eighteenth-century classical façades and twentieth-century Portakabins, an eclectic collection which has grown in response to the constant demands placed on 'the London'. Most East Enders at some stage in their lives owe a debt of gratitude to this place, and anyone working at the hospital today gets 'served well' by the local stallholders on Whitechapel Waste.[1]

When it was first opened along Whitechapel Road in the 1750s, the London Hospital stood not in the middle of a busy and densely populated district but surrounded by fields and farms. Engravings of that time depict an almost rural idyll with the hospital gazing out like some stately home over the neighbouring countryside. The decision to build here on Whitechapel Road was deliberate. Originally founded in 1740 by a group of public-spirited individuals concerned that the growth of London's population was unmatched by any increase in medical facilities, its first home was a small house in Featherstone Street off the City Road. In the next year the London Infirmary, as it was initially called, moved further east to a building in Prestcot Street. Within a few years this in turn proved too small, and in 1751 the Building Committee bought up plots of land to the south of Whitechapel Road.

The site selected was by no means perfect. An open sewer still ran down the middle of Whitechapel Road, while a huge rubbish-dump over thirty yards high lay mouldering to one side. This 'Mount' was a familiar landmark; City-dwellers wandering eastwards usually turned back at this point.[2] Children often played on such tips, and it was eyesores like these which gave rise to the cry 'I'm the King of the Castle', to be met by the accurate retort 'Get down, you dirty rascal!' This rubbish-tip was eventually cleared away, but its legacy lives on in the names of nearby Mount Terrace and East Mount Street.

Patients were admitted into the London from 1757, and since then its development has offered a microcosm of East End history. For example, one of its first surgeons was a Huguenot refugee, Gabriel Risolière, an early example of just how much newcomers to the East End have contributed to their new home. In the nineteenth century the hospital specialised in dealing with the accident cases frequently brought in from the docks, and it also established a Jewish ward serviced by its own kitchens, cooks and plates. At Passover time the food was served on special dishes kept all the year round for this single purpose.[3]

Not surprisingly, several well-known East End figures have had links with the London Hospital. One was a twenty-one-year-old Dubliner who arrived at the London in April

An eighteenth-century view of the London Hospital, Whitechapel Road, in its then rural setting.

1866, intending to take a medical degree before working as a missionary in China. While he was a student the young man, Thomas Barnardo, found himself drawn into charitable work in the East End, being appointed the superintendent of a ragged school in Ernest Street. It was soon clear to Barnardo that China would have to wait. In the East End of a city which had but recently hosted the Great Exhibition and was recognised as the 'workshop of the world', there was unbelievable poverty and suffering, especially amongst homeless children. That same year Barnardo established a shelter just off Ben Jonson Road (a plaque on the side of 58 Solent House marks its site), in what had once been a donkey-shed. One of the little boys who visited the shelter was Jim Jarvis, a waif who introduced Barnardo to countless other urchins sleeping out. In December 1870, Barnardo opened his first home at 18 Stepney Causeway under the patronage of Lord Shaftesbury. On one occasion Barnardo had to turn away a young boy called 'Carrots' because there was simply no more accommodation. Carrots died of exposure, and from then on Barnardo adopted a charter which read 'No Destitute Child Ever Refused Admission'. For the next thirty-five years Barnardo devoted his life to the children of East London, establishing his headquarters in Rhodeswell Road at the Edinburgh Castle, a once notorious pub which he bought in 1872 for £4,200.[4] He got rid of the drink and opened it as the Edinburgh Castle Coffee Palace, adorning the counter with the maxim 'Wine is a mocker, Strong drink is raging'. By the time of his death in 1905 from overwork, Barnardo had rescued and trained nearly 60,000 destitute children and assisted 250,000 more in want.[5]

Also at the London, but this time as an

inmate rather than as a would-be doctor, was Joseph Merrick, the so-called 'Elephant Man' who had been exhibited as a freak at 123 Whitechapel Road, directly opposite the London Hospital. The consulting surgeon, Frederick Treves, was horrified by this exploitation and he took Merrick under the protection of the hospital. For the last five years of his life, until April 1890, Merrick had his own room here.

Until 1948 when the London Hospital was integrated into the National Health Service, it was financed purely out of voluntary effort. In the 1890s, for instance, it required nearly £30,000 every year from public subscriptions and donations, and in a poor area such as the East End it was always difficult to raise these vital funds. It is doubtful if the London would have survived without the untiring efforts of Lord Knutsford, who was chairman of the hospital from 1896 until his death in 1931. Known affectionately as 'The King of Beggars' because of his ingenious efforts to raise money, Knutsford is estimated to have brought in £5 million to the hospital.[6] Many pages in A. E. Clark-Kennedy's excellent history of the London Hospital are devoted to this desperate struggle to keep afloat. How sad that future histories of the hospital in the 1980s will have a similar story to tell since money-boxes are once again being shaken in the streets in an effort to raise essential funds.

David Garrick in the East End

The end of the Theatre and the Curtain by no means concluded the East End's importance in the annals of English theatre. When Charles II was restored to the throne in 1660 he granted royal patents to two companies, which finally became the two theatres of Covent Garden and Drury Lane. Legally, these two playhouses alone were permitted to put on plays, but gradually they found themselves challenged by a number of smaller playhouses, one of which was built in Goodman's Fields, Whitechapel, in 1729. The two patents launched a series of legal complaints against the Goodman's Fields theatre, but the magistrates threw out the case. Henry Giffard, its proprietor, staged several plays by Henry Fielding, who was later to be known as a magistrate and a novelist. These plays attacked the Whig government of the day led by Sir Robert Walpole, Britain's first prime minister. The latter responded in June 1737 with the Stage Licensing Act which reinforced the legal control of Covent Garden and Drury Lane as

David Garrick, the leading eighteenth-century actor who made his London début in the East End.

well as instituting stage censorship under the Lord Chamberlain, a fact of theatrical life until 1968.

Yet Giffard managed to keep his East End theatre going by cleverly exploiting a loophole in the 1737 Act which prohibited the staging of plays 'for Hire, Gain, or Reward'; but what if the public paid for a musical concert and just happened to see the rehearsal of a play thrown in free? Or if tickets were purchased at nearby shops which entitled customers to admittance to a place which was at that very moment putting on the private showing of a play? For several years Giffard was successful in this stratagem, arousing the wrath of the patents but remaining unpersecuted by the authorities. He was eventually undone by his own success.[1]

On 9 October 1741 the young and unknown David Garrick made his professional London début at the Goodman's Fields theatre, playing the rôle of Richard III. Within days the news of this startling new perfor-mer's histrionic gifts had spread all over London and the theatre was besieged by wealthy patrons demanding seats. One contemporary observer wrote that 'There are a dozen dukes of a night at Goodman's Fields sometimes'.[2] The patents brought all possible pressure to bear on this serious threat to their continued existence, and when the Goodman's Fields theatre closed at the end of the season it was never to reopen. There is still a Goodman Street and a Goodman's Stile, but the site of the theatre is now covered by a complex of modern buildings belonging to the National Westminster Bank. As for David Garrick, he quickly became eighteenth-century London's most famous actor as well as being the manager of the Drury Lane Theatre for nearly thirty years. One of his most famous roles was as King Lear, and legend has it that he based his performance on the distraught father whose two-year-old daughter fell to her death from a window in Leman Street.[3]

More Newcomers to the East End: Scandinavians, Germans, Irish and Chinese

London's position as a world port ensured that many sailors of different nationalities spent some time in the East End, while a few settled here. William Wordsworth, in *The Prelude* (1805), depicted London's exotic internationalism:

> . . . The mighty concourse I surveyed
> With no unthinking mind, well pleased
>   to note
> Among the crowd all specimens of man,
> Through all the colours which the sun
>   bestows
> And every character of form and face:
> The Swede, the Russian; from the genial
>   south,

> The Frenchman, and the Spaniard; from
>   remote
> America, the Hunter-Indian; Moors,
> Malays, Lascars, the Tartar, the Chinese,
> And Negro ladies in white muslin
>   gowns . . . .

One substantial community which had settled in the East End was the Scandinavians, drawn to London because of the demand for their timber needed for the rebuilding of the capital after the Great Fire of 1666. There was even a saying current that 'the Norwe-gians warmed themselves comfortably by the Fire of London'.[1] In 1696 the Danish and

Norwegian settlers in Wellclose Square built themselves a church, paid for by Christian V of Denmark. A friend of the London observer Ned Ward remarked cruelly of the congregation soon after this church was opened that they were

> such a parcel of wainscot-fac'd Christians they were enough to scare an English parson out of the pulpit, were he to ascend amongst 'em, and stunk so of pitch and tar that as soon as ever he had clap'd his nose into the church he thought himself between decks. Their uncomb'd locks, tobacco breaths, and seafaring apparel, added such further fragrancy to the former that no rats that had taken sanctuary in a Cheshire cheese could have smelt more frowzily.[2]

A Swedish church was built nearby in Prince's Square in 1729. The Danish church was pulled down in 1869 and replaced by the school now in Wellclose Square, while the Swedish church survived until after the First World War. Its site is now called Swedenborg Gardens, although the land was auctioned off in March 1988 and will doubtless quickly be developed. Both churches had become marooned on the 'wrong' side of the river: it was the Surrey Docks in Rotherhithe which handled the Scandinavian timber from the middle of the nineteenth century, and the Finnish, Norwegian and Swedish churches are today in Rotherhithe.

Another foreign community based in the East End were the Germans, most of whom originated from Hamburg and worked in the district's sugar-refineries. They lived in or near Shadwell. Thomas Burke estimated that by 1708 the German settlement numbered some 2,000 people, a substantial figure even though little is known of their history.[3] Sugar-bounties finally ruined the trade in the 1860s. The German legacy today rests on the two German churches in Whitechapel, the German Sailors' Home in Poplar and, until it

was recently closed, the German Hospital in Ritson Road, Hackney, which was originally founded in 1845. One German enterprise does, however, remain a well-known East End landmark, namely the little shop founded by Mr Spiegelhalter, the jeweller and watchmaker who set up in Whitechapel in 1828 after leaving the Black Forest in Germany. In 1880, Spiegelhalter's moved to 81 Mile End Road, and there the shop remains, despite the fact that in the 1930s the directors of Wickham's wanted to build a huge department store on the site. The impressive building plans would have meant the removal of Spiegelhalter's. The Mr Spiegelhalter of those days refused all offers to vacate his premises, and finally the grand facade of Wickham's had to be built around the little firm of jewellers. This architectural compromise remains today to amuse those with a taste for visual oddity and to delight anyone who appreciates the triumph of the individual. Wickham's now contains the 'Direct Bargain Centre', and the Spiegelhalter business is carried on in Loughton in Essex. This incident gave rise to a new local and most expressive word: to 'spiegelhalt', meaning to put a spanner in the works![4]

The Germans often worked in the smelly and dangerous sugar-refineries because native Londoners shied away from accepting such labour. From the Germans to the Irish to the setting-up by London Transport of recruitment offices in the West Indies in the 1950s, this use of immigrants to do the dirty work is a less gratifying aspect of London life. For centuries the Irish have adopted this rôle. However hard their manual labour, whether as 'navvies', building workers or coal-heavers, it was almost certainly better than conditions back in Ireland. In some cases their willingness to undercut usual rates of pay led to disturbances and riots, the most serious occurring in August 1736 over the rebuilding of St Leonard's, Shoreditch, the church whose towering 192-foot steeple built of Portland stone still dominates the neighbourhood. The contractor had sacked his English workmen, taking in their place Irish labourers prepared to work for half or a third of the wages. The Prime Minister, Sir Robert Walpole, described what happened next: 'On the second evening, the mob was thought to be about 2,000 in number. They now grew more riotous – they attacked a public house kept by an Irishman, where the Irish resorted and victualled, broke down all the doors and windows, and quite gutted the house.' The Riot Act was read by the magistrates, to no effect, after which the Guards were called out from the Tower of London: 'Upon the appearance of the guards, the mob retired, shifted from one street and alley to another, and gave no resistance, and by break of day all were dispersed.'[5] The Guards had to be called out the next night as well.

For years to come the Irish in London functioned as convenient scapegoats, even though Daniel Defoe pointed out that there were 'ten thousand stout fellows that would spend the last drop of their blood against Popery that did not know whether it be a man or a horse'.[6] During the Gordon Riots (1780) the mob demolished two Catholic chapels in Stepney. The Government paid compensation for the chapel demolished in Virginia Street, Wapping; its replacement is now St Mary's Commercial Road. Not all the anti-Irish feeling sprang from ignorant bigotry. There were some cultural differences which caused problems. The historian Dorothy George has mentioned three insanitary Irish customs common in London which must have aroused much anger in their non-Irish neighbours: the sharing of rooms with pigs and other animals; the habit of tenants of single rooms letting space either permanently or for the night; and the Irish wake during which the burial of the corpse was frequently delayed for days.[7]

In the eighteenth century the Irish population congregrated in Rosemary Lane, now Royal Mint Street. By the Victorian period the unceasing demand for labourers to work on the construction of both the railways and the Underground, as well as the housing required to accommodate the rapid expansion of the East End's population, led to a marked increase in the number of Irish people in London. The famine in Ireland in the 1840s meant that nowhere else in the world could possibly be as bad as at home, and each year saw the migration of thousands of its people. So many came to the East End that there were soon more Irish here than in the whole of Dublin. As migrants had done before them and were to do again later, the Irish preferred to stick together, especially in Wapping and the district around Devons Road in Bow.

Today the distinctive Irish presence is most graphically demonstrated by the number of Catholic churches sprinkled liberally throughout the East End. They range from the massive buildings in North Street, Poplar, and in Underwood Road, Spitalfields, to the medium-sized St Patrick's in Wapping and the much smaller Our Lady of Sienna on Bow Road and Our Lady of the Assumption in Victoria Park Square. One colourful feature of these churches which is often mentioned in memoirs of the East End was the annual processions through the neighbouring streets.[8]

There was some antagonism displayed towards the Chinese community based in Limehouse, mainly because of the popular prejudice which assumed their numbers to be much greater than they actually were. Thomas Burke and Sax Rohmer were the two main culprits; in their writings they gave the impression that the East End was being overrun by some 'Yellow Peril'. The historian Sir Walter Besant, however, put the Chinese population in Limehouse a hundred years ago at less than 100, while the rector of St Anne's Limehouse, estimated that at their peak after the First World War there were never more than 300 Chinese people in Limehouse, living around Limehouse Causeway and Pennyfields.[9]

These streets were both heavily bombed during the Blitz and have never been rebuilt in a nondescript fashion. Nevertheless there are street-names evocative of the Chinese community – Canton Street, Oriental Street, Mandarin Street, Pekin Street, Nankin Street – and also a number of excellent Chinese restaurants, such as the Good Friends in Salmon Lane. Now plans have been drawn up to create a 'Chinatown' in Limehouse on a nine-acre site, containing a Chinese food-court, a Pagoda cinema, a floating restaurant and an oriental-style hotel. The project will cost £180 million. If it does in fact take place then, notwithstanding the small numbers of Chinese who lived in Limehouse in the past, life will imitate fiction and give us another example of 'East End myth' at work.[10]

'The First Godfather': The Career of Joseph Merceron (1764–1839)

One explanation for the public's enduring interest in Ronnie and Reggie Kray is that Reggie, the 'brains' behind the team, realised the importance of 'image', just as politicians do now. The Krays exploited the familiar 'Robin Hood' myth of stealing from the rich to give to the poor – with a judicious share for the middle men! The Krays supported charities such as the British Empire Cancer Campaign as well as the boys' clubs in which they themselves had learnt to become useful boxers. In this respect they were simply following in a well-established tradition, a line of 'kind-hearted' crooks which goes back to Joseph Merceron, the area's first King of Crime.

Merceron was born in 1764 and worked initially as a silk-weaver, being of Huguenot descent. He lived at the north end of Brick Lane. However, he realised that despite the growth of eighteenth-century East London the traditional forms of local government had not altered to keep pace. Based on the unit of the parish church, in this case St Matthew's, Bethnal Green, Merceron was soon able to 'pack' the open Vestry meetings with his own supporters. In any case this part of Bethnal Green was already notorious for its general dissoluteness; the Act of Parliament passed in 1745 in order to complete St Matthew's began: 'Whereas the want of a place for public worship of Almighty God hath been a great cause of increase of dissoluteness of morals and a disregard for religion, too apparent in the younger and poorer sort ... .'[1] Merceron was first elected a churchwarden of St Matthew's in the 1780s, whereupon he effectively ran Bethnal Green as his own personal kingdom, controlling funds intended for the poor simply by altering the rate-book. As a magistrate, too, Merceron put himself in charge of licensing pubs, allowing his own to operate – he controlled eleven and was the agent for another eleven – but closing down those of his rivals. No doubt this steady income enabled him to buy favours. He also curried favour with the local community by encouraging dog-fighting and bull-running in the streets of Bethnal Green.

In May 1818, Merceron was found guilty of stealing what was then the huge sum of £951 1s 3d from public funds. He was fined and imprisoned for eighteen months, but on his release he found that his only significant local adversary, the Reverend Joshua King, the rector of St Matthew's had left the district and Merceron was able to resume his criminal career. He finally died in 1839 at the age of seventy-five. Some historians have argued that Merceron was more of a public-spirited than a criminal-spirited man, suggesting that the ease with which he took up where he had left off in 1818 and his family's continued residence in the district after his death show his popularity. Until more research is done on Merceron it is impossible to say whether or not, like the Krays, he just had a good public-relations team working on his behalf. In the mean time the interested observer can still see the Merceron family tomb in the churchyard of the new St Matthew's, Bethnal Green, built to replace the church badly damaged during the Blitz which would have been familiar to Joseph Merceron. He is also commemorated today by Merceron Street near Cambridge Heath Road and by Merceron House at the junction of Globe Road and Old Ford Road.[2]

An East End Boxing Champion: 'Mendoza the Jew' (1764–1836)

In the 1930s the historian Thomas Burke referred to boxing in the East End as being almost 'a local industry',[1] and in his day the Wonderland and the Premierland were two of the main venues in London. In fact the East End could boast of a heavyweight champion at the end of the eighteenth century in the form of Daniel Mendoza, the boxer who was responsible for turning the vicious and brawling prize-fight into a reasonably well-ordered sport as well as showing that skill could sometimes make up for a lack of size. Being a relatively small man of 5 feet 7 inches, and therefore invariably matched against an opponent both taller and heavier, Mendoza had to rely on brains and not on brawn. Rather than adopting the toe-to-toe stance then common, he was the first boxer to move freely around the ring, tiring out his opponents with a barrage of quick punches.[2]

Mendoza was born in Aldgate in 1764 into a Jewish family. As a boy he passed through a number of jobs, from salesman to smuggler, but he first began to fight in the streets when he used to combat anti-Semitic abuse with his fists. He won his first professional fight at sixteen and then went on to contest matches with Richard Humphreys, who was the recognised champion of England. The three fights were held in 1788, 1789 and 1790, with Mendoza winning the last two – it seems that the first fight had been 'fixed'. The third contest lasted seventy-two rounds and was fought for well over an hour. Mendoza gained much popularity for not pulverising his obviously beaten opponent unnecessarily, and his victory was greeted by songs and ovations wherever he went. He was introduced to George III and the future George IV. He always fought under the title 'Mendoza the Jew', being particularly honoured by the Jewish community who called him 'the light of Israel'. He also set up a boxing school in order to train Jews to defend themselves – with such effect that one contemporary observer, Francis Place, noted that 'it was no longer safe to insult a Jew unless he was an old man and alone.'[3]

Despite the large sums of money which he won, Mendoza with his large family of eleven children soon accumulated debts which he tried to pay off by means of exhibition matches and tours around the country. Unfortunately he lost much prestige when challenged for his title in 1795 by 'Gentleman Jim' Jackson. In front of a crowd of 3,000 spectators.

The leading boxer of his day, Daniel Mendoza, in action.

Jackson proved himself to be no gentleman: he simply grabbed Mendoza's long hair, preventing him from moving around the ring, and then proceeded to pummel him systematically to defeat in seventeen minutes. The rest of Mendoza's long life throws up a familiar story of endless struggles to pay off his creditors. He ran a pub in Whitechapel and wrote two important books, *The Art of Boxing* and his *Memoirs*, but he also spent some time in the King's Bench debtors' prison. He died penniless in 1836 in an alley off Petticoat Lane. A plaque has recently been put on 3 Paradise Row, Bethnal Green, where he once lived. Notable East End boxers who have followed in Mendoza's footsteps this century have included Ted 'Kid' Lewis, who often drove around the streets of Whitechapel in an open car, flinging out silver coins to the children, but who blotted his copybook by getting involved with Mosley's blackshirts;[4] Jack 'Kid' Berg, born in Cable Street under the name Judah Bergman; John H. Stracey, Charlie Magri and Terry Marsh.

Nathan Mayer Rothschild (1777–1836) and Some Early Jews in London

Halfway up Brady Street in Whitechapel, behind a high wall, is a large Jewish cemetery. Often the cemetery keepers will allow the interested observer in to see the massed ranks of graves; amongst them can be found two splendid graves of white gleaming stone side by side, their magnificence telling a rather different story from the rise and fall of fellow-Jew Daniel Mendoza. Here lie Nathan Mayer Rothschild, whose inscription proclaims 'His Virtuous Deeds Bear Witness To His Worth', and Hannah his widow, 'Lived Beloved Died Lamented By All'.

N. M. Rothschild was born in Frankfurt in 1777 to a family of financiers which took their name from the *rothen Schilde*, or 'red shield', that hung outside the house. Rothschild's father was determined to expand the business and he sent four of his five sons to Manchester, Vienna, Paris and Naples in order to set up international branches. Nathan Mayer left Manchester for London in 1805 and there he made a name for his honesty and integrity, being entrusted by the Government with handling the payment of foreign subsidies during the Napoleonic Wars. One myth told about Rothschild is that with his efficient pigeon-post system he was the first person in England to know that Wellington had defeated Napoleon at the battle of Waterloo in 1815 and was able to use this information to make a 'killing' on the Stock Exchange. This is wrong: he would never have endangered his reputation as official bullion broker for the Government by such a short-term gain.[1]

By 1823, when Byron wrote *Don Juan*, he was able to refer to the collective might of the Rothschild and Baring businesses:

> ... every loan
> Is not merely a speculative hit,
> But seats a nation or upsets a throne.

One reason for the Rothschild wealth was that careful intermarriage between the branches of the family retained the dowries. When Nathan Mayer Rothschild died in 1836 he gave each of his seven children £100,000 each. His eldest son, Lionel Nathan, was elected Member of Parliament for the City of London in 1847 but was unable to take his seat because of the oath 'on the true faith of a Christian'. It was only after a battle of eleven years that this oath was finally dropped and he became in 1858 the first Jewish MP.[2]

The careers of the Rothschilds and of Mendoza challenge the popular misconception that the Jewish people only arrived in this country in the late nineteenth century. There have in fact been thousands of Jews in England since 1656 when Oliver Cromwell allowed them back after their expulsion by Edward II in 1290. An informative plaque on Albert Stern House at 253 Mile End Road recalls that this building once housed the hospital and old people's home of the Spanish and Portuguese congregation which was founded in 1656. This congregation claims to have been the first professing Jewish community to have been established in modern Britain and hence the parents of the present Jewish community in this country. Two early Jewish institutions were the Spanish and Portuguese synagogue which was rebuilt in Bevis Marks in the City in 1701 – the story has it that the builder, a Quaker, returned much of the money he was paid because he would not make a profit from building a House of God[3] – and the Jews' Free School founded in Bell Lane, Spitalfields, in 1817. Earlier this century it had 3,000 pupils on its roll, making it the largest school in Europe.

John Harriott and the River Police

By the end of the eighteenth century Britain's expanding overseas empire meant that the Port of London was always clogged with vessels waiting to load and unload. Access to the available quays and wharfs was so limited that ships would often have to wait for up to three months in order to discharge their goods. Nearly 15,000 ships passed in and out of the Port each year, an average of nearly fifty every day.

Quite apart from the costly delays, the process of unloading was in itself laborious and prolonged; the contents of the vessel were heaved into lighters which then in turn had to be unloaded on the riverside and the goods stored. Even the meanest criminal intelligence could see just how lucrative were the opportunities afforded by this method, and there was certainly no shortage of people more than willing to grasp their chance with both hands. Of the workforce of 37,000 employed on or about the Thames, some 11,000 were professional and full-time criminals. Crime on the river was something of an industry in itself, boasting its own categories and terminology. For example, 200 'Light Horsemen' worked hand in hand with the usually corrupt Revenue officers, while the 700 'Heavy Horsemen' were adept at concealing goods amongst the voluminous and multi-pocketed clothes which they wore. The 500 'Scuffle-Hunters' specialised in organising fights on badly managed and crowded quays which gave them the chance to steal whatever they wanted. The 100 'Mudlarks' hovered around the boats like gannets so as to snap up the goods dropped overboard to them.[1]

By 1797 the merchants of the West Indies companies had lost patience with this organised system of plunder which was costing them nearly £1 million a year. Fortunately for them, two quite dissimilar men had both been calling for the creation of a professional body of 'thieftakers' which would concentrate on preventing such wide-scale robbery. One was Thomas Colquhoun, an energetic Glaswegian merchant who spent much of his life agitating for the introduction of a police force both on the Thames and inland. The other was the extraordinary John Harriott, a swashbuckling figure of a man whose earlier careers had seen him as a sailor, an underwriter, a chaplain, a wine merchant, a duellist, a farmer and an inventor of the 'road harrow' which levelled ruts in the street. He later wrote some vivid memoirs called *Struggles through Life*.[2]

Impressed by the plans put together by Colquhoun and Harriott, the West Indies merchants stumped up the necessary money and on 2 July 1798 the 'Marine Police' began work. Started thirty years before Sir Robert Peel created the more famous Metropolitan Police, they were the first ever uniformed police force anywhere in the world, and their motto today remains 'Primus Omnium' ('First of All'). There were eighty full-timers as well as several hundred 'Ship Guards' hired to supervise the unloading of vessels. John Harriott was based at the Wapping New Stairs headquarters in his role as resident magistrate, while Colquhoun had his office in Westminster. The Marine Police patrolled the river in rowing galleys, armed with cutlasses and the added security of knowing that blunderbusses were tucked away in the firearm-lockers. Their presence immediately made itself felt, as was graphically demonstrated after only three months when a crowd of hundreds of 'Horsemen', 'Scuffle-Hunters' and others suffering from the attentions of the Marine Police besieged the Wapping headquarters. Bricks were thrown, windows smashed and lighted torches thrown into the building. Harriott and the six men on duty escaped outside, firing their guns and beating back their attackers. The arrival of reinforcements saved the day.

In its first year the costs of the Marine Police amounted to £4,200; they were estimated to have saved the merchants over £100,000. Clearly they were here to stay, and in 1800 the force was officially recognised by an Act of Parliament. By the time of Harriott's death in 1817 the success of the Marine Police had led Peel and others to plan a similar organisation on land, leading to the Metropolitan Police Act of 1829. Ten years later the Marine Police were merged into this larger body and became known as 'Thames Division of the Metropolitan Police'.

Despite this new name the river police were still confined to their 'rowing galleys' in September 1878 when the paddle-steamer *Princess Alice* crowded with holidaying families, was sliced in two by a collier called *Byward Castle*. Over 600 people were drowned in the mêlée, and the river police took a long time to reach the scene. The terrible consequences of this delay led to the introduction of powered craft and steam-launches. Today Thames Division's 146 men and women have access to the latest technology, including the specialist Underwater Search Unit. The modern boatyard at Wapping is a distinctive landmark on the river, covered as it is with rather bizarre white moulded panels. Nearby is the Thames Police Museum (an appointment is needed for a visit) which is housed in an old carpenter's shop and tells the fascinating story of the river police. Its exhibits range from portraits of Colquhoun and Harriott to cutlasses, old uniforms, a sailmaker's needle, a ship's leg iron and a surgeon's chest of 1859.

Thames Division is responsible for fifty-four miles of the Thames stretching from Deptford Creek to Staines with its twenty-nine bridges, and it deals not only with the 5 million people using the river's pleasure-boats each year but also with drugs, theft, suicides and the threat of rabies from imported pets. Despite the changes in its work brought about by the closure of the docks, the river police maintain an active and busy presence on the Thames. The duty-boats with their distinctive blue and white quarterings are often to be seen scooting up and down the river.

The Building of London's Docks

By the end of the eighteenth century the ever more crowded Thames meant lengthy delays before ships were unloaded. Moored out in the river, the exposed vessels were vulnerable to storms, even though the construction of London's first enclosed 'wet' dock, the Howland Dock built in Rotherhithe in 1697, offered a much more secure method of discharging cargoes. During the Great Storm of November 1703 many ships anchored in the Thames were destroyed; only one vessel within the sanctuary of the Howland Dock was damaged at all.

Why did the merchant companies not emulate the Howland Dock and build more enclosed docks? They were held back by the law, which stated that ships had to unload at the legal quays or at the twenty-one 'sufferance' wharfs that had been introduced, chiefly on the Southwark side of the water. By the 1790s the clamour of the country's traders for a drastic extension of the port's facilities was overwhelming, especially when it became clear that the war against Napoleon would permit Britain to expand hugely her already large overseas empire. Far-sighted merchants like William Vaughan put forward convincing arguments in favour of the installation of

Many of the old wooden ships were built in London. The arrival of 'ironclads' meant the move of shipbuilding to the Clyde and Belfast.

additional wet docks, as in his pamphlet of 1793 called *On Wet Docks, Quays, and Warehouses for the Port of London, with Hints Respecting Trade*, in which he actually suggests suitable sites. Fortunately for Vaughan, he lived to the ripe old age of ninety-seven and saw his ideas finally implemented. This campaign for change was supported by the findings of the parliamentary committee which had been set up in 1796 in order 'to inquire into the best mode of providing accommodation for the increased trade and shipping of the Port of London'.[1] Certain vested interests fought hard against the installation of new docks, particularly the City

Corporation battling to prevent the eastward drift of the Port, fearful of losing revenue, and the proprietors of the old quays. At last, nearly a century behind Liverpool, seven enclosed docks were built between 1801 and 1860, with the consequence that vessels no longer had to unload precariously in the middle of the Thames.[2] These docks did more perhaps to transform the landscape of East London than anything before or since, including German bombing during the Second World War, and ensured that for the next 150 years the fortunes of the East End and its people were to be inextricably linked with those of the Thames itself.

Ships in Limehouse Basin. In the background is the viaduct of the London–Blackwall railway now used by the Docklands Light Railway.

The first of these docks, the West India Dock, opened in 1802 and was designed by the architect D. A. Alexander. Appropriately enough in view of the high and daunting fortress-like walls which enclosed the dock and may today be seen in part near West Ferry Road, one of Alexander's previous projects had been the construction of Dartmoor Prison. The West India Dock was followed by the opening of the London Docks in 1805, the East India Docks in 1806 (a rather pompous inscription can still be seen near the north approach to the Blackwall Tunnel) and St Katharine's Dock, closest to the City, in 1828.

The construction of these docks sometimes entailed the wholesale destruction of dwellings situated inconveniently in the path of 'progress'. For St Katharine's Dock, over 1,250 houses were pulled down and 11,300 people cleared from the 24-acre site. The Royal Hospital of St Katharine, which had been there since it was founded by Queen Matilda in 1148, was shifted to Regent's Park and there was much anger at this treatment of 'poor old Kate' as she was familiarly known by local people. At the last service held in the chapel there the chaplain condemned 'the unfeeling and encroaching hand of commerce'.[3] As for the West India Dock, the company was authorised to enclose a grand total of 295 acres. Fortunately most of the land was barely inhabited. The Isle of Dogs was virtually sealed off from the rest of London as a result of the introduction of the West India Dock at its northern end. Within the docks themselves rose the towering wharfs and warehouses which fronted the river and that are now being turned into smart apartments. A glance today into the Ivory Warehouse of St Katharine's built in the 1850s in brick in order to lessen the risk of fire, confirms the excellence of these nineteenth-century engineers and architects whose structures have lasted so well.

Perhaps the finest examples still to be seen are the recently renovated warehouses erected for the East India Company in Cutler Street, just off Bishopsgate, over two hundred years ago. As recently as the 1960s these Cutler Street premises offered 127 rooms catering solely for dealers in oriental carpets and rugs – a total of eight acres of floor-space.[4] Each of the docks specialised in certain commodities; for instance, the London Docks handled wool, wine, tobacco and spirits, the West India Dock sugar and coffee, while St Katharine's Dock dealt in tea and ivory – two grey elephants still flank its East Smithfield entrance. Yet the building of the warehouses also entailed some architectural loss, too; by the middle of the nineteenth century, as Millicent Rose noted, 'the varied waterfront with its old galleried houses was giving place to a wall of warehouses and factories, interrupted by the wooden bastions of the docks. The old stairs down to the water were beginning to fall into disrepair.'[5]

The dock companies were also determined to improve drastically the poor roads of the East End, which were little more than the country lanes quite adequate in the area's rural past. A programme of road-building was carried out with almost Roman vigour and ruthlessness. The centrepiece of the scheme was Commercial Road, laid out in the 1800s and still clogged with traffic as it has been throughout its existence. This was followed by West India Dock Road, East India Dock Road, the smaller Dock Street and later on Commercial Street – the two 'Commercial' thoroughfares are a source of much confusion to those who do not know the East End.

The opening of the docks strengthened the position of London as the leading trade centre of western Europe, guaranteeing that throughout the nineteenth century and much of the twentieth its port witnessed a ceaseless parade of activity as vessels entered, unloaded and then departed on their travels. Trade with India brought many benefits. Hippolyte Taine wrote in 1861 that the view from Greenwich park showed a horizon 'bounded with masts and ropes', while the Polish seaman Jozef Teodor Korzeniowski, later to be more widely celebrated as the novelist Joseph Conrad, wrote in the late nineteenth century of 'the days when, in the part called the Pool, just below London Bridge, the vessels moored stem and stern in the very strength of the tide formed one solid mass like an island covered with a forest of gaunt leafless trees'. The servicing of this giant port demanded virtually an army of workers, ranging from those labouring as dockers to the men and women supplying the necessary goods and equipment for the never-ending flow of ships. In the days before public transport, all these people had to live close to their place of work, underlining the existence of 'Docklands'. Recruits were sucked in from Essex, from East Anglia and from Ireland. It was owing to the docks, and therefore the Thames, that the East End was, within the space of half a century – within living memory – turned from a district which was still semi-rural in character to a densely populated city with rows and rows of cheap tenements covering what had once been fields and farmland.

The dock companies used the Thames, too, as a means of hydraulic power. Just opposite the Prospect of Whitby in Wapping stands an ivy-clad building erected in 1890 for the

The octagonal accumulator tower near Limehouse Basin, thought to be the world's oldest hydraulic station.

London Hydraulic Company. In use until 1976, it once not only serviced many dock-side needs but also operated the lifts at the Tower of London and the London Palladium, the movable dance-floor at the Savoy and many of the lifts in Kensington flats far to the west of the City.

Yet, looking back with all the undeniable advantages of hindsight, it is clear that the dock companies were not as prescient as they might or, perhaps, should have been. Just stand by the lock entrance to St Katharine's Dock, close by the grey concrete pile of the Tower Hotel. It is hard to believe that even a good-sized rowing boat could squeeze through this narrow little space, let alone a heavily laden trading vessel. In fact the 45-foot entrance was sufficient for the average merchant ship of the early nineteenth century weighing 500 tons, and could cater for vessels of up to 1,000 tons – but by the end of the century the Port was expected to handle ships

St Katharine's Dock with the Tower of London in the background. Some of the warehouses remain today. Already the dock entrance seems much too small for the ships.

of up to 7,000 tons. In other words, the new docks, built to meet increasingly onerous trading demands, were themselves soon made obsolete by new demands for larger bulk.[6]

Another major defect was that the first docks were built before the introduction of the railways. The dock companies certainly installed new roads, but the docks were isolated from the most important form of Victorian transport. The 'second generation' of docks were able to profit from the mistakes of their predecessors. Built on the other side of the River Lea, the 'Royals' (The Royal Victoria Dock opened in 1855, the Royal Albert in 1880) were, first, much larger – a walk around their quays today involves a round trip of ten miles – and, second, railway lines were incorporated which went right down to the waterside. As with the older docks, the Royals specialised in particular commodities – the Royal Victoria in tobacco, the Royal Albert in frozen meat and bananas. But the failings of the upstream docks ensured that the eastward drift of the Port of London would continue and that at some point in the future – which turned out to be the 1960s and 1970s – the 'first generation' of docks would become commercially redundant and liable to closure. Throughout the nineteenth century these first dock companies merged with their rivals: the East India Docks amalgamated with the West India Dock in 1838, and the London Docks with St Katharine's in 1864, the same year that the docks on the south side of the river were formed into the combined Surrey Docks. But the die had already been cast.

Murder Most Foul:
The Ratcliff Highway Murders of 1811 and Jack the Ripper

In the early nineteenth century the East End's population expanded dramatically – the number of people living in Shoreditch, for example, almost doubled between 1800 and 1830 and then again between 1830 and 1860, until the 1861 census gave a figure of 129,339.[1] The river police might have been in operation, but onshore methods of law and order remained primitive, as was clearly demonstrated by the Ratcliff Highway Murders of December 1811. The Marr household in Ratcliff Highway was massacred late one night, and a few days later it was the Williamsons in New Gravel Lane, Wapping. The assorted bunch of local magistrates and constables were baffled by the murders. Only the suicide of a suspect called Williams, who hanged himself in his cell, got the law agencies off the hook. As was customary with suicides, Williams's corpse was buried at a crossroads, in this case at the junction of Commercial Road and Cannon Street Road. But, first, the body was paraded through the streets in front of a crowd estimated at 10,000 people. P. D. James and T. A. Critchley in their account of the murders describe what happened next:

> Here a hole about four feet deep, three feet long and two feet wide, had been dug ready. The hole was too small for the body, deliberately so. There was no intention that these ignoble limbs should lie in the semblance of innocent sleep, or be decently disposed as if laid out for Christian burial. Williams's body was seized, tumbled roughly out of the cart, and forced into the hole. Immediately one of the escorts jumped down beside it and began to drive the stake through the heart. As the blood-stained maul thudded on the stake the silence of the crowd

The corpse of Williams, held responsible for the Ratcliff Highway Murders of 1811, being paraded through the streets.

was at last broken and the air became hideous with shouts and execrations. A quantity of unslaked lime was cast into the hole; it was then filled with earth, and the paving stones were immediately replaced and hammered down.[2]

This practice of burying suicides at cross-roads lasted until George IV was held up by such a burial and an Act was passed in 1823 forbidding the custom.[3]

But if these murders of 1811 showed the deficiencies of law and order in the East End, then the Jack the Ripper murders of 1888, well after the introduction of the Metropolitan Police in 1829, hardly suggest that things had got much better. Anyone who expects this book to provide yet another pet theory as to the identity of the murderer or a detailed anatomical account of the victims' dismemberment will have to turn elsewhere. Surely there are more than enough – too many – such works, and I find the misogynistic element in them repellent. It can be no coincidence that every single 'Ripperologist' is male. The Jack the Ripper pub just by Christ Church, Spitalfields, contains much 'memorabilia' and planned to 'celebrate' the centenary of the murders in 1988 by offering such delights as a reddish-coloured drink called a 'Ripper Tipple'. The pub was picketed by groups of women who justly pointed out: 'Could you imagine a Peter Sutcliffe pub, or a Hungerford Massacre?'[4] At the time of writing it does seem as if this pressure has paid off and that the pub's name may be changed.

What is revealing about the Jack the Ripper murders is the light which is undoubtedly shed on social conditions in the East End a century ago. For example, there were an estimated 12,000 prostitutes on the Whitechapel streets in the 1880s. Pubs were legally entitled to stay open until one o'clock in the morning. Street-lighting was virtually nonexistent, and even today a walk into a dingy and dark alley called Woods Buildings just by Whitechapel station is a frightening experience. It was pointed out at the time that the authorities proved slow in offering a reward; certainly, if Mayfair or Hampstead had been the scene of such outrages, action would have been taken sooner. Meetings were held in Victoria Park and on Mile End Waste calling for the resignation of the Home Secretary and the Commissioner of Police.

It is a sad reflection on the political process that it took a series of murders to stimulate such social reforms as the rebuilding of slums in Flower and Dean Street off Commercial Street. The socialist publication *Commonweal* argued that 'a fiend-murderer may become a more effective reformer than all the honest propagandists in the world', an argument with which the *Daily Telegraph* from the opposite end of the political spectrum agreed. After the death of one victim, that paper considered 'She has effected more by her death than many long speeches in Parliament and countless columns of letters to the newspapers could have brought about'.[5]

'The World on Wheels': The East End Fairs

Until the nineteenth century much of London's trade and entertainment centred on the annual fairs which were held all over the capital. The two largest were Bartholomew Fair in Smithfield and Southwark Fair in Borough High Street, but East London, too, had its share. In the early seventeenth century the poet and waterman John Taylor described the bacchanalia of Bow Fair:

> There is such a baking, rosting, broyling,
>   boyling;
> Such swearing, drubbing, dancing,
>   dicing, toiling;
> Such shifting, shanking, cheating,
>   smoaking, stinking;
> Such gormandising, cramming, guzzling,
>   drinking;
> As if all the world would run on wheels
>   away,
> Or else the devils in hell kept holiday.[1]

By the Victorian period the fairs were coming under increasing attack from the authorities, worried by the risks of thousands of people gathered together and often awash with alcohol. In 1823, Stepney Michaelmas and Bow Fair were shut down, although Bow Fair has left behind one legacy in the name of Fairfield Road. The remaining Stepney Fair continued, and on Easter Monday 1844 was attended by 200,000 people. But as the East End was being rapidly built on and over, so even this fair was gradually squeezed and it died out in 1860.[2]

Petticoats and Bull Hanks: East End Street Life

At times it seems that everyone in the East End is buying and selling. Wads of money change hands on street-corners or inside pubs, newsagents' windows are crammed with cards offering everything from secondhand cars to babies' prams as well as discreet and relaxing personal services. Everyone has a friend who can help you out – for a bit of cash in hand.

Then of course there are the street-markets. Visit Wentworth Street any day of the week and there, in an atmosphere pungent with the smell of chips and the thump of 'ghetto blasters', the stallholders shout 'You want something? We got it!' Surely it is these many street-markets which typify the vitality of traditional East End life. The ubiquity of the ever present market has its origins in the fact that until the recent introduction of fridges and freezers it was impossible to store perishable food for any length of time, which therefore meant a demand for almost daily shopping at conveniently placed markets.

Several East End markets go back centuries. Spitalfields Market, for instance, although now housed in buildings put up in the 1920s, was first granted its charter by Charles II in 1682 – charters being a good method by which monarchs could boost their income. It specialises in selling fruit and veg, as a walk around its vicinity makes perilously apparent in the late morning when the buyers have gone and the scavengers have moved in. There are squashed tomatoes and soggy bananas and sometimes the occasional box of artichokes – slightly mouldy but with distinct possibilities. If you have never been to this market, go now or it will be too late. Christ Church at the end of Brushfield Street has looked down on Spitalfields Market for over 250 years; soon it will look down on yet more offices as the tentacles of commerce edge across Bishopsgate and the market is moved further out into East London.

Some markets have already disappeared, such as the Whitechapel Hay Market which was held in Whitechapel High Street from the early 1600s. Every Tuesday, Thursday and Friday hay-wagons from Essex and Hertfordshire would throng the narrow thoroughfare. By 1928 the increased volume of motor traffic meant that the Hay Market was impracticable, and it was abolished by Act of Parliament. A colourful tiled mural in the hallway of Whitechapel Library depicts the Hay Market as it was in 1788.

Other markets have been rebuilt, like the Watney Street Market which before the Second World War was famous for its naphtha lights winking far into late evening but now struggles to retain its vigour in the bleak open space between a development of flats. Others have survived, almost identical now as in the past. The most famous is held each Sunday in Middlesex Street – except that no one calls it that. This is the official name of the street and has been since 1830 when it was widened, but it will always be known as Petticoat Lane. Its original name was Hog Lane, probably from the pigs kept in the fields during the Middle Ages. A description by John Stow towards the end of the sixteenth century is an eloquent reminder of 'the fields beneath' today's East End: ' ... within these forty years [Hog Lane] had on both sides fair hedge rows of elm trees, with bridges and easy stiles to pass over into the pleasant fields, very commodious for citizens therein to walk, shoot, and otherwise to recreate and refresh their dull spirits in the sweet and wholesome air .... '[1]

The name 'Petticoat' came from the clothes sold here during the seventeenth century. In the Victorian period the market was largely taken over by Jews who were not always too bothered as to where the goods had come from. One late-Victorian commentator wrote

Petticoat Lane market – still as busy today.

of Petticoat Lane that 'It is perhaps not so bad as it was a few years ago, but it is still one of the most disreputable quarters of the Metropolis.'[2] No doubt today some of what is on display has doubtful origins, but only the most strait-laced could fail to be drawn into the excitement and restlessness of Petticoat Lane, the East End's answer to a Far East bazaar. All over the East End the stallholders will tell you that it's nothing like the old days – but they were saying exactly that to Henry Mayhew 130 years ago.

Not all the East End's street-life took place at markets. Some activities in the past defied rules and regulations, such as the 'bull hanks' with which the young men of Whitechapel often amused themselves during the eight-eenth century.[3] They would set loose a bull at the junction of Brick Lane and Osborn Street, chasing it down Whitechapel Road. This custom was not stopped until the introduction of the police force in the early nineteenth century. But, even if the bulls were no longer loose, a multitude of stalls and booths occupied both sides of Whitechapel Road, attracting huge numbers of people; one writer a hundred years ago called it 'the greatest public pleasure-ground of the East End'.[4] Stepney alone had 2,229 streetsellers in 1911.[5] The young in particular strolled up and down Whitechapel Road in their finery, an activity described as 'the monkey parade'. Sadly the advent of the motor car changed all that.

The East End's Park: Victoria Park

The industrial expansion of East London in the nineteenth century, unchecked as it was by government, meant that parts of the area became thoroughly squalid and insanitary. Limehouse Cut, for example, was built in 1770 in order to allow barges to use the River Lea without having to sail right around the Isle of Dogs; it became so noxious that 'no bargee who fell in had any chance of surviving his ducking in the filthy water'.[1] Yet if the Government looked on unconcerned, preferring to leave it to market forces, the prosperous living in the West End of London were indeed worried about the danger of epidemics wafting their way. In 1840 a petition pointed out that in East London 'the mortality is more than double those parts of the Metropolis which are more effectually ventilated. Fever is constantly prevailing in these places .... Nor is it less revolting to contemplate the moral pestilence, which is partly produced, and greatly aggravated by the want of open spaces.'[2] Early in 1841 the Government decided to create a new park in the East End.

Financed by the sale of York (now Lancaster) House off The Mall, the architect James Pennethorne began to buy up the land adjoining Bonner's Fields, a notorious open space much frequented by criminals and political agitators. The dwellings nearby were referred to as 'Botany Bay', presumably because most of their inhabitants were eventually transported there! The purchase of the land was a slow business, costing more than £100,000, and by 1845 the public, exasperated by the delay, simply began using the park.

Gardens, boating on the lake, swimming, tennis, brass-band music and football were just some of the activities held within its 217 acres, and park users could always refresh themselves from Angela Burdett-Coutts's neo-Gothic drinking-fountain which was put up in 1862 and still stands in the eastern half of Victoria Park. Over on the eastern boundary

A dockers' meeting in Victoria Park. Angela Burdett-Coutts's drinking fountain is in the background.

stand two stone alcoves removed from old London Bridge when it was pulled down in the 1830s. Victoria Park even had its own cemetery, somewhat isolated on the south side of Roman Road and occupying nine acres. Millicent Rose has noted that the owners of this private cemetery 'specialized in cheap burials for children, victims of the atrociously high infantile mortality rate in the district. The little coffins were interred in layers, in common graves that each held about twenty bodies, and the number of funerals was estimated at a hundred on an average day, and one hundred and thirty on Sundays.'[3]

One adult buried there was King Cole, a member of the Aborigine cricket tour of England in 1868 who died of tuberculosis at Guy's Hospital. The cemetery was turned into Meath Gardens in 1895, and the graves were cleared. In the summer of 1988 there was another Aborigine cricket tour of England and a flower planted in Meath Gardens in memory of King Cole.[4]

The space to the east of Burdett-Coutts's drinking-fountain established itself as the East End's equivalent of Speakers' Corner, thousands of people crowding here every Sunday. William Morris spoke in August

Gustave Doré's image of the notorious Blue Gate Fields in Shadwell in the early 1870s.

1886, describing the park in a letter to his daughter as 'rather a pretty place with water (though dirty) and lots of trees'. He said that they enjoyed a good meeting despite the rivalry of neighbouring groups and a band. The Labour politician George Lansbury often took his family to the forum, and his son Edgar has recalled the wealth of characters who gathered: 'In particular I remember one [old soldier] who used to take his audience at a penny per head into an adjacent field where they might count his assegai wounds. He had twenty-eight of them altogether on various parts of his body. To our chagrin he would not allow young boys to examine any but the two or three wounds on his forearm.'[5]

This century the suffragettes, Mosley's British Union of Fascists and the dockers are some of the organisations which have met here regularly, but the Victoria Park forum faded away after the First World War. During the Second World War the park contained trenches, allotments, air-raid shelters and anti-aircraft guns as well as staging performances by the touring Sadler's Wells Ballet Company. Today as in the past Victoria Park offers an attractive place in which to walk, talk and relax, feeding the deer or the rabbits. The southern side of the park is marked by the Grand Union Canal (or Regent's Canal) and the Hertford Union Canal.

The Thames Tunnel and 'Great Eastern': Isambard Kingdom Brunel in the East End

One of the most remarkable of all Victorians was Isambard Kingdom Brunel, the man who built railways, bridges, harbours, docks, hotels, steamships and much else besides. Born in 1806, Isambard's father, Marc, was also an engineer, and together the two men worked on one of Victorian London's most amazing feats, the construction of the Thames Tunnel. It was to be the world's first ever tunnel under a major river.

The Act of Parliament passed in 1824 authorised 'Making and maintaining a Tunnel under the River Thames, from some Place in the Parish of Saint John of Wapping, in the County of Middlesex, to the Opposite Shore of the said River, in the Parish of Saint Mary Rotherhithe, in the County of Surrey, with sufficient Approaches thereto'. Marc Brunel estimated that the work would take three years. In fact it took eighteen years, and it was not until March 1843 that Queen Victoria opened the 400-yard tunnel between Wapping

Isambard Kingdom Brunel, the dynamic Victorian engineer who built the Thames Tunnel and the ship, *Great Eastern*.

and Rotherhithe, knighting Marc Brunel for his efforts. There were several reasons for the delay, some of them financial and others resulting from the hazards of the work itself. On several occasions the Thames broke into the tunnel. The river was still used as a sewer, causing terrible health problems for the workforce; an entry in Marc Brunel's diary for 1838 reads: 'Heywood died this morning [of typhus]. Two men on the sick list. Pages is sinking fast. It affects the eyes.'[1] Unsympathetic, *The Times* called the whole venture 'The Great Bore'.

Within twenty-four hours of its opening, 50,000 curious Victorians had walked along the Thames Tunnel at a penny a time.[2] After fifteen weeks the total had risen to 1 million. And yet, after the first flush of enthusiasm, the tunnel declined in character and became the haunt of prostitutes and thieves. In 1865 it was sold to the East London Railway for £200,000, and within three years there were trains using it. In 1913 the line was electrified and it is still in frequent use today as the East London section of the Metropolitan Railway. If you travel by Tube between Wapping and Rotherhithe you are in fact passing through the Brunels' tunnel. After 140 years it is still in remarkably good condition. An informative series of boards on the platform of Wapping Underground station recounts how the Thames Tunnel was constructed.

The Thames Tunnel was not Isambard Kingdom Brunel's only association with the East End. For centuries many of Britain's ships had been built here, particularly in the early nineteenth century by George Green who made a fortune from supplying whaling vessels and East Indiamen, and by his son Richard who built ships for Australia. The Greens were an influential East End family, and a charming statue of Richard Green with his dog is to be found along the East India Dock Road outside Poplar Baths. It was to Millwall Dock that Brunel came in 1853 to build the hull of his enormous ship *Great Eastern*.

Unfortunately, just as the ever growing size of ships brought problems for the East End's 'first generation' of docks, so, too, was the Thames too small for the new 'ironclads' or vessels with iron hulls. Brunel's hull was finished at the end of 1857, but it then took three months to inch it slowly towards the river. Not until hydraulic presses were used was 'The Monster' finally afloat.[3] The strain of this enterprise contributed to Brunel's early death in 1859 at the age of fifty-three. London's shipbuilding industry was to close down rapidly.[4] The capital was in addition some distance from supplies of iron and coal, and instead the shipbuilding industry transferred to Belfast and the Clyde. On the foreshore of the Isle of Dogs, near West Ferry Road, can be seen the remnants of the timber slipway built by Brunel for the abortive launch of *Great Eastern*.

'The Queen of the Poor': Angela Burdett-Coutts (1814–1906)

If one was able to step back into the East End of the nineteenth century, amongst the many differences between then and now would be the complete absence of government-sponsored buildings and services, from job centres to schools and hospitals. The dominant philosophy guiding governments of all persuasions until this century was that of *laissez-faire*: if something was not to do with defence or law and order, then it should be left to the influence of market forces. It was most certainly not the Government's responsibility to ensure minimum standards of health, housing and education. This simple attitude, clear-cut in principle, in practice resulted in millions of people being condemned to blighted and stunted lives. For example, there were no state schools in Britain until after the Education Act of 1870, many years behind France and Germany.

But if governments washed their hands of any concern for welfare, then who did that leave? There were the churches and the labour movement, both of which are covered elsewhere in this book. The middle classes abandoned the East End as rapidly as they could when it was clear that the area was sliding swiftly down the social scale during the nineteenth century. This left only private individuals possessed of a social conscience who did their best to alleviate distress and suffering; not always with success, certainly, but at least they tried. Today it is fashionable to sneer at such 'do-gooders', and from the left of the political spectrum there is sometimes criticism that such Lord and Lady Bountifuls were helping to prevent revolution by taking the edge off misery. After John Wesley had visited Bethnal Green in January 1777 he wrote in his journal: 'Many of them I found in such poverty as few can conceive without seeing it. O why do not all rich people that fear God constantly visit the poor?'[1] One who did so was Angela Burdett-Coutts, familiarly known as 'the Queen of the Poor'.

Her father was Sir Francis Burdett, for thirty years the Radical MP for Westminster and a staunch advocate of extending the right to vote. He was once imprisoned in the Tower of London from April to June 1810 for publishing a speech which he had delivered in the House of Commons, then an action considered to be in breach of parliamentary privilege. Angela was born in 1814, and her maternal grandfather was the wealthy City banker Thomas Coutts. When her step-

grandmother left the family fortune to Angela in 1837, she became at twenty-three the richest woman in England, possessing an annual income of £80,000 a year without even touching her capital.[2] Until 1870 any woman on marriage automatically lost control of her estate to her husband, who was then free to do with it as he wished. Burdett-Coutts, all too aware of the fact that, like Miss Dunstable in Trollope's Barchester novels, not all the male attention lavished on her was entirely unconnected with the size of her bank account, turned down innumerable marriage proposals – including one, it is said, from the Duke of Wellington himself.

Yet, instead of sitting smugly on her wealth, living a luxurious life at her sumptous London homes at 1 Stratton Street in Mayfair and Holly Lodge in Highgate, Burdett-Coutts threw herself and her wealth into an enormous range of charitable endeavours, extending from the construction of churches to the RSPCA and the NSPCC. She was particularly fond of the East End, setting up ragged schools there, usually on the advice of Charles Dickens, who dedicated *Martin Chuzzlewit* to her. After the Anglo-French Treaty of 1860 had demolished the silk-weaving industry by allowing in French goods duty-free, she founded the East End Weavers' Aid Association. Her three major projects in the area were the building of Columbia Square and Market, and the drinking-fountain in Victoria Park.

At the rear of St Leonard's Church, Shoreditch, in the early nineteenth century lay the infamous Nova Scotia Gardens, a particularly pestilential neighbourhood which had a huge mound of rotting refuse in the middle, rather like the Mount that once stood beside the London Hospital.[3] Burdett-Coutts bought this site in 1852 for £8,700 and, although the dust-contractor who owned the tip managed to play for time over the next seven years, it was eventually cleared and work began on building a five-storey block of flats. Completed in 1862, the rather grim and

Angela Burdett-Coutts's Gothic-style Columbia Market, which cost £200,000, and Columbia Square which housed 1,000 tenants.

fortress-like structure adopted as far as possible the principle that what the residents needed was as much ventilation as possible, the theory being that East Enders suffered most from a lack of personal hygiene. The stairs contained large glass-free windows, and even the doors of people's homes were deliberately constructed to be smaller than the frames in order to create a supposedly healthy draught.[4] Although the rents charged were high, from 2s 6d (12 ½p) to 5s (25p) a week, the dwellings at Columbia Square for a thousand tenants were always oversubscribed because of the housing shortage in the East End.

Burdett-Coutts's next initiative was the erection of Columbia Market, a huge covered market-hall that opened in 1869 at a cost of £200,000 and which has been described as 'a cross between a gothic cathedral and a medieval palace'.[5] Intended both for the employment of the street-traders of the East End and to supply cheap food to the people without the intervention of 'middle men', Columbia Market was one of Burdett-Coutts's few failures. Most street-traders preferred their traditional sites in Petticoat Lane and Roman Road, no doubt distrusting the didacticism which led the architect H. A. Darbishire to inscribe over one entrance the maxims 'Be Sober Be Vigilant Be Pitiful Be Courteous'. Wholesalers boycotted it, too, and the opposition from Billingsgate Market was too strong to overcome.

German bombing and postwar demolition have meant that neither of the Columbias can be seen today, but the third of Burdett-Coutts's East End initiatives has survived. It is also in the Gothic style she favoured, which meant that the marble and granite drinking-fountain in Victoria Park looks like a smaller version of the better-known Albert Memorial in Kensington Gardens. Learning that the users of the park had no convenient drinking-supply – presumably Miss Burdett-Coutts's informant ignored the pubs strategically placed close to many of the park's gates – she instructed Darbishire to build a drinking-fountain. But not just any drinking-fountain. Finished in 1862, her drinking-fountain cost £5,000 and came complete with four distinctly chubby cherubs perched on top of dolphins. Although now covered with graffiti and best viewed from a distance, the 58½-foot fountain still stands proudly erect in the eastern section of Victoria Park: ornate and useless, it is an unfair memorial to its sponsor.

In 1871, Burdett-Coutts received a peerage, the first time that a woman had been granted this title because of her own efforts and not those of a husband. The next year she received the Freedom of the City. In 1881 she married an American called William Ashmead-Bartlett who was nearly forty years younger than herself. It was by all accounts a happy marriage, and her husband followed in the footsteps of her father by becoming MP for Westminster. When Angela Burdett-Coutts died in 1906 at the age of ninety-two, 30,000 people came to pay their respects before she was buried in the nave of Westminster Abbey near the West Door. Her memory lives on in the East End in the names of Burdett Road, Baroness Road and Columbia Road.

'Model Dwellings':
East End Housing in the Nineteenth Century

Angela Burdett-Coutts's Columbia Square was only one of the philanthropic housing ventures built in the East End during the nineteenth century. No Victorian capitalist considered that the area offered an opportunity for a return on his investment, and so it was left to a few individuals and organisations to provide better housing. The most famous was that initiated by George Peabody, an American grocer from Massachusetts who took up a second career in London as a banker and lived in Eaton Square, Belgravia. Like Burdett-Coutts, he possessed wider sympathies, arguing that the possession of wealth brought with it responsibilities as well as pleasures. In 1862 he set up the Peabody Trust 'to ameliorate the condition of the poor and needy of this great metropolis, and to promote their comfort and happiness'. On his death in 1869 he left £½ million to the Trust. The first block of housing erected by the Trust was opened in 1864 on the corner of Commerical Street and Folgate Street. The architect was H. A. Darbishire. The block can still be seen today.[1]

Sir Sydney Waterlow, the printer who made his fortune from producing railway timetables, paid for the Waterlow Buildings in Bethnal Green and elsewhere, and an organisation called the 4% Industrial Dwellings Company also built blocks of flats. One was in Wentworth Street, Spitalfields, and although it has since been pulled down the old arch still fronts the new housing estate. Millicent Rose has pointed out that 'A speculative builder has, in some measure, to put up the houses people want; the philanthropist builds what he thinks people ought to have.'[2] It is certainly noticeable that 'model dwellings' bear several resemblances, often looking more like a barracks or a fortress for sheltering convicts than living-places. Bleak corridors, small windows, a large windswept public courtyard, high rents which excluded the less well-off members of the working classes at whom these flats were ostensibly directed – these features seem to be a common denominator. And yet when, by contrast, the Metropolitan Association for Improving the Dwellings of the Industrious Classes (the Victorians loved such grandiose titles) put up the Victoria Cottages in Deal Street, Spitalfields, in 1865, followed by the Albert Cottages on the other side of the road, they were criticised for not making better use of the space. They still form a pleasant and friendly contrast to the twentieth-century tower-blocks; or even to the blocks radiating out from Arnold Circus in Shoreditch. Built in the 1890s to replace 'the Jago', the notorious slum properites behind St Leonard's Church, the buildings are rather gloomy, relieved only by the bandstand high up in the gardens.

Minors and Gaffs:
East End Theatre in the Nineteenth Century

The patent theatres of Covent Garden and Drury Lane managed to close down Henry Giffard's theatre in Goodman's Fields, but nearly fifty years later another playhouse in the East End took on the power of the patents. The Royalty built in Wellclose Square was started by a popular actor called John Palmer whose easy-going nature had earned him the nickname 'Plausible Jack' from the playwright Sheridan.[1] His playhouse opened in 1787. Palmer argued that a licence from the Governor of the Tower of London – the Royalty was only a few hundred yards away from the Tower – and from the magistrates of the Hamlets meant that he was exempt from the jurisdiction of the patents. He was wrong, but Palmer's challenge was only the first in a whole wave which gradually wore down the patents. By the 1830s so many venues all over London, but particularly in the East End, were staging plays that the authorities decided to clear up the unsatisfactory state of the law. They did this by means of the Theatres Regulation Act of 1843, hardly an Act enshrined in popular memory but in fact the legislation which allowed the East End to create its own entertainment industry for the rest of the nineteenth century.

The 1843 Act took away the patents' duopoly. Instead the Lord Chamberlain gave all the myriad places of entertainment then in existence a choice. They should either put on 'legitimate' drama (that is, plays), while banishing drink from the auditorium, or permit alcohol but cease to stage plays. In a nutshell, they had to choose between becoming a theatre or a music-hall. About half the venues in the East End jumped one way and half the other. Those that became theatres were often referred to as 'minors' – although they were anything but minor in terms of their size and importance – in contrast to the old patents, or 'majors'.

The East End possessed eight minors which flourished for many years. There was the East London or 'Effingham' along Whitechapel Road, the Garrick in Leman Street (a reminder of the Goodman's Fields theatre's most famous performer), the Brunswick in Wellclose Square, the Grecian Theatre in the City Road, the City of London in Norton Folgate, the Pavilion also along Whitechapel Road, the Standard in Shoreditch High Street and finally the Britannia in Hoxton Street. It is a sad fact that none of these theatres has survived. Some were bigger than Drury Lane or Covent

The Pavilion, like 'the Brit', could easily hold well over three thousand spectators.

Garden, but not even a wall or a doorway is to be seen. Nor is there a single plaque or tablet to commemorate these vast places which gave such pleasure to thousands of East Enders. Of the three most significant, a new housing estate stands on the site of 'the Brit', the site of the Standard is occupied by a petrol station and garage, and the Pavilion's site is empty.

Burbage built his playhouse in the East End because it was outside the City. By the early nineteenth century, however, the district's commercial attraction for theatrical entrepreneurs lay in the massive potential audience which was continually expanding. The population of Shoreditch was 43,930 in 1811 and 124,009 in 1891; Hackney's population was 16,771 in 1811 and 198,606 by 1891. It might not have been a wealthy audience, but the East End's spectators were eager to enjoy themselves when not engaged in backbreaking and tedious manual labour. The building of the railways ensured that an even larger

The arrival of such 'Cine-Variety Theatres' before the First World War meant the end for the East End's minor theatres.

The Pavilion on Whitechapel Road, known as the 'Drury Lane of the East'. Jo Lyons began his catering career here, serving tea and coffee to the queues of theatregoers.

audience further north and east was within reach.

The minor theatre buildings were initially added to public houses. Such was the case with the Britannia and the Grecian, but by the 1860s the continuing success of these ventures saw most of them rebuilt on a lavish scale. When the Brit opened in 1858 at a cost of £28,000 it held nearly 4,000 spectators; the Pavilion held 3,500 and was popularly known as 'the Drury Lane of the East' with its massive stage (70 feet by 58 feet); and the Standard after its rebuilding in 1867 had room for an audience of over 4,000. From the small frontages of the playhouses no one would

have guessed the size of the interiors. Space on a main road was expensive, the land behind less so – therefore patrons usually walked along a narrow passage to reach the auditorium.

The managers of these minors had often been the landlords of the public houses on which the theatres had been grafted. Part of their success lay in the continuity of management; the Brit had three managers in fifty years, and the popular Sara Lane was commonly called 'the Queen of Hoxton'. Eight members of the Douglass family ran the Standard for forty years, and Isaac Cohen managed the Pavilion for nearly thirty years.

These impresarios realised the audiences wanted exciting escapist entertainment and they were happy to supply it. In the Victorian age this meant melodrama, in which Virtue eventually triumphed over Vice and where heroes were heroes, villains black-haired and mustachioed, and the heroines beautiful, helpless and impossibly good. The orchestra thumped, screeched and wailed in accompaniment – indeed, our very word 'melodrama' comes from this combination of music and action. Most minors specialised in particular types of melodrama. The Pavilion with its penchant for nautical 'Jolly Jack Tar' dramas was called 'the Great Nautical Theatre of the Metropolis'. The Brit was famous for its pantomimes, its Shakespearian productions and its festival held every year from 1858. The Standard was known for its spectaculars and special effects, which could include waterfalls, lakes and racehorses. One little boy has recalled how effective the dramas were: 'Many times I have lain awake after going to the Brit, terrified to open my eyes for fear of seeing the murdered lying next to me.'[2]

The usual programme offered two plays plus interludes, which might be brass bands, magicians, hornpipe dancers or competitions such as 'Great Wheelbarrow Contests' in which members of the audience would come up on stage and wheel their friends around. The drama was certainly no 'theatre of illusion' – spectators threw down bouquets and presents in the middle of performances and these were graciously acknowledged by the actors and actresses with no worry about theatrical continuity or realism.

The plays themselves were usually written by hacks who would turn out at least a piece a week. Few were ever published, but we know that T. W. Moncrieff wrote more than 180 plays in his lifetime. The performers had to be able to project themselves and their voices, especially as they were acting in large playhouses without microphones. Thus the acting style tended to the declamatory rather than to the subtle, with the words bellowed out. If performers and other staff fitted in well, then they tended to stay for years – the average length of service at the Brit was 12½ years. Sometimes families became dynasties; the Lupino family worked at the Brit for generations, supplying clowns, walk-ons and leading men. Most minors realised the publicity value of involving the local community in their productions. Over 500 schoolchildren applied for parts in the Standard pantomimes. Each playhouse had it own substantial backstage team; the Standard again had over forty people employed in its wardrobe room, and all the costumes and props were made on the premises. One local caterer began by supplying queues outside the Pavilion and established a national business: Jo Lyons.

Fortunately for us, several Victorian observers visited the minors. Charles Dickens went to the Brit in 1850 when it was still a saloon theatre and was mildly disapproving. However on his return in 1860 he was much more enthusiastic. He praised the ventilation and lighting and remarked upon the audience:

> Besides prowlers and idlers, we were mechanics, dock-labourers, costermongers, petty tradesmen, small clerks, milliners, stay-makers, shoe-binders, slop workers, poor workers in a hundred highways and byeways. Many of us – on the whole, the majority – were not at all clean, and not at all choice in our lives or conversation. But we had all come together in a place where our convenience was well consulted; and where we were well looked after, to enjoy an evening's entertainment in common. We were not going to lose any part of what we had paid for, through anybody's caprice, and as a community we had a character to lose. So, we were closely attentive, and kept excellent order; and let the man or boy who did otherwise instantly get out from this place, or we would get him out with the greatest expedition.

Dickens watched a pantomime and then a melodrama:

> Throughout the evening, I was pleased to observe Virtue quite as triumphant as she usually is out of doors, and indeed I thought rather more so. We all agreed (for the time) that honesty was the best policy, and we were as hard as iron upon Vice, and we wouldn't hear of Villainy getting on in the world – no, not on any consideration whatever. Between the pieces, we almost all of us went out and refreshed. Many of us went the length of drinking beer at the bar of the neighbouring public-house, some of us drank spirits, crowds of us had sandwiches and ginger-beer at the refreshment-bars established for us in the Theatre.'[3]

By the 1890s, when H. G. Hibbert went to the Brit, the need to go outside for a drink had been dropped: 'Men walked to and fro incessantly with trays groaning beneath the weight of pies in infinite variety, thick slices of bread plastered with jam, chunks of cheese, slabby sandwiches, fried fish, jellied eels. Gallons of ale washed down mountains of food.'[4]

The entrance prices for the minors ranged from 5s (25p) to 6d (2½p), and at these prices they attracted thousands of people each week. The minors have been almost completely ignored by theatre historians, even though over a third and probably a half of London's seating capacity at the Victorian theatre was located in the East End. But that was not all. For those not able to afford the minors, recourse could always be had to the penny gaffs, the scores of little fly-by-night theatres operating from converted shops and stables. At any one time in London there were up to a hundred gaffs in busy activity, with a daily attendance of about 30,000. Most of these were in the East End.

Penny gaffs derived their name from the penny which was the standard entrance fee, a 'gaff' being a showman's word for any kind of show or exhibition. Millicent Rose recalls once talking to a taxi-driver who referred to Shaftesbury Avenue as 'Gaff Street'.[5] Other non-London gaffs were sometimes called 'blood tubs' or 'bursts' from the habit of rowdy members of the audience bursting the paper bags from which they had been eating sweets. I once met a man who as a boy in Newcastle before the First World War had been a regular at the local 'lophouse', or licehouse, where it is probable more things were shared than simply entertainment!

The gaffs were invariably primitive. The stage was usually no more that a few planks resting on two beer-barrels, the lighting was provided by candles, and there was little scenery and few props. The seating was hard wooden benches. Generally the audience was young people, and what they demanded was the broadest melodrama – not finely tuned monologues or philosophical disquisitions but blood, thunder, violence, comedy and tragedy; a kind of animated strip cartoon. In forty minutes the audience might well see *two* Shakespeare plays. How could this be? All long windy speeches were excised, while prominence was given to the murders and duels which punctuate Shakespeare's plays. No doubt the groundlings at the original Globe also preferred these bits, too. With ten or twelve new pieces a week, the prompter was often the busiest member of the company – if, that is, the words had been written down in the first place.

Most Victorian commentators who visited the gaffs were horrified by what they saw as their immoral and evil character, denouncing them in terms very similar to those with which the City Fathers in 1597 had attacked the Elizabethan playhouses. Dr Barnardo went to one Whitechapel gaff and was so shocked that he paid the manager £5 in order to be allowed to address the audience. When he did so the manager proceeded to eject Barnardo, who left taking most of the audience with him.[6] Henry Mayhew verbally attacked the gaff he visited as 'cruellest debauchery', claiming that a girl of nine learns 'to understand the filthiest sayings and laugh at them as loudly as the grown-up lads around her'. He watched a drag act in which a fourteen-year-old girl danced 'with more energy than grace', and a comic in a battered hat whose song ended each stanza with a filthy word.[7] The audiences at gaffs believed in making its feelings known, and sometimes performers would leap into the auditorium to berate physically any particularly rude spectator. When the songwriter George Sims went to an East End gaff he found an audience loudly barracking a refined lady vocalist. Things got so bad that one spectator called out: 'Give the poor old cow a chance, can't you?' 'Thank God,' she called back gratefully, 'at least there is one gentleman in the house.'[8]

The penny gaffs have been almost totally ignored by theatre historians, to everyone's loss.

Towards the end of the nineteenth century the gaffs were dying out, harassed by the police for ignoring the new fire and safety regulations and threatened by new forms of entertainment such as seaside holidays and organised football matches. The minor theatres were also in trouble. Of the smaller venues, the City of London became a temperance hall in 1874, the Garrick closed in 1881, the same year that the Grecian was taken over by the Salvation Army. The Brit, Pavilion and Standard staggered on into the twentieth century, the Pavilion becoming a Yiddish theatre before it closed in 1934. The Brit became a cinema and was then destroyed during the Blitz, as was the Standard.

'The Handsomest Room in London': Wilton's and the East End Music-Halls

It has been estimated that a hundred years ago the area we now call Tower Hamlets boasted 150 music-halls.[1] In addition the man often referred to as 'the Father of the Halls', Charles Morton, was born in Bethnal Green in 1819, although his first enterprise, the Canterbury Hall, was opened on the other side of the river in Lambeth in 1852. Today the walker seeking out the East End's old music-halls is rather more fortunate than in a search for the minor theatres. Several buildings have survived substantially intact, such as the Varieties in Pitfield Street, Hoxton, built in 1870 to hold over 2,000 spectators. It became a cinema in 1910 before ceasing to be a place of entertainment and becoming a warehouse. Its elegant ornate façade remains, although at the time of writing a 'Sold' notice suggests that anyone interested in seeing it should pay a visit in the near future. Half a mile away is Hoxton Hall at

64 Hoxton Street. It is now a community centre but its little hall, which once held 1,000 spectators and has retained its distinctive double balcony, can still be seen and music-hall performances are sometimes staged here.[2]

Also standing, but empty and with new buildings encroaching upon it, is Wilton's on the north side of Wellclose Square by Cable Street. It is the oldest music-hall building in Britain. In 1850, John Wilton had taken over a pub called the Prince of Denmark; fitting it out in mahogany, the first pub in London to be so decorated, it became known as the Old Mahogany Bar. In 1853, Wilton decided to build a music-hall on the back. Rebuilding it five years later, he described it as 'the Handsomest Room in London'. The foundation stone, which sports a verse, probably by Wilton, can still be seen:

Wilton's Music Hall in one of its more genteel phases, as is evident from the evening dress of the performers.

The entrance to the music hall opened by John Wilton in Wellclose Square in 1858.

To Great Apollo, God of early morn,
Who wakes the song of birds from
  Eastern sky,
We consecrate this shrine of gentle
  music;
Music that alternates from smiles to
  tears;
Smiles emanating from the purest mirth,
And tears of sympathy that speak not
  sadness.[3]

The hall was fitted out with a lavish and colourful décor which included a sunburner lamp and massive gas-chandeliers, twisted iron columns and plaster decoration of flowers, roses and leaves 'in the Italian style'. The high stage offered spectators an excellent view. The intimate hall held 2,000 spectators, a figure hard to believe if one strolls around its compact exterior today.

Despite the range and excellence of the acts which performed on his tiny stage, Wilton was never able to attract the West End clientele for whom he was aiming. His successors failed to halt the decline of the hall. In 1877 the building was badly damaged by fire and when rebuilt it failed to satisfy the rigorous safety regulations in force from 1878 which had also shut down so many penny gaffs. Wilton's closed in 1880 and was then used as a Wesleyan mission-hall. In 1889 it was used for dispensing free meals to families during the Dock Strike. It was then used as a rag-warehouse. There are now plans to turn Wilton's into a Museum of Variety and Music-Hall.

Just like the minors, the East End music-halls came under pressure from other rival forms of entertainment. In any case the vast new 'theatres of variety' built in the West End were enticing away East End audiences. However, the architect of one of these build-

ings, Frank Matcham, who designed the Coliseum in St Martin's Lane, was in fact responsible for the Hackney Empire along Mare Street which opened in 1901. Marie Lloyd, Charlie Chaplin, W. C. Fields and 'Little Tich' were just some of the stars who once graced its boards. Although intervening years and its use as a bingo-hall have brought about some deterioration, notably the loss of the distinctive green domes, the Hackney Empire has retained enough of its original décor to give a splendid idea of what it must have been like to visit the Edwardian music-hall. One would have swept up its double staircase into an auditorium of marble, flanked by exotic plasterwork. It would have been a far cry — deliberately so — from most people's homes. The Hackney Empire is at present engaged in a fierce fund-raising struggle to survive as a venue of variety and music-hall.[4]

Some Turbulent Priests: The Church in the Victorian East End

For ten months from May 1859 until March 1860 an East End church was the scene of some of the most rowdy and bad-tempered behaviour ever witnessed inside a religious building in London. The clergy were jostled by the congregation, the choirboys were insulted and spat upon, the churchwardens mutilated the organ and paid the organist not to play, and dogs were deliberately brought into the service and encouraged to fight and howl. The climax came on 26 February 1860, as one observer recounted:

The whole service was interrupted by hissing, whistling, and shouting; songs were roared out during the sermon and lessons, and cushions, hassocks, and books were hurled at the altar and its

furniture; while the clergy were spat upon, hustled, and kicked within the church, and only protected from the greater outrages by the efforts of sixty or eighty gentlemen from different parts of London, who, unasked, came to the rescue.[1]

What was the reason for these riots at the church of St George's in the East, the lovely Hawksmoor building whose exterior still stands on the north side of the Highway? Why should the rector, Bryan King, and his colleagues have aroused so much bitter hostility in what was perhaps mid-Victorian London's poorest and most deprived parish? The answer has to do with the difficult problems facing the Church of England in the nineteenth-century East End, namely that of a population which was indifferent to the Established Church. As in all Victorian cities, people were simply ignoring the Church: the religious census of 1851 showed that less than one in ten people in the cities were attending church on Sundays. In addition many churches were suffering from 'absenteeism'; the rector before Bryan King had visited St George's in the East once in the previous seven years.

The Church of England's response to this alarming state of affairs was simply to erect more churches. Bishop Blomfield, Bishop of London from 1828 to 1856, referred to this proposed building as 'a work of prudence no less than charity'; its objects was 'to reclaim hundreds of thousands of the poor from practical heathenism, and to give increased efficiency and therefore stability to the Church'.[2] It was an attitude which placed a touching faith in the magnetic powers of bricks and mortar. In Bethnal Green alone, twelve new churches were consecrated, while in Stepney an extraordinary twenty-six new churches were built between 1823 and 1891. Even today, when so many buildings have been pulled down, almost every neighbourhood in the East End seems to contain the gloomy and derelict hulk of a Victorian church.

At times there were almost more churches in the East End than clergymen willing to come and work here. But in the middle of the nineteenth century a number of young men entered the church who could see quite clearly that the ecclesiastical authorities were doing little to bring the true church, as opposed to church buildings, to the people of the East End. Equipped with determination, selflessness and a social conscience which prompted them to act rather than to agonise, clergymen such as Charles Lowder and Stewart Headlam sought out East End livings. They argued in terms similar to the 'liberation theology' current in Latin America that the

Church had a special mission to the dispossessed. As Stewart Headlam put it, 'I have always deprecated other-worldliness, as it is called, morbid concern about self, hysterical visions of Heaven, as though earth were a place to be despaired of. I have always talked of the Kingdom of Heaven being fulfilled here and now on earth, and deprecated too much dwelling on a future life, fortified by the fact that Christ Himself said very little about the other world, and very much about this.'[3]

This movement has been classified under different names: some refer to it as 'Anglo-Catholicism', others as 'Christian Socialism'. But whatever it is called, its exponents agreed that the Gospels carried a social and political message of egalitarianism – that we are alike in the eyes of God, that we must love our neighbour, that the rich man is going to have problems entering the Kingdom of Heaven. Unlike some East End philanthropists, clergymen such as Lowder and Headlam lived in the district along with their parishioners, involving themselves in the day-to-day struggles of the local community. In the nineteenth century the parish church often operated as a welfare state, providing schools, clubs and soup-kitchens.

Within the movement there were two strands. The first was exemplified by Charles Lowder and emphasised the importance of ritual in services. Lowder had been educated at Oxford but he had known poverty after his father went bankrupt. His first job had been in Pimlico, the poorest part of West London. Then, in 1856, he was appointed to St George's in the East, Shadwell, where the rector, Bryan King, formerly the curate of St John's, Bethnal Green, was coping with a terribly deprived parish. By 1851 the 243 acres of St George's parish housed some 48,000 people, with 23 houses to an acre; the metropolitan average was 5½.[4] The East London Association carried out a survey around the church and found that of the 733 houses contained in the neighbouring four

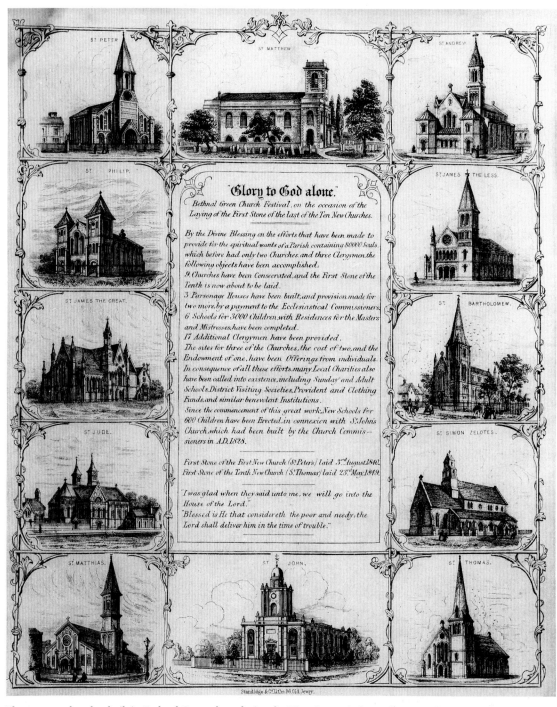

The ten new churches built in Bethnal Green alone during the Victorian period. St John (*centre bottom*) was designed by Sir John Soane.

streets 40 were public houses and beer-shops and 154 were houses of 'ill-fame'.[5]

In *London: A Pilgrimage* of 1872, the French artist Gustave Doré drew a picture of Bluegate Fields, Shadwell, which was just off Cable Street, and which is terrible in its gloom and depression. Unemployed men lounge around hopelessly outside slum dwellings, ragged children hang on to the tattered skirts of their mothers, muck and sewage lie stagnant in the middle of the street. The only light comes from the pub on the corner. In the commentary to the book, the journalist Blanchard Jerrold uses this depiction of Bluegate Fields to draw attention to what he saw as the root problem of Victorian poverty:

> If in the densely-packed haunts of poverty and crime – in the hideous tenements stacked far and wide, round such institutions as the Bluegate Fields Ragged School in Shadwell – there are hundreds who have never had the chance to escape to comfort and virtuous courses; there are – and they are the main body of the army – the victims of Drink, illustrators of every horror, form of suffering, and description of crime, to which the special curse of our land leads the poor. At the corner of every tumble-down street is the flaring public-house lamp – hateful as the fabled jewel in the loathsome toad's head.

In such conditions, King and Lowder tried to make their services as beautiful as possible. A colleague of Lowder claimed that by doing so 'it raises the hearts of the poor out of the miseries of their earthly lot into the majesty and peace of heaven. The beauty and the brightness of the services, the glorious music, the solemn dignity of the ritual, all these contrast with the squalidness and nakedness of their homes, and makes the church to them the very house of God, the gate of heaven.'[6] By comparing this remark with that of Headlam, one can see the differences between the two men: Headlam was much more of a political activist.

The ritualism of Lowder and others called for the use of vestments, processions, lights, incense, choral services, flowers, pictures and music. It was these elements which began to arouse opposition at St George's in the East towards the end of the 1850s. In October 1858, King and Lowder were joined by Father Mackonochie, another controversial High Churchman, and from this point onwards the hostility of some parishioners towards what they called 'Popery' started to take the form of disrupting the services. In March 1859 this opposition managed to get the Reverend Hugh Allen, a vociferous Low Churchman, elected to a post at the church, leading to the absurd situation whereby Allen forcibly occupied the pulpit and urged on his supporters in the congregation to wreak havoc during the service being taken by King, Lowder and Mackonochie. On 25 September 1859, Lowder was confronted by a mob as he walked along Old Gravel Lane which wanted to throw him off the dock bridge, but his friends managed to get him away. The church was closed for six weeks; on reopening things carried on as rowdily as before. By January 1860, 180 policemen were stationed in the church each Sunday morning and evening. Allen's supporters soon attracted followers who cared little for the religious issues but who recognised the opportunity for a good fight. It was noted that the area's brothel-owners and pub-keepers, who stood to lose most from any religious revival, were organising the riots. By the end of February 1860 events had reached such a stage that it seemed as if sooner rather than later the church would go up in flames.

At this point the respected Thomas Hughes, best-known as the author of *Tom Brown's Schooldays*, intervened with a compromise plan which involved the departure of King, whose health had broken down, supposedly temporarily. In fact he never came back, accepting a parish in the country. Father Mackonochie eventually left for the church of St Alban's, Holborn, where he continued to be the centre of much similar furore, whilst Lowder managed to establish his own church, St Peter's, London Docks, in Wapping Lane. There he gained a loyal following because of his fearless work during the cholera epidemic of 1866–7. St Peter's is still very much alive – a visit to the church finds one enveloped in an atmosphere of warmth and mystery. Two stained-glass windows portray Lowder and Mackonochie, while the charming little Chapel of the Resurrection is a memorial to Lowder. Other images represent Wapping dock scenes. The uncompromising 'Notes to Visitors' are blunt and explicit: 'Some people will tell you that at the Reformation the Church of England ceased to be Catholic and became Protestant. Do not believe them.'

Stewart Headlam was an Old Etonian whose radical political views ensured that he spent his life in conflict with his ecclesiastical superiors. He was never offered a parish, and for eleven years was deprived of his licence by the Bishop of London. While still a curate at St Matthew's in Bethnal Green he founded the Guild of St Matthew in 1877. This date is often taken to mark the beginning of Christian Socialism. A resolution passed by the Guild in Trafalgar Square in October 1884 gives some idea of its political stance:

Whereas the present contrast between the great body of the workers who produce much and consume little, and of those classes which produce little and consume much is contrary to the Christian doctrines of brotherhood and justice, this meeting urges on all Churchmen the duty of supporting such measures as will tend – a) To restore to the people the value which they give to the land; b) to bring about a better distribution of the wealth created by labour; c) to give the whole body of the people a voice in their own government; d) to abolish false standards of worth and dignity.[7]

Headlam was similar to Lowder in both his commanding presence and his bravery. He was one of the very few public figures to stand by Oscar Wilde during the playwright's trial and imprisonment and offered bail for Wilde even though he knew that several 'friends' would disown him for doing so, and the mob threatened his house with stoning. At an election meeting after Wilde's trial a heckler shouted out: 'Isn't this the man that went bail for the notorious convict, Wilde?' Headlam jumped up and replied: 'Yes, I am the man, and by the laws of England everyone is reckoned innocent until he is proved guilty. And I would do it again.' George Bernard Shaw tried to get up a petition calling for the reprieve of Wilde, but he could find only one man brave enough to put his name to the document: Stewart Headlam. It was Headlam, too, who greeted Wilde on his release from Wandsworth Prison in May 1897.[8]

Headlam acted as he did even though he knew that his actions would cost the Guild members. He also faced disapproval by founding the Church and Stage Guild in 1879, seeking to reverse the pulpit's traditional disapproval of the theatre. Although the rector of St Matthew's, Bethnal Green, forced Headlam out of his curacy because of his involvement with this organisation, Headlam maintained his connections with the area. For seventeen years he represented Bethnal Green as a councillor on the London County Council. He was especially interested in education, throwing himself into the task of making sure that East End schools and evening classes were as good as anywhere else in the capital.

A colleague of Headlam wrote that 'To join him in a walk through its streets was to be in the company of a Pied Piper of Bethnal Green. The children had a welcome for him as soon as he appeared; out they rushed from their houses or from their play and held on to his coat-tails.' The Liberal MP for Bethnal Green, Sir Percy Harris, summed up: ' ... if ever there was an unselfish public servant, devoted to the cause of mankind, it was Stewart Headlam.'[9] After his death in November 1924 he was and is remembered by the name of Headlam Street which leads off Cambridge Heath Road.

The Museum of Childhood, Bethnal Green

Lying away on what were once the outskirts of London, Bethnal Green was famous for its fields and farms. Samuel Pepys visited his friend Sir William Rider whose house lay just to the south of our Roman Road; the diarist had too much to drink: 'We drank great store of wine, and a beer glass at last which made me almost sick.' In September 1666, Pepys returned to Rider's house where he stored his valuables during the Great Fire of London, most valuable of all being his diary.

The Green itself was gradually formed during the seventeenth century out of what was called 'Poor's Ground', and it covered several acres. The only building which survives from this period is Netteswell House at the back of the Museum and occupied by the curator. Later Bethnal Green was noted for its mental asylums, which explains why the middle section is still known locally as 'Barmy Park'.[1] The Bethnal Green Library, opened in 1922, occupies the site of the largest asylum; inside it contains portraits of Wagner, Marx, Morris and Darwin.

Slowly the fringes of the Green were built over. The most important development was Sir John Soane's St John's Church of 1828, which still stands facing Bethnal Green Road with its unusual 'beehive' tower. In the 1860s the Museum at South Kensington (now the Victoria and Albert) offered its iron structure, built originally for the Great Exhibition of 1851 and known familiarly as the 'Brompton Boilers', to any London district wishing to start a museum. Encased in a new brick covering, the Bethnal Green Museum opened in 1872.

Some critics had prophesied that few East Enders would ever make much use of such an institution; in fact there were 850,000 visitors in the first six months alone.[2] It provided the first home for what became the Wallace Collection and also the nucleus of the National Portrait Gallery. In 1895 the public was allowed access to Bethnal Green Gardens, the remnants of the old Green. Today the Bethnal Green Museum of Childhood is a branch of the Victoria and Albert and houses a fine collection of toys, dolls and puppets as well as clothes and dresses, the last including examples of the work of the Spitalfields weavers. In the forecourt of the Museum is a cast-iron statue called 'The Eagle Slayer' which was also once exhibited at the Great Exhibition.

The Jewish Soup Kitchen in Brune Street, Spitalfields. Contrary to popular belief, not all Jewish people became wealthy.

The Jewish Community in the East End

A major influx of Jewish people into London took place during the last decades of the nineteenth century in the wake of the pogroms launched by the authorities in Poland and Tsarist Russia.[1] In 1881–2 alone, for example, 225,000 Jewish families fled Russia. Between 1870 and 1914 about 120,000 Jewish people came to London, though some remained here only briefly before setting off for the United States.

They sometimes received a cool reception from Londoners, and an undercurrent of anti-Semitism finally resulted in the passage of the Aliens Act of 1906 which restricted entry to Britain – although this measure was not stringently enforced by the new Liberal government. Moreover the established Jewish community was fearful that these penniless, jobless and Yiddish-speaking refugees might tarnish the carefully cultivated and respectable image of Anglo-Jewry. In addition these newcomers were Ashkenazi Jews from eastern Europe and therefore looked down on by the Sephardi Jews of Spanish and Portuguese origin. The then Lord Rothschild summed up these anxieties at a meeting of the Jewish Board of Guardians when he warned: 'We have now a new Poland on our hands in East London. Our first business is to humanise our Jewish immigrants, and then to Anglicise them.'[2]

In 1900, C. Russell and H. S. Lewis published a book called *The Jew in London* which included a map showing the proportion of Jewish people in the East End.[3] A black band along a street indicated a proportion of 95–100 per cent, and the map reveals just how quickly parts of Spitalfields and Whitechapel were indeed turned into 'new Polands'. Most of the black bands are concentrated in the streets to the north of Wentworth Street, both sides of Old Montague Street, the vicinity of Tenter Street to the north of Prescot Street, and the neighbourhoods around Plumber's Row and Fieldgate Street and to the west of Cannon Street Road. Here, virtually everyone was Jewish. Why were there such close groupings? Jerry White has pointed out that these newcomers had of necessity to be near to a synagogue, a kosher butcher and a communal baths.[4] In any case, the East End was already so crowded that no available room existed for the Jewish immigrants to spread out.[5]

One of these newcomers was Israel Zangwill, who was educated at the Jews' Free School in the 1870s and went on to write a series of novels of which the most famous, *Children of the Ghetto*, was published in 1892. Although unfairly neglected today, Zangwill's books bring out the extraordinary resilience of the Jewish immigrants who stamped their own way of life here on the East End. A recent study by Jerry White of the Rothschild Dwellings erected in Flower and Dean Street, Spitalfields, in 1887 has shown how, despite the rigorous list of rules imposed by the Superintendent and the urban surroundings unfamiliar to those raised in the vast wastes of the Ukraine, the residents still retained a sense of communal life and togetherness based around the quarter-acre courtyard which became a kind of village green.

The new Jewish settlers were also helped by their possession of a distinctive language, Yiddish. This bastardised, mongrel but highly expressive dialect had originated in North

Rhineland in the Middle Ages. As Jewish people had moved eastwards it had gained Polish and Russian elements as well as some Hebrew. Yiddish was, and still is, a living language of the lower classes which has evolved over the centuries. Twentieth-century English has taken over some of its vocabulary; for instance, words like 'kosher' and 'gazump' are now in common use.

The Jewish refugees soon developed their own networks of self-help and support, such as the Jewish Friendly Society movement first founded in 1885 and already numbering 176 societies by 1901. The Jewish Working Men's Club was founded in 1872, moving to new premises in Great Alie Street eleven years later which could accommodate 1,300 adults and 300 young men. The Workers' Friend Club in Jubilee Street, opened in February 1906, was a later addition – as, too, was the Workers' Circle, which had its own library and reading-room. As this list suggests, a strong emphasis was placed on broadly educational and cultural activities. Sometimes existing 'Gentile' institutions were virtually appropriated, such as the Whitechapel Library whose reading-room provided intellectual stimulation, warmth and a place to meet. The poet and artist Isaac Rosenberg, killed in the trenches in 1918, was the most famous of the Library's frequenters – there is a plaque outside in his honour – but it plays a large part in virtually all the autobiographies and memoirs of the Jewish East End.

Although the top floors were badly damaged during the Blitz, the Whitechapel Library has survived, which is more than can be said of the Yiddish theatres that once abounded in the East End. The first was opened in 1886 for the actor Jacob Adler and his troupe which had fled from Russia in December 1883. Although Adler, nicknamed 'the Jewish Irving' and 'the Great Eagle', was undoubtedly the most famous Jewish actor of his generation and was related to the Chief Rabbi who is commemorated by the name of the street which links Whitechapel Road with Commercial Road, there was much opposition amongst Anglo-Jewry to the Yiddish theatre. In one way it reminded those already here too vividly of the East European world which they had left behind decades before. Adler's troupe also used actresses and sometimes played on a Friday in direct contravention of Hebrew teaching.[6]

In 1886 a wealthy butcher called David Smith raised £3,000 for the construction of a permanent Yiddish theatre which was installed at the back of 3 Prince's (now 6–10 Princelet) Street. It contained an orchestra pit, a gallery and a library. The company's repertoire ranged from Yiddish classics by Abraham Goldfaden to versions of Shakespeare, Ibsen and Gogol. In January 1887, however, at a packed Prince's Street Theatre, a cry of 'Fire!' – false, as it turned out – led to a panic, and in the stampede seventeen people died. The *Jewish Chronicle*, voice of respectable Anglo-Jewry, drew the moral that the disaster 'ought to be a lesson to avoid such performances of strolling minstrels acting in the jargon [Yiddish], and helping to keep up the alienation of the foreign contingent'.[7]

Although Adler and his troupe left for America the following month, the Jewish passion for dramatic excitement did not lessen. Often companies staged Yiddish plays at the established East End theatres like the Standard in Shoreditch and, from 1905, Yiddish drama was a permanent feature at the Pavilion along Whitechapel Road. This huge playhouse held 3,500 spectators. There were new venues, too: the Manor Yiddish Theatre in Hackney, the Jewish Music-Hall in Christian Street, and from 1912 another purpose-built Yiddish theatre called the Temple which was in Commercial Road and held 900 spectators. Its first performance included a Jewish opera called *King Ahaz*, followed by a Yiddish *Rigoletto*. Unfortunately it was unable to sustain the demands of putting on both

operas and plays, and the Temple closed within six months.

One constant factor was the histrionic quality of the Jewish audiences, graphically described by Harry Blacker in his account of performances at the Pavilion:

Here, the Yiddish theatre flourished in all its sentimental glory, offering the romance-deprived audiences improbable slices of life where virtue always triumphed over vice. At predictable intervals during each performance the actors broke into ballads that wrung the hearts and brought tears to the eyes of the audience, already smarting from the pall of tobacco smoke that partially obscured the stage. Upstairs, in the overcrowded gallery, and looking amazingly like an animated Hogarth cartoon, were the mums and dads who watched the action and at the same time consumed gargantuan snacks of schmaltz herring, fish and chips, pieces of cold chicken, oranges, pineapple chunks and monkey nuts, all openly carried into the theatre in shopping baskets. The unconsumed portions of the repast were tossed over the rails onto the heads of the 'Capitalists' in the pit below. The remote verbal exchanges that followed the bombardment often provided better entertainment than the advertised play.[8]

As well as the Yiddish theatres there were also of course the religious houses built in the East End. Jerry White has listed just those within walking distance a hundred years ago of the Rothschild Dwellings in Flower and Dean Street, Spitalfields:

The believer had a choice of shuls in Artillery Lane, Cutler St, Duke's Place, Fournier Street (the Machzikei HaDath), Goulston St, Hanbury St, New Court Row, Spital Sq, Union St and White's Row. In Thrawl St there was a Rabbinical seminary at the Etz Chaim Yeshiva or Tree of Life College. And at the Great

The (in)famous Petticoat Lane market a century ago. The positioning of the clothes explains why they are called 'hand-me-downs'.

Assembly Hall, Mile End Rd, the tenants of the Four Per Cent could have free tickets for special services held during the High Holidays. All of this was apart from the numberless nameless stiebels, local synagogues organised on the old village community basis.[9]

If the Jewish immigrants brought with them their own culture and religion, what they did not bring were jobs. Instead they found themselves forced into street-selling, tailoring and bootmaking, all of them trades requiring little capital with which to get started. Usually the conditions were abominable, and workers were packed away in tiny overcrowded 'sweatshops' labouring for inordinately long hours. Few of these workshops were registered, as the law demanded, but in any event a shortage of inspectors meant that they effectively existed outside the law.

Tailoring was the most important source of work, mainly because it offered chances to unskilled labour. As one London tailor pointed out in the 1880s, 'our trade, unfortunately being an easy trade to obtain a small knowledge of, is one to which they [foreign immigrants] rush in very large numbers'.[10] Piecework drove down wage rates, and in any case the seasonal nature of the trade meant that there was little work between August and November, a mad rush before Christmas, then slack again afterwards. The 'sweatshops' were at the mercy of the wholesalers, and with such small units of production it was almost impossible to set up trade unions. It is not surprising that so many Jewish settlers should have been imbued with a burning desire to better themselves and to move on elsewhere.

The 'People's Palace' and Toynbee Hall

One East End philanthropist of the nineteenth century was the entrepreneur and businessman 'Barber' Beaumont, who established a Philosophic Institute in Beaumont Street, to the south of Mile End Road. After his death in 1841 the trustees were uncertain how to continue Beaumont's venture, but their opportunity came in the 1880s after the publication of Walter Besant's novel *All Sorts and Conditions of Men*. Subtitled 'An Impossible Story', Besant's book tells the story of Angela Messenger, a wealthy heiress who comes to the East End to help the poor needleworkers and ends up marrying Harry Gosling in St Dunstan's, Stepney Green. In the course of the novel Besant portrayed a social and cultural centre which he called the 'Palace of Delights'.

This provided the stimulus for the plan that the East End, supposedly a cultural desert, should indeed have just such an institution, and the Beaumont Trust bought up some land to the north of Mile End Road administered by the Drapers' Company whose Bancroft Hospital included almshouses and a school. On 14 May 1887, Queen Victoria was enticed down to the East End to open this 'People's Palace', with not altogether pleasant results to the Queen as she passed along Whitechapel Road and Mile End Road. She noted in her journal: ' ... what rather damped the effect of the really general and very enthusiastic reception, to me, was the booing and hooting, of perhaps only two or three, now and again, all along the route, evidently sent there on purpose, and frequently the same people, probably Socialists and the worst Irish.'[1]

There were two aspects to the work of the People's Palace, the educational and recreational. Out of the first developed the East London College which eventually became a part of the University of London, obtaining its charter and the name Queen Mary College in

1934. As for entertainment, the Queen's Hall hosted lectures and concerts, the latter often conducted by Sir Malcolm Sargent and remembered with great affection by those present. In 1931 it was burnt down but opened again after rebuilding in 1937. After the Second World War the Queen's Hall was absorbed into Queen Mary College.

The People's Palace was only one of the educational institutions opened at this time. Another was Toynbee Hall, started in 1884 by Canon Samuel Barnett and his wife Henrietta (who also was the driving force behind the creation of Hampstead Garden Suburb), based at St Jude's Church, Commercial Street. It was named after Arnold Toynbee, the writer and philosopher who had worked in Whitechapel from 1875 until his early death in 1883. With Barnett as Warden and fourteen Oxbridge graduates in residence, the hall soon attracted young middle-class socialists and liberals, such as William Beveridge, later to produce the famous report which fathered the Welfare State, who felt that they should get to know the working classes. This sometimes patronising attitude towards 'the deserving poor' was satirised by Arthur Morrison in his novel *A Child of the Jago*.

However, Barnett's radical sympathies were always evident, such as when he entertained the Central Strike Committee here after the victorious Dock Strike of 1889. The Whitechapel Art Gallery's first exhibitions were held at Toynbee Hall as were the early meetings of what became the Workers' Educational Association (WEA) and also the Youth Hostels Association. In 1910 the Secretary of Toynbee Hall was Clement Attlee, later to be MP for Limehouse from 1922 and then the Labour Prime Minister after the Second World War. Although it was badly bombed during the Blitz, Toynbee Hall was rebuilt, unlike St Jude's. A survey carried out for the Bishop of

London after the First World War indicated that of St Jude's parish 8,000 people were Jews and foreigners and only 200 were Christians. The church was demolished in 1929.[2]

Some East End Benefactors: William Booth, John Passmore Edwards, Andrew Carnegie and the Reverend William ('Hang Theology') Rogers

The poverty of the Victorian East End attracted several benefactors other than Angela Burdett-Coutts. In July 1865, William Booth, born in Nottingham and for a number of years a pawnbroker, began his 'Christian Mission' in Whitechapel, first addressing pedestrians on Mile End Waste near Wren's Trinity Almshouses. A statue of Booth stands there today. Booth struggled long and hard against initial indifference and hostility, but his undoubted sincerity and the provision of relief to the poor gradually won him supporters. In 1878 a slip of the tongue led to the movement being renamed the Salvation Army, and subsequently military titles and uniforms were used. Booth became 'General' Booth. Particularly striking was the decision to adapt hit tunes into Salvation Army songs: 'Within a year of their Musical Department opening up, there were four hundred Salvation Army bands crashing into a repertoire of eighty-eight hit tunes.'[1] One especially valuable facet of the Salvation Army's work was their attention to the plight of women.

One facility which until recently was taken for granted was this country's excellent public library system. Yet before the First World War there were few public libraries in Britain; although the Libraries Act of 1850 empowered borough councils to introduce them, few ratepayers welcomed this additional expenditure. In the East End, libraries had to be provided by two individuals: John Passmore Edwards and Andrew Carnegie.

A statue of William Booth, founder of the Salvation Army, who began his campaign in Whitechapel in July 1865.

89

Passmore Edwards was a Cornishman who became a journalist, a newspaper proprietor and a Liberal MP. From the 1890s he began to use his wealth to build educational institutions in the East End and in Cornwall. He helped to pay for the establishment of the Whitechapel Art Gallery as well as for a number of 'free libraries' in Shoreditch, Hoxton, Whitechapel and Poplar. A fine example of a Passmore Edwards building is Limehouse Library in Commercial Road; look up towards the roof and you will see two open books in stone. The museum in Stratford, opened in 1900, is also named after Passmore Edwards who contributed half of its £6,000 cost.[2]

Andrew Carnegie was a Scot who emigrated to America in 1848 as a young boy. He amassed a fortune as an iron and steel magnate. In his book *The Gospel of Wealth* (1900), Carnegie refreshingly argued that 'a man who dies rich dies disgraced', and in accordance with this maxim he spent the rest of his life giving away his wealth. By the time of his death in 1919, Carnegie had financed the setting-up of 2,505 libraries all over the world. Two good examples of Carnegie-endowed libraries can still be seen in the East End: in Pitfield Street, Hoxton, and in Cubitt Town on the Isle of Dogs.

Finally, one major asset of the East End is the Bishopsgate Institute founded in 1894 by the splendidly named Reverend William ('Hang Theology') Rogers. Housed in an art nouveau building designed by C. H. Townsend, it contains a lecture-hall and an excellent reference library with a marvellous London collection.[3]

Matchgirls and Dockers: The Strikes of 1888 and 1889

In the 1840s a doctor called Hector Gavin conducted a careful and detailed study of Bethnal Green, publishing his research under the title *Sanitary Ramblings* in 1848. Even today, at a distance of nearly 150 years, Dr Gavin's book still has the power to shock. He found 30,000 people living in half a square mile or, to turn the microscope round the other way, eight people living and sleeping in a room 10 feet long by 6 feet wide by 9 feet high. Pleasant Place turned out to be a misnomer: 'The street is nothing more or less than an elongated lake or canal; only, in place of water, we have a black, slimy, muddy compost of clay and putrescent animal and vegetable remains.' Pleasant Place has gone; Three Colts Lane remains: ' . . . at a distance of about 230 feet, and from 40 to 60 feet in width, was one enormous ditch or stagnant lake of thickened putrefying matter; in this Pandora's box dead cats and dogs were profusely scattered, exhibiting every stage of disgusting decomposition.'[1] Dr Gavin found one household too poor to bury a corpse, which was therefore kept on the premises. Nearly sixty years later the American Jack London found a similar case:

> When a child dies, and some are always bound to die, since fifty-five per cent of the East End children die before they are five years old, the body is laid out in the same room. And if they are very poor, it is kept for some time until they bury it. During the day it lies on the bed; during the night when the living take the bed, the dead occupies the table, from which, in the morning, when the dead is put back into the bed, they eat their breakfast. Sometimes the body is placed on the shelf which serves as a pantry for their

Some of the Bryant and May matchgirls who successfully went on strike in the summer of 1888.

food. Only a couple of weeks ago, an East End woman was in trouble, because, in this fashion, being unable to bury it, she had kept her dead child three weeks.[2]

One major reason for this dire poverty lay in the very low wages paid in the East End. The 'New Model' unions formed in the middle of the nineteenth century called for high subscriptions from their members, which assured them of generous 'friendly' benefits relating to sickness, death and unemployment, but which excluded the less well off, even if they had not already been excluded by rules barring non-craftsmen from the trade. The absence of employee organisation meant that, with every man out for himself, and forced to compete against everyone else for work that would feed his wife and children, brutal callousness was commonplace. There were terrible instances of this on the docks where in any case the work was seasonal: if the Thames was frozen, then there was no work – and no dole. Ben Tillett has left a graphic description in his pamphlet *A Dock Labourer's Bitter Cry* of what it was like to be herded into a shed called the 'Cage' where the foreman 'walks up and down with the air of a dealer in a cattle-market, picking and choosing from a crowd of men who, in their eagerness to obtain employment, trample each other under foot, and where like beasts they fight for the chance of a day's work'. Presumably such scenes never intruded upon the perceptions of those middle-class Victorian writers who claimed, from the comfort of their drawing-rooms, that the root problem of the East End was laziness on the part of its inhabitants.

Conditions of work in the East End were often horrific, especially for matchgirls. The manufacture of matches in England had started in the 1820s; within a few years evidence piled up demonstrating the ill-effects on the matchgirls of the phosphorus used in the process. Most

debilitating was a condition known as 'phossy jaw' in which the lower half of the face was gradually eaten away. Photographs of girls suffering from this complaint are often horrendous. One of the largest firms involved was Bryant & May, which opened a new factory in Fairfield Road, Bow, during 1860. Within a few years they were producing nearly 2 million matches a year, but at what cost to the girls?[3] Quite apart from the terrible working conditions, the directors of Bryant & May were not exactly renowned for their generosity. Being enthusiastic supporters of the Liberal Party, they decided to put up a statue to William Gladstone, the party's leader, in 1882. But who was to pay for it? Why, the matchgirls themselves would surely be only too delighted, and therefore money was docked from their already meagre wages. At the unveiling of the statue the girls rushed forward and smeared blood from their arms on the base of the statue. Gladstone's statue is still there, outside St Mary's Church, Bow. Six years after this protest, the matchgirls were to prove for a second time that they had ideas of their own.

On 23 June 1888 the campaigner Annie Besant published an article called 'White Slavery in London', revealing that, notwithstanding the substantial profits made each year by Bryant & May, many of their matchgirls earned as little as four shillings a week, and even then fines were regularly deducted for offences such as unpunctuality. The company proceeded to sack the girls suspected of giving Besant her information; but, to the consternation of both employers and the 'New Model' unions which regarded unskilled workers as being incapable of organised action, the rest of the workforce walked out in sympathy. For the next month the 1,400 matchgirls threw themselves into trying to publicise the terrible conditions in which they were required to work. Two of their favourite meeting-places were the Assembly Hall just beside the Trinity Almshouses on the north

A barefooted boy selling the Bryant and May matches which were to be the cause of the famous dispute in 1888.

side of Mile End Road, and Christchurch Hall in Hanbury Street, Spitalfields.

An independent Toynbee Hall report was published which largely supported the match-girls' case. With public opinion turning against them, the directors of Bryant & May finally gave in, reinstated the girls and increased their wages. It was a victory with enormous consequences for working people. If the unorganised matchgirls could mount such a successful campaign and remain united to the end, then surely other groups of workers in the East End could also do something about their rates of pay and working conditions. Bryant & May closed down their Bow factory in 1971, but the gloomy buildings still stand on the east side of Fairfield Road with the letters B and M visible on the entrance columns.

Later in 1888 gasworkers based at the Beckton works in West Ham went on strike and they, too, were successful, achieving an eight-hour day, albeit for six days a week. Next year saw the biggest dispute of all, the Dock Strike of 1889. That August a confrontation over the very existence of unions at the South-West India Dock escalated and the dockers came out on strike. Like the match-girls, dockers had been regarded as being too primitive and individualistic for the formation of trade unions, yet now their solidarity proved powerful. They demanded two main improvements: payment of sixpence an hour (the docker's tanner) and employment of not less than four hours at a stretch, rather than fragments here and there which prevented them from looking for another job that day.

Having set up their headquarters at the Wade's Arms in Jeremiah Street in Poplar, the leaders of the strike – amongst them John Burns, Ben Tillett, Tom Mann and Eleanor Marx, Karl's daughter, who was secretary of the strike committee – realised that public support for their case was essential. They set out to win this by means of an imaginative campaign which included daily marches along Commercial Road to the dock owners' offices in Leadenhall Street in the heart of the City of London. The first march, for example, boasted some forty-one banners; on some of these banners the dockers stuck stinking onions, old fish-heads and mouldy pieces of meat in order to show the City magnates what the dockers had to live on.[4] Two contemporaries, H. L. Smith and Vaughan Nash, have provided a lengthy description of the marches which brings out their colour and flamboyance and explains why they were called 'a kind of caricature of the Lord Mayor's show':

First came a posse of police, behind whom the marshals of the procession, with axes and scarves, reserved a clear space for the leaders. With them some-times walked Superintendent Forster, a familiar figure in the strike. His solici-tude for the comfort and safe passage of his convoy were unmistakable, and the man in the straw hat at his side [John Burns], deep in consultation, might have been a brother officer in plain clothes. Next came the brass band of the steve-dores, following which streamed the multitude whose calling lay at the docks and riverside. Such finery as they boasted in the way of flags and banners had been lent by friendly and trade societies, and this gave the procession the appearance of a great church parade or demonstration of foresters. There were burly stevedores, lightermen, ship painters, sailors and firemen, riggers, scrapers, engineers, shipwrights, perma-nent men got up respectably, preferables cleaned up to look like permanents, and unmistakable casuals with vari-coloured patches on their faded greenish gar-ments; Foresters and Sons of the Phoenix in gaudy scarves; Doggett's prize winners, a stalwart battalion of watermen marching proudly in long scarlet coats, pink stockings, and velvet caps, with huge pewter badges on their breasts, like decorated amphibious huntsmen; coalies in wagons fishing

An example of the imaginative tableaux used by the dockers to present their case during the 1889 strike.

aggressively for coppers with bags tied to the end of poles, a brother coalie in effigy attached as figure-head to one of their vehicles, placarded with the announcement that he wouldn't go a step higher up the ladder on which he sprawled till the docker had got his tanner; skiffs mounted on wheels manned by stolid watermen; ballast heavers laboriously winding and tipping an empty basket, Father Neptune on his car in tinsel crown and flowing locks, surrounded by his suite.... Emblems quaint and pathetic were carried in the ranks, the docker's cat and the sweater's cat, the docker's dinner and the sweater's dinner, the docker's baby and the sweater's baby, diminutive and ample, respectively.... The brass dressers, locked out for forming a union, brought up the rear, carrying their brass brooms like lictors.

Such was the strike procession. It had its moods – was merry on some days, taciturn on others, laughed at the Dock House sometimes, howled at it at others, but it never lost command over itself or caused serious anxiety to its leaders or the citizens of London.[5]

Enlivened by such pageants, by bands – the strikers spent some £1,000 on the musicians – and by tableaux, the marchers finished up either on Tower Hill or at Hyde Park. Within a few weeks £50,000 had been raised from the public in Britain, a sum boosted by an additional £30,000 from the Australian trade unions. Gradually the dock-owners began to wilt under the pressure of public opinion, and in mid-September 1889 the dockers returned to work having gained nearly all their demands. The discipline of the strikers is highlighted by the fact that, despite employers' attempts to incite violence by bringing in 'blackleg' labour, less than twenty police-court cases arose from the dispute.[6]

95

'The Sheer Joy of Living':
The Life and Songs of Marie Lloyd (1870–1922)

On 9 May 1885 a fifteen-year-old girl called Matilda Wood, the daughter of a man who worked as a part-time barman at night and an artificial-flower seller by day, made her stage début at the Grecian Saloon in City Road. She soon showed that her natural vivacity appealed immensely to audiences, actually taking the spectators' mind and attention away from the food and drink consumed so copiously in the halls during performances. Matilda Wood began to tour the country's music-halls, still appearing under the stage-name 'Bella Delmere'.[1] It was the typically arduous apprenticeship undergone by all would-be music-hall stars, trying to raise a laugh or flicker of interest amongst often indifferent audiences seated in cold and draughty venues and touring with every kind of weird and wonderful act. In September 1886, for instance, the sixteen-year-old girl was at the Sebright Music-Hall in London sharing a bill with Sergeant Simms' Zouave Troupe, the King of Egypt and a 'one-legged champion'.

The same year saw her change her name to 'Marie Lloyd' – Marie because she liked it, and Lloyd from the publication *Lloyd's Weekly News*. With her new identity she found 'stardom', earning more than £100 a week as a top-of-the-bill attraction. She was still just sixteen.

Born in Shepherdess Walk, Hoxton, in 1870, Marie Lloyd was just one of the famous entertainers who have come from the East End. There was Charles Coborn, who scored a great success with 'The Man Who Broke the Bank at Monte Carlo', who took his stage-name from Coborn Road in Bow, and also Bud Flanagan, born in Whitechapel in 1896 as Chaim Reuben Weintrop, who later teamed up with Chesney Allen. But it was Marie

Lloyd who somehow epitomised the cockney spirit and humour, as she still does. Her married life was a disaster with three husbands: a tout, a coster singer called Alec Hurley and finally a young jockey who had won the Derby in 1910. None of the marriages lasted. Towards the end of her life the demon drink began to take over – a not uncommon occurrence when music-hall performers relied upon alcohol to enable them to appear at three or even four halls in an evening. They were also expected to drink with customers at the bar after their act.

Marie Lloyd suffered, too, from the changes pioneered by Edward Moss and Oswald Stoll, the proprietors of the Empire chain and others, who were transforming the intimate and rowdy old music-hall into the more refined and respectable 'theatre of variety', and also from the coming of radio and the cinema. She was never forgiven by the Establishment for her part in the music-hall strike of January 1907. There had been no need for her to get involved. Stars like Marie Lloyd did very nicely, unlike the artistes who propped up the rest of the bill. The managers thought that they had got their own back when they excluded her in 1912 from the first Royal Command Performance.[2] That night Marie Lloyd was performing at the London Pavilion and someone pasted special strips across the posters, proclaiming that 'Every Performance by Marie Lloyd is a Command Performance. By Order of the British Public'. On her death in October 1922 a huge funeral procession followed her coffin, while pubs in the East End were draped in black crêpe as a mark of respect.

The explanation for Marie Lloyd's popularity – more so in London than in the provinces – lay in her unpretentious vitality. She might have earned thousands of pounds but she never lost an impulsive generosity which reminds one of Nell Gwyn. Max Beerbohm observed that 'sheer joy of living was always her strongest point', while another admirer, T. S. Eliot, wrote an essay about her: '... whereas other comedians amuse their audiences as much and sometimes more than Marie Lloyd, no other comedian succeeded so well in giving expression to the life of that audience, in raising it to a kind of art. It was, I think, this capacity for expressing the soul of the people that made Marie Lloyd unique, and that made her audiences, even when they joined in the chorus, not so much hilarious as happy.'[3]

Marie Lloyd's songs reflected the troubles and travails of everyday London life, from 'Don't Dilly Dally' and 'A Little of What You Fancy Does You Good' to 'One of the Ruins That Cromwell Knocked About a Bit'. She was sometimes accused of crudity – 'The Railroad Song' was known as 'The Girl Who'd Never Had Her Ticket Punched Before'.[4] If her winks and pauses suggested that there was more to the lyrics of the song than seemed apparent at first glance, she was never coarse or vulgar. Her genuine honesty and lack of pomposity shone though her performances, and the few scratched recordings of her voice do not do her justice. There is a plaque on 55 Graham Road, Hackney, where she once lived. A pub in Chart Street, Hoxton, has been named after her, and its sign carries a portrait.

Originally opened as a Yiddish art theatre in March 1912, this building became the Palaseum cinema.

Troxies and ABCs: Cinemas in the East End

That three famous East End theatres – the Britannia, the Standard and the Pavilion – became at some point cinemas underlines the impact of moving pictures on the entertainment business. At first films were shown in temporary makeshift surroundings, rather like the penny gaffs, with live acts often interspersed between the films – in fact some of the early 'fleapits' were also called 'penny winkles'.

Gradually, however, as more investment was attracted to this new and profitable form of entertainment, the cinemas became increasingly grand. And, as Emanuel Litvinoff has recalled, the cinema was better value than the theatre at 4*d* (2p) for three hours' worth.[1] The Paragon Theatre of Varieties in Mile End Road, once visited by Little Tich and Charlie Chaplin, became the Mile End Empire in 1912, and gradually the live acts were pushed out. It was rebuilt in 1939 and eventually became the ABC Mile End.[2]

Perhaps the most splendid East End cinema was the Troxy in Commercial Road, which was opened in 1933 and had 3,250 seats. Its manager, Maurice Cheepen, was a real showman and once kept live vultures in the foyer. One sign of the changing times is that when the Prime Minister, Clement Attlee, came to the Troxy once after the war he arrived and left by bus![3] As with so many other cinemas, the Troxy found itself in trouble with the coming of television, and in 1963 the building became the home of the London Opera Centre. It is still to be found on the south side of Commercial Road, slightly tatty and faded. Today there are very few cinemas in the East End.

The East End Furniture Trade

At the City end of Commercial Road sits a modern six-storey building. Inside are the discordant sounds of musical instruments being made and also the intriguing sight of rows of would-be piano-tuners hermit-like in their individual cells with their ears pressed against a piano. This is the London College of Furniture, situated appropriately enough in the East End – for it was Shoreditch and Bethnal Green which for decades furnished not just London and the provinces but also much of the world.

Why should Shoreditch, and more particularly Curtain Road, have been the centre of the furniture trade? The first reason was geographical. Shoreditch was not only close to the Regent's Canal but close, too, to the docks which provided imports of timber and then exported the finished products. Second, the furniture trade needed a huge pool of cheap labour, just as tailoring did. And where better than the Victorian East End to draw upon such a pool? The demand for furniture was certainly present: 200 miles of new streets were built in London between 1839 and 1850 alone, which meant in turn thousands of new houses requiring to be furnished.[1]

The long and comparatively broad Curtain Road established itself as the furniture trade's 'High Street', and a stroll down it today still introduces the walker to several old showrooms.[2] There is Vaughan's, built in 1877 and containing a 'hospitality room' for customers, and the five-storey C. & R. Light on the corner of Old Street with an impressive facade. Of the 135 firms in Curtain Road in 1901, 102 were in the trade. Just to the west of Curtain Road is Charlotte Street, and to pass down between its high storerooms is like walking through a canyon. At the pub called the London Apprentice, still in Old Street, cheques were cashed.

From this angle, the East End furniture industry appears solid and impressive. In fact Curtain Road was the home of the 'middle men' who sold to such retailers as Maples in Tottenham Court Road. A very different story emerges when one looks at the appalling conditions in which the furniture was actually made. It was a classic 'sweated trade' of long hours, cut-throat competition and low wages, of endless subcontracting and families toiling ceaselessly in garrets. A recent book emphasised what this could mean in practice:

> These small masters frequently worked in their own homes, all too often only a room or garret, hence the term 'garret master' by which they were known.

They sometimes made to orders given by the 'warehousemen'; sometimes they worked without orders, speculatively 'hawking' their goods on a barrow from one warehouse to another until they were sold. The later it was on a Saturday, the more desperate they became. It was common for goods to be sold at a loss, so desperate were the garret masters to pay their assistants, buy new materials to keep them in business, as well as to buy food for their families in the coming week.[3]

Again like tailoring, it was almost impossible to organise this diverse workforce into trade unions. Between the wars several important firms moved out to the Lea Valley where land was cheap and there was room to expand, unlike in Shoreditch. In 1951, 5,092 people were employed in the furniture industry in Shoreditch and 4,040 in Bethnal Green;[4] but now, as the City of London expands northwards and eastwards, rents are rising and the remnants of the furniture trade face a grim struggle to survive.

'May the Imperial Port Prosper': The Rise and Fall of the Port of London Authority

Until the beginning of the twentieth century the remaining dock companies competed strenuously against each other in a struggle which resulted in the failure to carry out such fundamental activities as the dredging of the river simply because there was no immediate profit to be gained. Necessary improvements such as the enlargement of the dock entrances were also neglected on the grounds of expense, while the Dock Strike of 1889 revealed that it was most certainly not high wage costs which were at the root of the port's financial failings. As in the 1790s, an official inquiry was clearly required.

In 1902 a Royal Commission on the Port of London recommended that a new self-governing public trust should be constituted which would supersede the private dock companies. In March 1909 the Port of London Authority (PLA) duly took over the entire 2,700-acre dock area and embarked upon a much needed improvement programme under the chairmanship of Lord Devonport. Acutely aware of its international and imperial links, the PLA adopted as its house motto 'Floreat imperii portus', 'May the Imperial

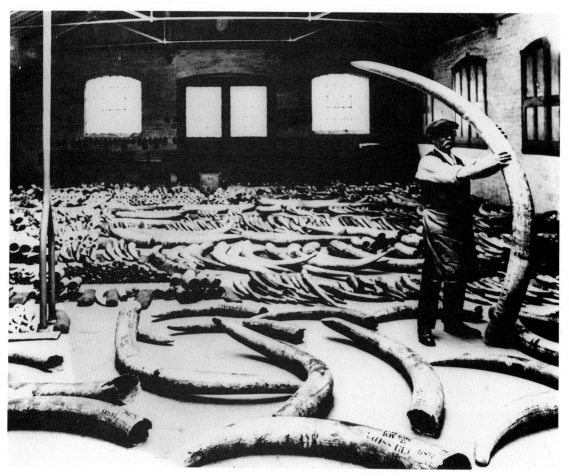

The ivory stored at St Katharine's Dock. Two model elephants still flank the entrance off East Smithfield.

Port Prosper'.[1] Even today the international flavour of the Port of London is demonstrated by exotic street-names such as Cuba, Manilla, Tobago and Trinidad. In 1922 the PLA moved into its new headquarters overlooking Trinity Square and the Tower of London, an awesome stone building which Sir Nikolaus Pevsner described as 'a super-palace for an international exhibition, showy, happily vulgar and extremely impressive'.[2]

Between the wars the PLA was responsible for updating many of the dock's facilities, and its investment led to an expansion in the tonnage using the Port as well as in the annual value of imports and exports, from £322 million in 1909 to over £450 million by 1939.[3] Much of the PLA's work, however, was destroyed by severe German bombing during the Second World War. Ironically, the Luftwaffe was guided to the docks by following the Thames from the North Sea. For fifty-seven consecutive nights London's docks were attacked, and eye-witnesses such as the lawyer and writer A. P. Herbert have described the onslaught as leaving the Thames 'like a river in hell'. The timber-storage yards of the Surrey Commercial Docks, for instance, blazed non-stop for nearly a week. The docks

The construction of the Rotherhithe Tunnel, built between 1904 and 1908.

did to some extent get their own back; the Mulberry Harbours used on 'D-Day' in June 1944 which allowed ship-to-shore landings had been built over a six-month period in the East India Docks. But by 1945 damage of £13½ million at 1939 prices included the loss or damage of a third of the Port's warehouses and transit sheds as well as the destruction of half of its total storage accommodation. For example, the still impressive North Quay warehouses of 1802 which stretch along the Import Dock of the West India Dock were originally twice as long. In addition the river was in danger of silting up owing to a six-year absence of dredging.

After the war the upstream docks briefly enjoyed an Indian summer: trade with the Commonwealth peaked during the 1950s. But all this was rapidly to change. By the 1960s trade with the Commonwealth had halved, and the worst-affected were the 'first generation' of docks because they were geared to Commonwealth trade.[4] Second, changing methods of loading and unloading ensured that the Port of London's centuries-old shift eastwards would accelerate. The introduction of mobile cranes, electric-quay cranes and also fork-lift trucks which were able to use stan-

Dockers waiting by the entrance to East India Dock, hoping for work.

dardised pallets all lessened the need for dockers. Perhaps most revolutionary of all was the impact of 'containerisation'. As John Pudney has observed, these containers 'need space, large areas of land for marshalling and stacking – up to 25 acres for each berth. Transit sheds and warehousing became redundant: the container itself is protection enough from the elements.'[5] No longer did the ships have to unload at the inconvenient docks close to the City, especially when the Tilbury Docks, though twenty-six miles downstream from London Bridge, had quick and easy access to the railway. Air and road traffic was growing, and often the new coastal ports, free from the trade unions, attracted the trade which would once have gone without question to the Port of London. By the end of the 1960s, after years of rumour and denial, the PLA began to close down the old docks. The gates were padlocked and the vast expanses of water seemingly forgotten.

The Siege of Sidney Street, 3 January 1911

In his novel *The Woman in White*, published in 1860, Wilkie Collins made much of the anonymity of the East End, arguing that it was an ideal spot to go to ground. Such attractions explain in part why so many political refugees have resided briefly in Whitechapel, amongst them Lenin and, even more surprisingly, Joseph Stalin who in May 1907 stayed at Tower House in Fieldgate Street, the gloomy lodging-house which is still there.[1] Stalin was here for the Bolshevik Congress held in Islington at the Brotherhood Church. Groups of anarchists, on the other hand, set themselves up permanently in the East End, forming clubs, establishing newspapers and sometimes living in communes, one of which was at Dunstan House overlooking Stepney Green Gardens. Invariably short of funds and unable, or unwilling, to secure jobs, a few groups turned to theft and armed robbery to support themselves. It was such activities which gave rise to one of the most famous incidents in East End history.

Late in December 1910 the inhabitants of Cutler Street, Houndsditch, reported hearing suspicious noises one night at the back of a jeweller's. The police went to investigate and surprised the intruders, who attempted to shoot their way out, killing three policemen and leaving two badly wounded. The gang split up, but most were soon captured. A reward of £500 was offered for information leading to the arrest of the remaining members, and on 3 January 1911 the last two were discovered in their lodgings at 100 Sidney Street, a thoroughfare which joins Mile End Road and Commercial Road. Surrounded by police and ordered to give themselves up, they responded by firing round after round from their Mauser pistols out of the windows. *The Times* reported the scene in graphic detail:

On the roof of the Rising Sun, a public-house overlooking the Commercial Road end of Sidney Street, was a crowd of armed police and spectators. Every few minutes shots rang out, and every now and then a ricochet from the brick walls went whistling or sighing overhead. Men armed with revolvers were peeping out from behind the van gates of the brewery entrance. The major part of the fire, however, was taking place from the windows, directly opposite those of No. 100. Here expert shots were hidden, and at the suspicion of a movement within the first floor windows they fired point blank into them. The damp haze of the morning made the burning cordite visible. At intervals the sharp cracks of the service rifles were punctuated by the savage snaps of the automatic pistols that returned the fire, and it was possible to see the striking bullets as they chipped the masonry of the windows behind which the police and soldiers were ensconced.[2]

The Scots Guards from the Tower of London were called out, and on arrival suggested a bayonet attack on 100 Sidney Street, a proposal which was turned down. The Liberal Home Secretary of the day, a certain Winston Churchill, could not keep away from the action and ordered artillery to be moved here from the barracks in St John's Wood. In the event the two 13-pound guns arrived too late. An observation-post was set up on the roof of the nearby London Hospital. As the bullets ricocheted all over the neighbouring streets, perhaps the most amazing sight was the inquisitive crowd craning their necks out of adjoining buildings in order to get a better view of proceedings, while some of the more foolhardy perilously clung on to lamp-posts, chimneys and drainpipes.[3] Throughout the siege an elderly postman continued to deliver mail to addresses in Sidney Street![4] Amongst

Top-hatted Winston Churchill, Liberal Home Secretary, surveys the proceedings at the Siege of Sidney Street in January 1911.

the bystanders, so they both claimed in their autobiographies, were a young journalist called Edgar Wallace and a future prime minister, Clement Attlee.[5]

After nearly 2,000 rounds of ammunition had been fired – although there was not one single important civilian casualty throughout the siege – and a battle which had lasted from dawn until nearly two o'clock in the afternoon, 100 Sidney Street was seen to be on fire. This may have been started on purpose by the two men inside, Fritz Svaars and 'Josef', who could see that there was no possible escape. When the police came to sift through the charred remains they found two corpses. But fiction is often more compelling than fact, and word soon got around that there had been a third man present at 100 Sidney Street called 'Peter the Painter' who had miraculously escaped the blazing inferno. For years to come East End parents used to threaten recalcitrant children with a visit from 'Peter the Painter' if they didn't start behaving themselves. Today 100 Sidney Street is no more, but it stood roughly between Lindley Street and Wolsey Street on the east side. Almost opposite is a new block of flats which is called Siege House in memory of this episode.

'The John Bull of Poplar': George Lansbury (1859–1940)

One of the most enormous developments built in the East End since the Second World War is the Lansbury Estate, which was put up for the Festival of Britain in 1951. This vast concrete expanse commemorates the Labour politician George Lansbury, one of the best-loved figures in East End history, a man whose political opponents never questioned his honesty or integrity. He realised that the building up of a radical and socialist movement in the area could only be done slowly and painstakingly, and accordingly he gave special attention to the everyday problems of local people. Before Lansbury, the labour movement's only political success in East London had been Keir Hardie's time as MP for West Ham between 1892 and 1895. Lansbury's dogged determination to right wrongs led him to be affectionately called 'the John Bull of Poplar'.[1]

In fact Lansbury was born in 1859 in Suffolk, but he moved to the East End when still a boy and, apart from a brief and disastrous spell when he emigrated to Australia, spent the rest of his life here. Although he was at first active in the Liberal Party, then in the Marxist Social Democratic Federation and finally in the Labour Party, Lansbury's prime love was local politics.

His first post came in 1892 when he was elected to the Board of Guardians responsible for supervising conditions in the workhouses in the East End and elsewhere. Lansbury recalled that Poplar's workhouse was like Dante's *Inferno*:

Sick and aged, mentally deficient, lunatics, babies and children, able-bodied and tramps all herded together in one huge range of buildings. Officers, both men and women, looked upon these people as a nuisance, and treated them accordingly. Food was mainly skilly, bread, margarine, cheese, and hard, tough meat and vegetables, and occasionally doses of salted, dried fish. Clothing was of the usual workhouse type, plenty of corduroy and blue cloth. No undergarments for either men or women, no sanitary clothes of any sort or kind for women of any age, boots were worn till they fell off.... On one visit I inspected the supper of oatmeal porridge. On this occasion the food was served up with pieces of black stuff floating around. On examination we discovered it to be rat and mice manure.[2]

In 1910, Lansbury was elected to Parliament as MP for Bow and Bromley, but in 1912 his ardent support for the suffragette movement and especially for Sylvia Pankhurst who had formed the East London Federation led him to resign his seat and fight for it again on the issue of 'Votes for Women'. In spite of his popularity he lost, indicating the strength of the prejudices against which the suffragettes had to battle. Lansbury did not regain his seat until 1922, but his energies in the intervening period were channelled into the Labour newspaper the *Daily Herald* which he founded and then edited for several years.

After the First World War, Lansbury was elected the leader of Poplar Borough Council. In the 1920s and 1930s Poplar was the poorest district in London, yet it still had to pay the same sums to central government and the London County Council as much wealthier boroughs such as Westminster and Kensington in addition to providing local services. In 1921, for instance, West London had a rateable value of £15 million and had 4,800 unemployed; Poplar with a rateable value of £4 million had 86,500 out of work.[3] In Lansbury's words, 'the poor had to keep the poor'. Poplar Council decided to stop collecting the rates for outside bodies, and on 29 July

A wonderful picture of George Lansbury opening the Chapel House Street estate on the Isle of Dogs in January 1920.

1921 the councillors marched five miles to the Law Courts in the Strand to put their case. As George Lansbury expressed it, 'If we have to choose between contempt of the poor and contempt of Court, it will be contempt of Court.' The Poplar councillors were found guilty and in September 1921 they were taken to prison. The male councillors were put in Brixton, the women in Holloway. For the next six weeks daily processions were held outside both prisons by supporters of 'Poplarism', and George Lansbury often addressed the crowds through the bars of his cell. Finally, after six weeks, he and his colleagues were released and a measure of 'rates equalisation' enacted.[4]

From the end of the First World War Lansbury and his wife Bessie lived at 39 Bow Road, and their home, prominently situated on a busy highway, became a convenient meeting-place and discussion-centre for socialists from all over the world. Lansbury claimed that if too many bricks started to come through his windows, then he knew he was doing something wrong! As a committed Christian Socialist, for many years Lansbury walked down Bow Road each Sunday to attend St Mary's Church where he also took the Bible-study class every Sunday afternoon.

In the 1931 general election the Labour Party won only forty-six seats, and Lansbury became the leader of this depleted band, encouraging them with his tremendous vigour and spirit. In 1935 he resigned this post because as a convinced pacifist he was at odds with the Labour Party's acceptance of the need for rearmament. Lansbury died in 1940, virtually penniless as a result of his unfailing generosity to those in need. His ashes were scattered off Land's End: 'I desire this because although I love England very dearly and consider this lovely island the best spot in the world, I am a convinced internationalist.' A few weeks later 39 Bow Road was hit by German bombs, causing such severe damage that only the doorway was left intact. A small garden paid for by public subscription now stands there, and a plaque honours 'A Great Servant of the People'. There is also a plaque on 203 East India Dock Road commemorating the march of the Poplar councillors on their way to the High Court on 29 July 1921.

Sir Percy Harris and Dr Alfred Salter

George Lansbury was not the only East End politician with a loyal following. Percy Harris was the Liberal MP for South and West Bethnal Green between 1922 and 1945, winning six elections. This was a remarkable tribute to the jovial and tolerant Harris; for most of that time he was not only the one Liberal MP in London but also the only Liberal MP with a seat within a hundred miles of Westminster. His warm and generous autobiography, *Forty Years in and out of Parliament*, provides the explanation why. It also gives glimpses of times when election meetings really were rough. At the 1922 election Harris was being persistently heckled by a spectator, who suddenly went silent. The next day a burly street-trader came up to Harris and remarked casually: 'I says to him, hold your noise and he wouldn't stop. Unlucky I didn't have me beetle crushers on, only me pumps, but you'll never hear him again.'[1]

On the other side of the river there was Dr Alfred Salter, a Quaker who represented Bermondsey between the wars. In 1900, Salter had begun work as a general practitioner in Jamaica Road, Bermondsey, and was soon a familiar figure going about his rounds on a bicycle. He and his wife, Ada, were heavily involved in local issues. Salter's greatest ambition was to make Bermondsey, traditionally one of London's most deprived areas, into 'a garden city'. The council lacked the resources to carry out all his plans, but the tree-lined and well-designed roads of Wilson Grove, Scott Lidgett Crescent, Janeway Street and Emba Street, created out of a neighbourhood which Salter had described as 'a death trap and fever den', indicate what could have been done.[2] They are also infinitely preferable to the tower-blocks foisted on many East End people after the Second World War. The lengthy Salter Road winds around the Surrey Docks.

'The North-West Passage': The Jewish Dispersal

Although some Jewish people returned to Russia after the 1917 Revolutions, the East End between the wars still retained a heavily Jewish presence, numbering in all over 80,000 people. Spitalfields and Whitechapel, for instance, remained predominantly Jewish ghettos. Yet, as with the Huguenots 150 years earlier, each passing decade saw the newcomers of 1870–1914 increasingly integrated into 'the English way of life', a process of 'Anglicisation' accelerated by the state elementary schools introduced by the Education Act of 1870. First-generation parents would speak in Yiddish and be answered in English by their children.

In addition, a number of Jews from outside the East End were also keen to turn Jewish boys into Englishmen first, Jews second. Sir Basil Henriques was an Old Harrovian who stayed briefly at Toynbee Hall but then, in 1914, set up his Oxford and St George's Jewish Club in Cannon Street Road. In 1930 the Club moved to a huge 125-room establishment in Berner Street off Commercial Road which cost £65,000 and was paid for by the Jewish philanthropist Bernard Baron. The building is still there. The tall Henriques, known as 'the Long 'Un' because of his height, ran the Club on public school lines with 'houses' and captains. His wife Bunny ran the adjoining Girls' Club, but Henriques was adamantly opposed to the idea of 'mixed' clubs. Some boys hero-worshipped Henriques, others were more distrustful, but his influence was immense. After his death in 1961, Berner Street's name was changed to Henriques Street.[1]

Bloom's on Whitechapel Road was founded in 1920, and the lively argumentative Jewish presence continued throughout the interwar period. One custom was the daily 'Petticoat Lane Parliament'.[2] It took place in the large underground gentlemen's toilets which are still to be found in Leyden Street just off Petticoat Lane – although the stench is such that it is advisable to clap a handkerchief over your nose. Here, Jewish men would gather to put the world to rights. And yet, during the 1930s, Jewish people began to disperse out of the East End, embarking on what was called 'the North-West Passage': Stoke Newington and Clapton, then Golders Green and Finchley, and then Ilford and Newbury Park. The movement northwards was reinforced by the effects of evacuation during the Second World War and by the impact of the motor car which lessened the need for families to live in the same streets. Two symbols of the fading Jewish East End: the Pavilion theatre closed down for good in 1934, and the Yiddish newspaper *Die Zeit* ended in 1950.

Today a walk in search of the Jewish East End is fragmentary yet still rewarding. The Temple of 1912, briefly the home of Jewish opera, became a cinema called the Palaseum and is now empty. The Pavilion, which stood near the corner of Whitechapel Road and Vallance Road, was pulled down in 1962; only a stroll around the back indicates its former size and traces of the red paint so beloved by theatrical decorators. The numerous fish and chip shops in Vallance Road which serviced the 'Pav's' customers are much reduced in number. The Russian Vapour Baths in Brick Lane opposite the turning into Fournier Street were closed down during the Second World War, and not a brick or stone now remains. Yet another home of the Yiddish theatre, the Grand Palais, held out until 1970. On the north side of Commercial Road at numbers 133–9, it now houses Flick Fashions.

The famous Bloom's survives, Kasler Hall in Greatorex Street is an excellent cheap Jewish restaurant, and in Osborn Street is to be found a Jewish 'monumental mason' and a Jewish bookshop. There are synagogues in Nelson

Street, Fieldgate Street and Commercial Road. But the 25,000-strong Jewish community in Stepney during the 1950s has now shrunk to less than 7,000. It is entirely fitting that the Museum of the Jewish East End is not to be found in, say, Whitechapel or Spitalfields but in Finchley. One ironic postscript is that the Canary Wharf project on the Isle of Dogs is being largely financed by three devoutly Jewish brothers and as a result the Transport and General Workers' Union has signed an agreement under which their members will observe the Jewish holiday, from soon after noon on Friday until dusk on Saturday. Otherwise, however, the Jewish newcomers are newcomers no more; most have moved on and become newcomers to other, more salubrious parts of London. But their legacy is lasting; it is the voluble, excitable, hardworking and generous Jewish presence which has been responsible for much of what is best in East End life.

The Battle of Cable Street, 4 October 1936

In the early nineteenth century the London observer J. P. Malcolm could not bring himself to describe the slums of Shadwell: 'Thousands of useful tradesmen, artisans and mechanicks, and numerous watermen inhabit [Shadwell], but their homes and workshops will not bear description; nor are the streets, courts, lanes and alleys, by any means inviting.'[1] Even 150 years later the reputation of Cable Street, the long thoroughfare which bisects Shadwell, was no better: a local petition put together in October 1947 to complain about living conditions referred to the area between Leman Street and Christian Street as 'a pestilence',[2] and journalists in search of sensational copy were often to be found writing up Cable Street's cafés, gambling-dens and prostitutes in the most lurid terms. Joseph Williamson, the vicar of St Paul's, Dock Street, in the 1950s and 1960s, provides in his autobiographies horrific accounts of Cable Street's active vice trade.

Today a walk down Cable Street is a comparatively sedate affair. Much of the old slum property was demolished during the 1960s, forcing the gamblers and 'street-waitresses' to ply their trade elsewhere and giving the street a sense of spaciousness which it never before possessed. Now the Docklands Light Railway passes along the north side of Cable Street, while at the west end near Wellclose Square, on the site of what was until recently a ship's chandler and supplier of marine engines, is the new four-storey Leybourne House, smart, clean and expensive. A mere £100,000 buys the client not only a flat but also access to the heated swimming-pool in the basement and the roof garden with its sweeping views over the East End.

Yet Cable Street is more than just another example of a changing East End street busily discarding unwanted associations. 'Cable Street' (in quotation marks) is a symbol of the East End tradition of political activity; of simply not just lying down and taking it. Halfway down Cable Street, close to the local library and the impressive old St George's Town Hall, is a splendid mural by Ray Walker which rears up colourfully at the bystander and whose swirling figures include policemen on horses, men in black shirts and people waving red banners. The mural commemorates what is now known as the 'Battle of Cable Street' when, on 4 October 1936, a huge crowd prevented Oswald Mosley's British Union of Fascists (BUF) from marching

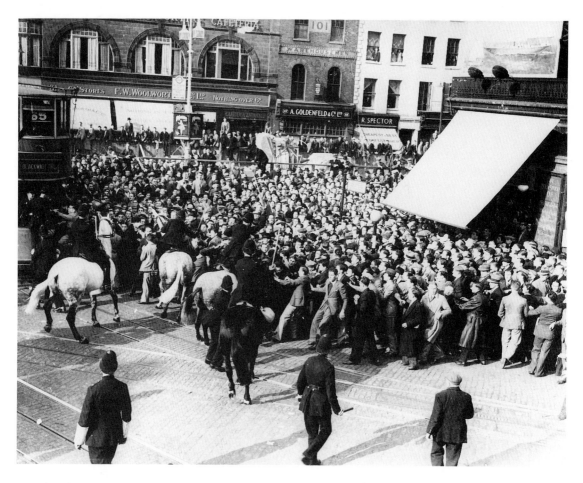

Crowds gathering at Gardiner's Corner in October 1936 to prevent Oswald Mosley's 'Blackshirts' from marching through the East End.

through Shadwell.

Why was Mosley trying to march through the East End in the first place? Mainly because parts of the East End – Bethnal Green, Shoreditch, Limehouse – were strongholds of the BUF and Mosley was hoping to extend his influence in Shadwell and Wapping.[3] His head-quarters were in Pitfield Street, many recruits came from Duckett Street, and Victoria Park Gardens were a favourite meeting-place. Although once a member of the Labour Party, Mosley had resigned his post in the government of 1929–31 and then veered rapidly towards the political right. His BUF

was modelled on the organisations headed by Mussolini in Italy and Hitler in Germany. Mosley insisted on being called 'Leader', introduced the fascist salute and housed his followers in a barracks in Chelsea. By the middle of the 1930s Mosley was deliberately stirring up anti-Semitism in an attempt to attract recruits, and where better than the East End to try to make the Jews scapegoats for the poor economic conditions which were none of their making? In the summer of 1936, Mosley announced that he would lead a parade early in October through Stepney, intending to assemble in Royal Mint Street and then march up Leman Street and along Commercial Road.

The cautious Labour Party decided to combat Mosley by advising its members to remain at home on Sunday, 4 October. It was advice largely ignored. As the *News Chronicle* reported. 'The greatest East End crowd in living memory – one estimate is three hundred thousand – awaited the fascists.'[4] Scuffles and then pitched fights broke out as the police desperately tried to clear a path through the streets by means of baton charges. The crowd shouted out, 'They shall not pass,' a slogan borrowed from the Spanish Civil War which had broken out a few months before.

The sheer volume of people massed at Gardiner's Corner at the top of Commercial Road meant that it was quite impossible for the 3,000-strong BUF to march along its planned route, particularly as drivers had deliberately abandoned their trams at strategic points. An alternative way down Cable Street was proposed, but here the narrowness of the road meant that hastily thrown up barricades were highly successful in blocking the highway, obstacles supplemented by a human and impenetrable barrier. In the face of such overwhelming opposition, the Metropolitan Commissioner of Police had to tell Mosley that the march simply could not take place. Instead the BUF marched through the empty streets of the City and along the Embankment. On the following Sunday, 11 October, the BUF sought a token of petty revenge by smashing the windows of Jewish shops along Mile End Road.

The 'Battle of Cable Street' does indeed deserve to be remembered and commemorated. Its significance lies in the manner in which the East Enders of all political and religious views, and none, united to ward off a highly provocative and insulting march. After October 1936 the BUF declined rapidly, a process helped by the country's partial economic recovery and by the Public Order Act of 1936 which banned the use of uniforms and other militaristic paraphernalia. It is difficult to find a memoir or autobiography of the East End in the 1930s in which the writer was not at Cable Street on 4 October 1936. After fifty years, to have 'been there' is still worn as a justifiable badge of honour.

The Blitz

The 'Blitz' on London began on 7 September 1940 and continued for the next seventy-six consecutive nights. Between September 1940 and May 1941 nearly 20,000 tons of bombs were dropped on the capital, 30,000 people were killed, 220,000 homes totally destroyed and hundreds of thousands more badly damaged. Deliberately, the Luftwaffe ensured that the East End bore the brunt of the attacks, if only because it contained the docks. Stepney and Poplar were particularly badly damaged – the modern window in St Dunstan's church depicts the devastated neighbourhood.

When the Blitz started East Enders found themselves their own shelters, often in the face of official disapproval. One huge shelter was the railway arches sandwiched between Leman Street and Commercial Road. Known as the Tilbury Shelter because the nearby yards and sidings were used by traffic from the Tilbury Docks, on some nights over 10,000 people crammed in here. At first conditions were primitive, especially in the 'overflow' parts, as Angus Calder has described: 'Great stocks of margarine were stored in the "unofficial" section. There was sanitation only for

The remains of Hughes Mansions, Vallance Road after being struck by a German bomb which killed 13 people in March 1945.

the handful of workmen usually employed here. Children slept among trodden faeces and soiled margarine; so did Indians, Lascars, Negroes, spivs, prostitutes and Jewish refugees. Parties of sightseers from the West End would make the Tilbury Arches the highlight of their tour of black spots.'[1] Gradually, however, in the wake of much campaigning in the press and by local figures such as Father John Groser, the sanitary conditions improved and, like many shelters, it developed its own communal loyalty.

In Bethnal Green the Tube station was turned into a massive shelter capable of holding 10,000 people; it even had its own canteen, a library and a concert-hall. Tragically it was also the scene of one of the Blitz's most terrible disasters. On 3 March 1943, as the sirens were wailing and people making their way down to the shelter, a woman slipped on the stairs and in the ensuing panic 173 people were crushed to death and another 62 seriously injured.[2] Also in Bethnal Green, 27 March 1945 became known as 'Black Tuesday' after a V2 bomb demolished Hughes Mansions in Vallance Road, killing 130 people. A garden now stands on the site of Hughes Mansions.

There are two memorials in the East End to the German bombing. One is a plaque on the railway bridge in Grove Road which remembers the first V1, or 'doodlebug', which crashed here in June 1944, killing six people. The other stands outside Bethnal Green Library and honours the fortitude and bravery of East Enders during the Second World War.

Father John Groser and the Church in the East End in the Twentieth Century

In the nineteenth century clergymen such as Headlam and Lowder were looked up to by local people because they provided leadership for the community at a time when many middle-class residents were fleeing the East End and leaving London. Apart from a few doctors, it was the clergymen who had to deal with the manifold political, social and personal problems of the area. Almost always this meant conflict with the authorities. One such clergyman who carried on the tradition in this century was Father John Groser, a curate at St Michael's, Poplar, from 1922 and then vicar of Christ Church, Watney Street, from 1929 to 1948. With his abundant energy and determination Groser threw himself into the struggle to right wrong. He was heavily involved in the General Strike of 1926, heading marches wearing a billowing cassock and carrying a six-foot crucifix, and in the late 1930s he was the President of the Stepney Tenants' Defence League which launched a series of rent strikes in protest at slum landlords who pocketed the rent but left their properties in a vile state.[1] Groser presided over lengthy strikes in Langdale Buildings, Brady Street Mansions and Alexandra Buildings in Commercial Street. He always paid tribute to the women in these places who provided the backbone of the strike.[2]

Staying in the East End throughout the Blitz, Groser was a prominent figure, his tall and imposing presence striding through the wrecked streets and making sure that local and national authorities did their bit for the injured and homeless. His own church of Christ Church was wrecked by a land-mine in April 1941. After the war Groser became the Master of the Royal Foundation of St Katharine when it moved back to the East End from Regent's Park and was sited in the bombed

Father John Groser, the formidable East End churchman based in Shadwell between the wars who became Master of the Royal Foundation of St Katharine.

wreck of St James, Ratcliff. Fortunately, the lovely Georgian vicarage survived. The house was built in 1798 for a West Indies sugar merchant and is supposed to be haunted by the ghost of a young Italian artist who hanged himself when refused permission to marry his daughter, but his frescos are still to be seen.[3] The house looks out on to a lovely cloistered garden which exists as an oasis of tranquillity despite the traffic careering past in Butcher's Row. The Foundation offers a good place for conferences and retreats. Inside the new chapel are some exquisitely carved fourteenth-century choir-stalls, a hanging lamp which traditionally was presented by Henry VII, and a beautiful seventeenth-century pulpit which it is a pleasure to run one's hands over and feel the craftsmanship. John Groser retired as Master in 1962, but his influence and memory are still strong in the East End.

Groser was by no means the last in the line of campaigning priests. Apart from Trevor Huddleston, the former Bishop of Stepney and well known for his involvement in the anti-apartheid movement, there was 'Father Joe' Williamson who was brought up in the slums of Poplar. At the turn of this century, when Britain ruled a worldwide empire, Williamson and his family of nine lived in two upstairs rooms and, in his words, 'One room of 9 feet by 6 would be a good sized room in Poplar.' Overcoming objections made by some of the church authorities that his working-class background debarred him from being a clergyman, he was ordained in 1925. After serving various parishes outside London, in 1952 he was appointed to the church of St Paul's, Dock Street, which then stood in one of the most squalid parts of Stepney. In the 1950s and early 1960s the west end of Cable Street was full of slum properties which contained sleazy cafés, gambling-joints and brothels, the last being so obvious that men could often be found queuing outside in the street. 'Father Joe' set up a sanctuary in Church House, Ensign Street, for prostitutes, striving to raise funds in the face of what was often official church indifference. Williamson was another in the line of East End Anglo-Catholic priests, and he knew full well the value of theatre in attracting recruits to church; always clad in his cassock and biretta, he once wrote: 'Drama forces the message home: I have found myself on my knees in the gutter of Cable Street, demonstrating how the Lord washed the dirty feet of His disciples.'[4] By the end of the 1960s much of Father Joe's work had been achieved with the large-scale demolition of parts of Cable Street, although of course this meant that the problem was simply pushed on to someone else's patch. Father Joe died in March 1988 at the age of ninety-two. Sadly, his church of St Paul's, Dock Street, is now redundant and is to be sold.

The massive decline in the population of the borough of Stepney and then of Tower Hamlets, combined with the drop in churchgoing, meant that there were far too many churches for the congregations to support and maintain. Since 1969, twenty-eight churches in Stepney have been closed; St Augustine's with St Philip's, for instance, the largest church in the East End, stands empty and neglected in Newark Street near the London Hospital. Some of the churches have been turned into flats, others have been taken over by squatters.[5] In a period of uncertainty and confusion in the East End, the Church, too, is struggling to find a role. What is sure is that, unless the Church of England can once again attract men of the leadership and dedication characterised by Lowder, Headlam, Groser and Williamson and others, it will remain peripheral to the lives of East Enders.

'Mean Streets' and Tower-blocks: East End Housing in the Twentieth Century

If you walk or drive around the East End today, occasionally, on turning a corner, you chance upon fine Georgian terraced housing or an early nineteenth-century square. For a moment you might think you have ended up in the West End by mistake. For example, there is Tredegar Square, a grand construction of the 1830s which is only a stone's throw away from the busy Mile End Road.[1] It was built by Lord Tredegar in an unsuccessful attempt to dilute the increasingly working-class character of the East End. Hackney contains the elegant Hackney Terrace.[2] Built in the 1790s, its exterior conveys a sense of spaciousness and ease. It is now numbers 20–54 Cassland Road. Sutton House on the corner of Homerton High Street was built nearly 500 years ago, although it has been much altered. Today it is administered by the National Trust.

These fine buildings, however, are exceptional. On the whole, during the nineteenth century the East End was covered either with barrack-like 'model dwellings' or street after street of cheap, often badly built terraced housing. Although born and brought up in Poplar, the novelist Arthur Morrison was wrong when, in his collection of short stories, *Tales of Mean Streets*, he equated the uniformity of the streets with a uniformity in their residents. Virginia Woolf's view of urban life was more generous and accurate: 'The fascination of the London street is that no two people are ever alike, each seems bound on some private affair of his own.'[3]

Today these densely populated streets are the objects of much nostalgia. People remember the ever open front doors, the neighbourliness, the children able to play outside in the street because of the lack of traffic. They recall the street-parties which were pioneered after the First World War by a Poplar Methodist minister called W. H. Lax (a block of flats on East India Dock Road is named after him), and the celebrations for the Jubilee in 1935 and for the coronation of George VI in 1937. Life was not always as pleasant as these images suggest, mainly because of the terrible overcrowding. The 1921 census showed that 62,921 people in Stepney lived more than two to a room, 184 more than six to a room, and

that 3,697 houses were occupied by three or more families.[4] Ten years later little had changed: 'The overall density of population for the whole borough [of Stepney], 127.5 people per acre in 1931, was twice the average for the whole County of London, which was itself very high, at 58.7 people per acre, compared with the figures for other large cities.'[5]

The Second World War changed much of this. German bombs laid waste these 'mean streets', and people left the East End never to return. The question was, how was the East End to be rebuilt for those who remained? Surveys immediately after the war revealed that most people preferred the prospect of a house to a flat, not liking a flat's lack of a garden or the absence of privacy.[6] But what did they know? Contemporary architects decreed that twenty-first-century Man should live in tower-blocks. It was of course irrelevant that the architects themselves seemed to prefer Georgian houses in Hampstead and Highgate. Governments of the time agreed, subsidising the creation of these concrete slabs. Indeed, the higher the block, the higher the subsidy received. The councils, worried about a possible shortage of land, acquiesced. It did not seem to matter that a flat cost, on average, 50 per cent more to build than a house, nor that completion took longer because the first family could not move in until the whole block was completed.[7]

The tower-block changed the face of the East End and the life of its community. Unfortunately they, and their deleterious social consequences, will be with us for a long time to come, if only because it is so difficult to demolish them. Up to the 1970s the horizon in the East End was dominated by dock cranes; today it is tower-blocks.

The funeral of Charlie Brown in 1932. He ran a pub-cum-museum in West India Dock Road which today still carries his name.

The Kray Twins and East End Crime

For many people mention of 'the East End' summons up, however unfairly, images of crime and gangland, of beatings-up down dark alleys, razor blades and broken bottles, slashed faces and bodies entombed within motorway bridges. Much of this image has been deliberately and ignorantly sensational-ised, as we saw in the earlier section 'The East End in Myth and Legend'. Often, too, the name 'Kray' is mentioned, though it is over twenty years since the Kray twins, Ronnie and Reggie, were imprisoned. As with Jack the Ripper, time does not seem to diminish popular interest in their exploits. Reggie Kray still receives twenty letters a day at Parkhurst from members of the public. Some nostalgia surrounds the Krays, partly because it is

widely believed that when they controlled the East End in the 1950s and 1960s the streets were safer than they are now. The *Daily Telegraph* of 14 November 1986 reported the case of a publican in Stratford, plagued by hooliganism and physical violence, who thought that 'compared with some of the villains today they [the Krays] were thorough gentlemen, respected and even admired by many people. They were nasty to their own kind, but they left ordinary people alone. Today's villains are nasty to everyone, old, young, middle-aged. They make no distinc-tions.' Reggie Kray has recently claimed that 'we were not killing women and children. We have never hurt the public.'[1] Public interest in the twins is likely to grow. A campaign has

116

been launched which includes the sale of calendars, badges and T-shirts and is based around the slogan 'Parole, it's about time', and a £5 million film – ironically enough valued at far more than the Krays ever made in their criminal careers – called *The Profession of Violence* is currently in production.

A walk today around the East End familiar to the Krays reveals that several of the pubs they patronised remain, most notably the Blind Beggar in Whitechapel Road where Ronnie Kray shot George Cornell dead in broad daylight. So does the church of St James the Great on Bethnal Green Road where Reggie Kray married Frances Shea in April 1965. But Stean Street in Hoxton where they were born in 1933 has altered beyond recognition, the Regal Billiard Hall in Eric Street behind Mile End Tube station where they started their 'business career' after the Second World War has gone, as has 178 Vallance Road, the 'Fort Vallance' where they lived for many years with their mother Violet. Only the grubby back-to-back terraced housing in nearby Voss Street and Derbyshire Street suggests what 178 Vallance Road must have looked like. As for the rest of the houses and businesses in the vicinity, most are festooned with the burglar alarms of the upwardly mobile.

The rise and fall of the Krays might be said to mirror many recent changes in the East End and the way in which it has been 'discovered' and 'opened up' to outside influences, whether these be television, the City or property speculators. The Krays were the last in the line of East End gangsters who, like feudal lords, ruled their patch or 'manor' – the latter word a reminder that the East End was originally a collection of tight-knit communities with codes of loyalty akin to those in Sicilian villages. They were 'self-policing' and it was a transgression of the unwritten law to go elsewhere for help – 'People in the East End don't go to the police for help. It's not done' (Reggie Kray). It is interesting that the Krays were always unsuccessful when they stepped outside the environment in which they were born and bred; for example, they were unable to develop international links or to move out of London, and their nightclub in Wilton Place, Knightsbridge, failed. In comparison with Mafia bosses the Krays seem absurdly unsophisticated; it is inconceivable that a 'Godfather' would personally shoot someone in a pub or hack to death an underling, as happened to Jack McVitie in a poky Stoke Newington flat. Somehow the demise of the Krays suggests the end, too, of 'the old underworld'; as Reggie Kray has observed recently, seemingly without a trace of irony: 'Today there is no longer such a thing as the underworld. Crime has touched all areas of society. A heroin case the other day involved a stockbroker's son. You get these types of people in crime today. They are not of the criminal fraternity. That's why you get so much mugging and raping going on today. Crime is for people in all walks of life.' Here we have an East End gangster complaining about what might be called the 'new egalitarianism' of crime!

Looking back at the history of crime in the East End, the available statistics are of little help because they are notoriously unreliable, depending so much on what is actually reported to the police. Charles Booth in his monumental study *Life and Labour of the People of London* published at the end of the nineteenth century, considered Hoxton to be the foremost criminal quarter in London. It is difficult to know how much of this criminal activity took place within the East End itself. Robert Barltrop and Jim Wolveridge have argued that before 1945 East Enders never stole from each other, but it is hard to reconcile this view with Arthur Morrison's novel *A Child of the Jago* in which everyone steals from everyone else. Incidentally Morrison also hints at the appalling treatment of women in the East End; the rest of the Jago women distrust Hannah Perrott because she is not regularly beaten by her husband. It is also revealing that Arthur Harding, the Jago criminal extensively interviewed by Raphael Samuel, rarely seems to have ventured to the West End for suitable 'work' – 'We didn't go far out of our manor.'[2]

Harding's account demonstrates two other characteristics of East End crime during the first half of this century. First, there is the comparatively well-behaved approach of both sides, crooks and police. At one point Harding proudly states: 'As an Englishman, I would never use a knife.' Fists and boots, yes; knives, no. Care was also taken not to assault a policeman. A later East End gangster, Jack 'Spot' Comer, was another who apparently had certain principles, content to make his money from gambling but refusing to get involved in brothels or 'white slave' traffic.[3] Second, Harding indicates that the underworld at the end of the nineteenth century and the start of the twentieth was not well organised. Some pickpockets worked in gangs, such as the 'Spread Eagle' mob from Hoxton Street or the 'Titanic' from Shepherdess Walk. The latter even had an insurance fund in case members were caught and imprisoned.[4] Otherwise, however, East End individualism seems to have made the setting up and control of gangs difficult.

Certain areas of London were recognised as specialising in various criminal trades.[5] Apparently the police thought of thieves as coming from King's Cross, cat burglars from Hackney, small-time con-men from Stepney, and 'villains' from Bethnal Green and Whitechapel. But until the 1950s and 1960s the East End underworld appears rather tame, certainly when compared with organised crime in the United States. Attempts at political corruption seem to have been beyond the capabilities of these gangland 'bosses'. Jack 'Spot' Comer was even bankrupted in 1957.

Comer and the Krays were the representatives of the old-style East End underworld, amateur and often bungling. It is impossible to imagine them handling the £26 million from the Brinks-Mat raid. The disintegration of their old 'manors' and the fragmentation of former loyalties has reflected the opening up of the East End. Today's criminals think on a much larger scale, developing networks right across Europe for disposing of stolen cars, merchandise from hijacked lorries, or drugs and pornography.[6] In many ways, what is happening to the East End in relation to Docklands is occurring twenty years after similar changes within the underworld. The Stratford publican's nostalgia for the days of the Krays mirrors opposition to the 'brave new world' being ushered in by the London Docklands Development Corporation.

Yet More Newcomers

Scandinavians, Germans, Huguenots, Irish, Jews – all these peoples have settled in the East End over the past five centuries, and today this tradition of East End cosmopolitanism continues. Most of these groups have in fact been here in London for generations. It is revealing to note that of the capital's population of 670,000 in the eighteenth century as many as 20,000 were black. Virtually all were servants, and therefore little is known of them, other than fleeting glimpses in the works of the artist William Hogarth.

The largest West Indian influx came in the 1950s after the United States prohibited immigration there. It has been estimated that 132,000 coloured people arrived in Britain

An East End delicacy, jellied eels.

between 1955 and 1957 alone, more in three years than in forty years of Jewish immigration before the First World War.[1] Why should there have been this sudden surge? In the 1950s Western Europe experienced an economic boom, based in large part upon the availability of cheap and often 'foreign' labour – Turks and Yugoslavs in West Germany, Algerians and Moroccans in France. Britain was no exception, and it should be emphasised that the newcomers were quite entitled to enter Britain under the terms of the Nationality Act of 1948 which gave British citizenship to members of Britain's colonies and former colonies. Confined to poorly paid jobs and bad accommodation, the new arrivals often occupied those same East End areas recently vacated by Jewish people.

In recent years it has been the Asians who have entered the East End, following the pattern of the Jewish arrival a hundred years ago. There are the same sweatshops, the same protective banding-together, the same emphasis on religion, hard work and the family. Figures suggest that there are no more than 15,000 Bangladeshis in Tower Hamlets today, barely 20 per cent of the population, but already their presence in Whitechapel and Spitalfields is obvious. Shops display their exotic produce, and around Brick Lane are to be found wonderful restaurants, sweetshops, schools and mosques. Stand in Fieldgate Street on a fine day and you will see multi-coloured saris hung out to dry on washing-lines between the flats, like brilliant flags. No doubt in fifty years' time this community, too, will have moved on, leaving historians to try to piece together the 'Asian East End'.

The East End in the 1980s and 1990s: The LDDC and All That

Books written on or about the East End before 1939 generally stress two things: namely, the overcrowding and the rôle of the docks. Today, neither of these factors applies. During the nineteenth century the East End's population grew at an enormous pace as villages on the eastern outskirts of London were swallowed up. Bow, for example, was transformed from a village of 2,500 inhabitants in 1820 to a suburb of 50,000 people in 1908. Yet this century the East End's population has dwindled, a fact recognised in 1965 when the three Metropolitan Boroughs of Bethnal Green, Stepney and Poplar were merged into the single unit of the London Borough of Tower Hamlets. In 1901 the area now covered by Tower Hamlets held 570,000 people; in 1931 the figure had fallen to 489,000; and in 1951 to 231,000. Today it is less than 140,000.[1]

As for the docks, the most immediate impact of their reduced trade was on the dockers themselves. The 22,815 East London dockers of 1967 had declined to 7,120 in 1980 – and this before the closure of the 'Royals'. But of course these figures show only part of the problem: three times as many jobs were lost in dock-related trades.[2]

The startling decline in population and the closure of the docks ensured that walks around the East End in the 1970s were tinged with gloom. Local firms moved to areas where they could build bigger factories and recruit more highly skilled labour. There was depression and a lack of spirit everywhere. It was a state of affairs surely symbolised by the thirty miles of corrugated-iron sheeting hiding Tower Hamlets' acres of derelict land, which actually totalled 1½ times the size of Hyde Park.[3] A walk along the riverside was no better. Weeds sprang up on once busy quays, the water became stagnant and full of rubbish, and cranes rusted. After 2,000 years the

decline of the Thames's commercial resources meant that the East End had lost its life-blood. It was difficult to see what could fill the vacuum for this declining area. The East End became a kind of 'Land That Time Forgot'. It seemed a sad end for a place once bursting with vitality.

In many respects, of course, this was a grossly simplistic picture. In reality, the East End had always been much more than just the docks. Moreover St Katharine's Dock, the one nearest to the City and the Tower of London, was quickly redeveloped. It was transformed into a marina, dominated by the Tower Hotel, a conference centre, restaurants and shops. Most extraordinary is the Coronarium, or open-air chapel, whose circle of seven cast-iron columns originally came from a warehouse which stood on the site of the hotel. This chapel was placed as near as possible to the site of the old church which had for centuries served the Royal Hospital of St Katharine.[4]

Various pressure groups put forward plans for reviving small businesses based on and around the quays, but none of them offered any prospect of the profit needed to attract the necessary private investment. The three main councils concerned, Tower Hamlets and Newham on the north and Southwark on the south, were unable or unwilling to attract private capital – ever since 1945 they had discouraged 'Business'. Nor did they themselves possess sufficient resources to carry out developments on their own. It was an impasse. All this was to change, however, along with much else outside the East End, after the election of Margaret Thatcher's Conservative government in 1979. Two years later the London Docklands Development Corporation (LDDC) was set up.

Some people (for example the Conservative

government, property developers and builders) greet mention of the LDDC with cheers and applause. Others, among whom are many local residents, are more inclined to boo and jeer. At times it almost seems as though discussion of the LDDC is taking place in some giant Christmas pantomime with the Corporation cast as either the Fairy Godmother or the Wicked Stepmother. What is indisputable is that the LDDC has triggered off a series of far-reaching changes, effecting a transformation of this part of the East End as startling in its way as that achieved when the first enclosed docks were built at the beginning of the nineteenth century. Whereas the wet docks were built over the course of decades, the LDDC's impact is as if someone has pressed the 'fast forward' button on a video-recorder. Roads appear and disappear in a weekend, new flats are suddenly to be found on waste land derelict since the Blitz, cranes and scaffolding dominate the horizon. Almost everyone in the East End seems to be wearing a 'hard hat'. For the unwary walker, yesterday's through road is today's cul-de-sac and tomorrow's 'No Public Right of Way'. A few months ago I was turned back, not very politely, from a road which was clearly marked on the latest *A-Z* and informed that it had now 'gone'. Gone where? I could still see the road, but it had now been translated from the public to the private and had therefore, for all intents and purposes, indeed 'gone'.

Vibrant 1980s Docklands is very different from the derelict and decaying place of the 1970s. Yet, whereas the old docks had depended upon the commercial opportunities of the Thames, the LDDC has calculated that the river's value today is primarily aesthetic. A 'riverbus' service is planned, but in the main the Thames is now considered to be something to look out over, not to work on. The Victorian warehouses are to become dwelling-places; their residents will usually be employed somewhere else. Nearby are brightly coloured offices; somehow the architects seem to have been allowed only primary colours for their work. Even Marsh Wall, the new road running around inside the perimeter of the Isle of Dogs, is now popularly known as the 'Red Brick Road' because of its colour. Huge developments such as the twenty-storey Cascades on the western edge of the Isle of Dogs have turned much of the East End into a gigantic building site, giving visitors the impression of having landed suddenly on the moon as they survey bleak windswept spaces and craters waiting to be filled. This upheaval has occurred in advance of the £4 billion Canary Wharf project which is to provide a tower 200 feet higher than that on the National Westminster building in the City. There will also be 12 million square feet of office space here in the middle of the Isle of Dogs in an attempt to profit from deregulation of the City in the wake of the 'Big Bang'.

For the first time ever, the East End has become fashionable. The centuries-old westward drift has to some extent been halted. And yet the LDDC, under whose aegis much of this rapid change has taken place, is one of the most controversial organisations in London. The Government sees it as a pioneer in creating a new 'enterprise culture' which will take Britain into the future, echoing the LDDC's own claim that it is giving birth to a 'Metropolitan Water City of the Twenty-First Century'.[5] Critics such as Stephen Gardiner, architectural correspondent of the *Observer*, claim that the LDDC has functioned as 'no more than a Government estate agent, selling off land to the first buyer, and displaying minimal, if any, regard for its huge responsibilities to the city, to the special character of the area, and thus to its people.' Gardiner also calls it a 'free-for-all gone mad'.[6] One of the finest views in the East End is to stand in Island Gardens and look across the river to Sir Christopher Wren's Naval Hospital, now the Royal Naval College. Wren refused to accept payment for his work, saying that he wished to 'have some share in this work of mercy' in providing a home for retired sailors. Wren's altruism contrasts sharply with the greed which seems to permeate much of Docklands today.

Many local residents have complained about the manner in which the Government 'gave' the unelected LDDC 657 acres in an almost feudal manner, absolving the Corporation from the usual planning inquiries. Its powers of compulsory purchase have often been used, leaving people homeless or offering them merely 'pre-boom' compensation for their homes.[7] The LDDC responds by arguing that the failure to do anything with the docks in the 1970s – 'There was a Docklands Joint Committee in existence for nearly three years and what did it do? It did not build a toilet. All it did was to talk and pass stupid resolutions' (Lord Mellish)[8] – meant that only drastic action could revive the dock areas. As one of the LDDC officials has bluntly put it, 'If you're not prepared to close business, demolish buildings, use compulsory purchase orders and persuade people to move, you will never get anywhere.'[9] No doubt similar sentiments were heard when the residents were moved to make way for St Katharine's Dock in the 1820s.

One undoubted success of the LDDC has been the Docklands Light Railway, built at a cost of £77 million.[10] Since the summer of 1987 it has 'opened out' the East End, giving passengers panoramic views over the old docks before depositing them at the attractive Island Gardens on the southern tip of the Isle of Dogs. The section of the railway between Tower Gateway and Westferry is built on the bridges and viaducts of the old Fenchurch Street-Blackwall line opened in 1840. It allowed Londoners access to the Brunswick Pier and the steamers which took them to Southend for the day. This line was closed to passenger traffic in 1926. The most spectacular views from the specially designed 'picture windows' in the carriages are over the Isle of Dogs. Not even the most virulent critic of the

LDDC could deny the pleasures and the ease of movement offered by the Light Railway. It is to be extended west to the Bank and east to Beckton in East London. There are also suggestions to take it across the river to Lewisham.

The LDDC has undoubtedly attracted private investment to the area. This amounted to some £2.2 billion by December 1987 even before the Canary Wharf development. But 'the good old British taxpayer', about whose interests the present government is normally so concerned, has not escaped unscathed. A particular attraction for companies moving into this designated 'Enterprise Zone' is that it is rate-free for six years, while capital allowances can also be written off against tax. Over £220 million of public money has gone into improving the infrastructure of Docklands, an investment of more obvious benefit to offices and businesses than to residents. This has led to some extraordinary juxtapositions; for example, the new printing site of the *Financial Times* in East India Dock faces a particularly run-down council estate.

Local people claim that little of the new housing put up is for them, although the LDDC counter-claims that of 3,263 houses and flats completed so far 1,842 have gone to locals at 'affordable' prices of £40,000 or less.[11] Nevertheless it seems that few new jobs will go to the locals. Most incoming businesses will bring their own staff with them – it is unlikely that the editor of *The Times* or the *Daily Telegraph* will recruit reporters from Isle of Dogs residents. A recent report by a firm of accountants criticised the LDDC for failing to produce clear and effective policies to deal with training and rising unemployment. The number of jobless in Docklands has risen by over 30 per cent since 1981. It seems as if the new chief executive of the LDDC, Michael Honey, will attempt to improve the Corporation's efforts in this respect.[12]

The LDDC's plans to develop the second generation of docks, namely the 'Royals' in

East London which it calls 'the jewel in the Docklands crown', are still at a planning stage.[13] Rival schemes worth £750 million and £1,000 million have been submitted for the Royal Albert Dock, while the scheme for the Royal Victoria Dock is worth £545 million and the one to redevelop the Silvertown area is valued at around £400 million. These massive figures indicate that private capital is sure of the future and that the eastward drift of the City is not a passing fashion, even if the recent stock-market fluctuations and the suspension of flights between the London City Airport and Paris in December 1987 on the grounds of safety indicate that all will not be plain sailing.

Newham Borough Council at least seems to have accepted the fact that the LDDC is here to stay for the foreseeable future and that it is probably better to negotiate and win concessions than to be ignored. Newham has just signed an agreement with the LDDC in which its reward for co-operation is the provision of 1,500 homes for its tenants: ' ... the price of the LDDC having us with them from the start was having local people planned in, not planned out.'[14] Although such a remark is of little consolation here and now to local people whose lives are being disrupted, the achievement or otherwise of the LDDC will best be judged by generations to come. One word of warning; in his book *The Shape of Things to Come* (1933), H. G. Wells wrote of 'the great London landslip of 1968, due to the weight of new buildings piled up on the northern slope, when the bed of the Thames buckled up and the Second Fire of London ensued'.[15]

The massive changes taking place in Docklands can divert attention away from the rest of the East End where the future seems much more bleak. A recent report by the London Planning Advisory Committee points to the 'Two Londons' in which the western half is prospering at the expense of the east: 'The economy of east London is very much weaker than that of west London and the disparity is growing.'[16] It looks as if not only will there be 'Two Nations' (north and south) and 'Two Londons' (west and east) but in addition 'Two East Ends': the 'old' and the 'new' Docklands. The danger is not just that those trapped in the 'old' will become little more than servants or menial help to the newcomers, but that the Government will split the Isle of Dogs from Tower Hamlets to form a separate borough. At the moment 'Yuppies' – although I don't like this word and have tried not to use it – are for some an imperial class imposing their own culture on the local residents. Could it be that resentment of these 'foreigners' will lead to incidents like the burning of holiday cottages in rural Wales? There is little evidence that the newcomers – from the west and not from abroad as has traditionally been the case – have the kind of social conscience exemplified by Angela Burdett-Coutts.

In his book *The Streets of East London* (1979), Professor Bill Fishman referred to 'the unchanging essence of East End life'. The last nine years have seen tremendous changes in the area. And yet something unique still remains about the East End. In 1897 the East London clergyman the Reverend J. G. Adderley wrote that 'Chelseans and Maryleboners have no marked individuality, but East Londoners have.'[17] This, I think, remains true of the East End. Whatever the consequences of the LDDC or any other organisation, it will remain true in the future.

A reminder of the East End's rural past when its farms fed and watered much of London.

TEN EAST END WALKS

> Travelling is a wonderful way of reading history. I often start from a base point, and walk or take a bus or even a canal trip. You can see more easily the societies which have produced the landscape. The trouble with the way history is taught in schools is that children do not learn to observe in this way, and understand what they are looking at.
>
> ASA BRIGGS in the *Sunday Times*, 21 August 1983

These ten walks introduce anyone interested in the East End to the area's many and varied pleasures. Starting either from an Underground station or a station on the Docklands Light Railway, they should take about 1½–2 hours each, although if you stop off in Victoria Park or Shadwell Park, as you should, they will obviously take longer. All ten are tried and tested in that I have taken hundreds of my groups over these routes in the past five years.

As everyone knows, the East End is changing very rapidly. The walks were up-to-date in the summer of 1988, but there will have been changes before this book is published. I have made the directions as explicit as possible, but as a precaution it is advisable to take a London *A-Z* with you. The information in these walks is self-contained, but you will get more out of all ten if you have read the rest of the book first. Happy walking!

Note: **N** = north; **S** = south; **E** = east; **W** = west; **R** = right; **L** = left.

Bethnal Green and Victoria Park

Start: Bethnal Green station (Underground)
Finish: Bethnal Green station (Underground)

Arriving at **Bethnal Green station**, remember the terrible tragedy of 3 March 1943 when 173 people died here after a panic during a German raid. Come out of the **SE** exit by **Roman Road**. The major part of **Bethnal Green Gardens**, sometimes known as 'Barmy Park' because of the asylum which stood here, stretches **S**. Its site is now occupied by the local library. Outside the **library** is the **memorial** commemorating East Enders' bravery during the Blitz. The **asylum** occupied the site of **Sir William Rider's** house, where **Samuel Pepys** stored his diary during the **Great Fire of September 1666**.

Cross **Roman Road** to **Sir John Soane's St John's** Church of 1828 with its distinctive 'beehive' dome. Turn into the attractive and always well-kept **Victoria Park Square Gardens** on the **R**. On the **N** side is **Museum Passage** with four Victorian lamps. Dominating the **N** section is the **Bethnal Green Museum of Childhood** to which we will return at the end of the walk. Cross the Gardens into **Victoria Park Square**. Here is a lovely early **eighteenth-century terrace**. Turn **L** and walk past the **Roman Catholic church**, into **Old Ford Road**. Opposite are more Georgian houses, recently renovated — newcomers when compared with the seventeenth-century **Netteswell House** at the back of the Museum. Turn **R** down Old Ford Road, following the path of the Roman legions on their way to the ford over the **River Lea**.

Turn **L** down **Approach Road**. A hundred yards along on the **R** is the **London Chest Hospital**, founded in the Victorian period for tubercular patients. It stands on the site of the former country house of the Bishops of London, one of whom was the notorious **Bishop Bonner**. Enter **Victoria Park** be-

Angela Burdett-Coutts's drinking fountain in Victoria Park, built in 1862 at a cost of £5,000.

tween the impressive columns. Unfortunately the equally impressive lodge was destroyed in the Second World War. To **L** and **R** flows the **Regent's** or **Grand Union Canal**. We are now in the **W** section of Victoria Park, with some nice houses on the **N** boundary. Worth exploring here are the **rabbit compound**, the **deer park** and the **lake**. By crossing over **Grove Road** one reaches the large **E** part of the park. Immediately visible is **Burdett-Coutts's drinking-fountain**. In this section is another **lake**, a **rose garden**, a well laid out **children's adventure-playground**, an **athletics track** and on the **E** boundary the two **stone alcoves** from old London Bridge. Also worth a look is the pretty **lock** by **Parnell Road**. It is worth devoting at least one sunny day to exploring Victoria Park.

Go back down Approach Road and **R** along Old Ford Road. Just by the junction with **Cambridge Heath Road** is **York Hall** on the **R**, a public bath on the spot of **St Winifred's Well** which once supplied water

to the district from 1160 until the spring was closed down in the mid-eighteenth century. Turn **L** at Cambridge Heath Road, once called **Dogs' Row**, and walk into the **Bethnal Green Museum of Childhood**, opened in 1872. It houses a fine collection of toys, dolls, puppets and dresses, including the work of the Spitalfields weavers. To return to the Underground keep down Cambridge Heath Road. On the other side of the road is the now attractive **Paradise Row**. Number 3 bears a plaque showing that the boxer **Daniel Mendoza** once lived here.

Hoxton and Shoreditch

Start: Old Street station (Underground)
Finish: Old Street station (Underground)

A small arcade of shops is grouped around the entrance to **Old Street station**. Leave by the **SE** exit. **Old Street**, an 'old' Roman road, heads off **E**, while **City Road**, which leads to the **N** and **S**, was built in the 1760s to link up the City with Islington and the North. Turn down **Great Eastern Street**. On the **L** is **Curtain Road**; a plaque on numbers 86–88 indicates that this was London's first 'theatreland'. In the late nineteenth and early twentieth century Curtain Road was the home of East London's furniture trade, and some of the imposing warehouses and showrooms built then can still be seen on either side of the road.

Turn **R** down **New Inn Yard** into **Shoreditch High Street**. On the **R** is a petrol station which stands on the site of one of Victorian London's grandest theatres, the **Standard**. Cross Shoreditch High Street into **Bethnal Green Road** and walk **L** up **Club Row**, once the venue for an animal market.

At the end is **Arnold Circus**. This was the location of the infamous Nichol, which appears as '**the Jago**' in Arthur Morrison's novel. It was cleared by the London County Council in 1986. A bandstand can be found up several flights of steps. Walk down **Calvert Avenue** on the **L** to the front of the impressive **St Leonard's** which was built in the 1730s, although there has been a church on this prominent site for centuries. The steeple of nearly 200 feet dominates Shoreditch. Number 118½ to the side was formerly the **Clerk's House**, built in 1735. Inside the church is a memorial to several Elizabethan men of the theatre, a beautifully carved clock-case of the eighteenth century, and the 'Poor Cupboard' from which fifty loaves were dispensed each Sunday to the poor.

The church is surrounded by an attractive garden which contains the old wooden stocks and the parish whipping-post. Angela Burdett-Coutts's '**Columbia**' projects were further to

the **E**. Walk up **Kingsland Road**, another broad and straight road of Roman origin, and after a few hundred yards on the **R** will be the exquisite almshouses of 1714 which now house the **Geffrye Museum of Furniture**. Do not fail to visit this gem of a museum. A statue of Geffrye stands by the exterior of what was once the chapel. Retrace your steps along Kingsland Road and then turn **R** down **Falkirk Street** which leads into **Hoxton High Street**. Turn **L** down the High Street, which is often full of market-stalls. On the **L** at 64 High Street, is **Hoxton Hall**, now a community centre but first opened in 1863 as a music-hall. Ask to see the hall with its distinctive double balcony. Keep down the High Street. On the **R**, by **Myrtle Walk**, is a new block of housing. Here until 1940 was to be found the **Britannia**, one of London's best-loved theatres.

Turn **R** off the High Street into **Mundy Street** which takes you to **Hoxton Square**, an unexpected delight. On the **W** side is a plaque commemorating the local Shoreditch doctor **James Parkinson**, discoverer of the disease which bears his name. Walk along **Bowling Green Lane** into **Pitfield Street**. Down to the **R** is **St John's**, built in the 1820s to accommodate Shoreditch's rapidly growing population. Almost opposite the end of Bowling Green Lane is the former **Theatre of Varieties** erected in 1870; a music-hall, then a cinema and finally a warehouse, it awaits redevelopment. Also on the other side of Pitfield Street is the early nineteenth-century building put up for the Haberdashers' Company but now the home of the **East London College**. Immediately on the **L** is the library, in a building paid for by the philanthropist **Andrew Carnegie**. On this side of the road is a pub, now closed, which remembers the East Enders who went hop-picking in Kent each year. Turn **R** past **Parkinson House** into **Charles Square**, unfortunately devastated in the storm of October 1987. On the **R** is **Baches Street** which contains the **Marie Lloyd** pub. At the end of **Brunswick Place** is the City Road. Turn **L** and there is Old Street station.

The Isle of Dogs and Greenwich

Start: Island Gardens station (Docklands Light Railway)
Finish: Island Gardens station (Docklands Light Railway)

It is well worth making the trip to **Island Gardens** whether you intend to do the walk or not. The railway line passes high over the **West India Dock** and gives the passenger panoramic views over the **Isle of Dogs**. All around new buildings are springing up – and this before the massive **Canary Wharf** development. As the train nears Island Gardens you will see on the **L Mudchute Park and Farm**. The name comes from the earth shot across here from the excavation of **Millwall Docks**. Also on this side is **Millwall Park**, the original home of the football team whose base is now **S** of the river. On the **R** is the **Chapel House Estate**, London's first 'garden city' built after the First World War. Its intimacy will in years to come provide a contrast to Canary Wharf.

On leaving Island Gardens station most people head straight for the Gardens themselves with their magnificent view over the Thames to **Wren's Naval Hospital**, now the

A Victorian clipper with St Anne's, Limehouse, in the background.

Royal Naval College, with Inigo Jones's **Queen's House** sandwiched in between. However, it is well worth making a detour either to the **R** to see the **Ferry House** pub whose name recalls the ferry which once crossed to and fro; or to the **L** and **William Cubitt's Christ Church** of 1857, **Newcastle Draw Dock** right on the edge of the river, or the **Waterman's Arms** pub in **Glenaffric Avenue**.

The **Greenwich Foot Tunnel** was built in 1902 for those dockworkers living on the **S** side of the Thames but who worked on the Isle of Dogs. Its coming meant the end for the ferry. The pedestrian goes down in the lift (if working, that is), between 200,000 white tiles

and then up in the lift at the other end and out near the **Cutty Sark**. This tea-clipper of the mid-nineteenth century often unloaded at the East India Docks. To the **R** is Sir Francis Chichester's minute **Gipsy Moth IV** – hard to believe it could negotiate the Serpentine, let alone go right around the world. In the Middle Ages, Greenwich was a fishermen's village and in parts today, despite the traffic, it still retains a semi-rural air. **Greenwich Church Street** in front of you is notable more for the number and range of its eating-places than for any architectural distinction, but on the **R** is Nicholas Hawksmoor's **St Alphege's**. It bears many striking resemblances to the architect's three East End churches. The churchyard to the rear has been turned into an attractive garden.

Go back along Greenwich Church Street, but cross it at the zebra crossing and go **R** down **Turnpin Lane** into the market. A plaque by the main entrance informs you that the market has been trading here under a charter since 1737. Turn **R** down **College Approach** and **R** again down **King William Walk**. On the **L** are the fine buildings of the **Royal Naval College** and the **National Maritime Museum**. Pedestrians might care to stop off for a visit to the museum or to see the **Painted Hall** sometimes open in the Naval College. King William Walk takes you to the statue of **King William IV**, 'Sailor Bill', which once stood in the City. You are now on the edge of the lovely **Greenwich Park**. The fit and curious are advised to clamber up the hill and enjoy the view from **General Wolfe's statue**. You look down over the East End. Amongst the buildings nearby are **Flamsteed House** and the **Old Royal Observatory**.

Leave **Greenwich Park** by the **NE** entrance on to **Naval Row** and walk towards the river, crossing **Romney Road** again. On the **R** is the charming **Trafalgar Tavern** of 1837, although largely rebuilt in the 1960s. Upstairs is the **Nelson Room**. Walk down **Crane Street** at the rear of the Trafalgar

Tavern and a hundred yards on the **R** are the small fortress-like almshouses of **Trinity House**. Since 1617 they have been the home for '21 retired gentlemen of Greenwich'. Blotting out the sky is the **Greenwich Power Station** which once provided the power for London's trams. Return to the Trafalgar

Tavern and walk along the footpath in front of the Royal Naval College. On the other side of the Thames are Island Gardens. **Greenwich Pier** on the **R** is to be radically overhauled. Go back through the Foot Tunnel to Island Gardens station.

Limehouse

Start: Limehouse station (Docklands Light Railway)
Finish: Limehouse station (Docklands Light Railway)

On leaving the station, admire the arches of the former **London-Blackwall railway**, built in 1840, which now carry this section of the Light Railway. Make your way through to the always busy **Commercial Road**, laid out by the dock companies in the early nineteenth century. Turn **L** down **Butcher Row** and come to the **Royal Foundation of St Katharine's**. As an institution it dates back to 1148 but has been here only since the Second World War. An appointment is needed to visit the lovely little garden and chapel. However, you can see the Georgian **vicarage** of what was once **St James, Ratcliff**, and the public garden to the **S**. Keep down Butcher Row, passing over the entrance to the **Rotherhithe Tunnel**, and walk into the appropriately narrow **Narrow Street**

This was once a path through canyon-like warehouses. Much new development is taking place. Walk down it, passing **Limehouse Basin** on the **L**, to which we will return, and the old generating station. Halfway down Narrow Street on the **R** is the famous eighteenth-century **Grapes** pub with its excellent riverside views. Alongside it is a strip of Georgian housing, where Limehouse's most famous resident, **David Owen**, lives. Keep along Narrow Street. On the **L** is the

distinctive '**House That Was Left Behind**' and on the **R** some still active wharfs. **Dunstan's Wharf** has blacksmith's tools depicted on the front.

Narrow Street leads into **Limehouse Causeway** and in turn into **West India Dock Road** and **Pennyfields**. This was the heart of the old **Chinese quarter**, although there were never so many Chinese here as Sax Rohmer made out. It has been largely rebuilt after German bombing. Turn **R** down West India Dock Road. On the **R** is **Charlie Brown's**, the famous pub once run by a sailor who turned it into an informal museum. When he died in 1932 huge crowds followed the funeral to Tower Hamlets Cemetery. On the **R** is **Garford Street**. Go down it a little way and there on the **L** are the houses built in the early nineteenth century for the **dock police**; the sergeant naturally had the largest in the middle, the four constables those on either side.

Return to West India Dock Road and turn **R**, walking to the old **entrance** to the **West India Dock** itself, London's first enclosed dock, which was opened in 1802. On the **R** is the large **Salvation Army hostel**, once for Scandinavian seamen, and the former **Dock Master's House** of 1807. Directly in front of

Chinese people in the East End established their own organisations. This society was at 48 Poplar High Street.

you are the **sugar-warehouses** of 1802 which once stretched along **North Quay**. You can see the bars on the windows to prevent pilfering. After bombing, only half survive. The new '**Red Brick Road**' was built to open up the **Isle of Dogs**. Go down it to the **R** to the **lock-up**, where drunken dockers were incarcerated. It once had a companion. The more energetic can follow the 'Red Brick Road' round to **Cascades**, a smart new project on the **R** with wonderful views over the City, and on the **L** will be **Canary Wharf**, the multi-billion-pound development which will dominate the Isle of Dogs.

Return to Charlie Brown's and walk up West India Dock Road. A hundred yards up on

the **R**, on the other side of the road, is the former **ship chandler and sail-maker's**, in a building of 1860. At the top is a noisy junction of roads. On the **L** is the former sailors' home, the '**Sailors Palace**', erected in 1903. Over the entrance Britannia holds two ships. Turn **L** along Commercial Road and then **L** again down **Three Colt Street**. Pass into the churchyard of **St Anne's**, another fine Hawksmoor church which has recently been cleaned. The church clock is the highest in London. The mysterious **pyramid** is in the **NW** corner. Cross **Newell Street** to the little garden laid out beside **Limehouse Cut**. Originally opened in 1770 to speed up traffic between the Thames and the Lea, the Cut is

The destruction of St Anne's, Limehouse, in April 1850. Fortunately fire insurance had been taken out just weeks before the fire.

less smelly and noxious than it once was. Return to Newell Street. Number **12** is the curved house in what was then Church Row, once occupied by **Christopher Huffam, Charles Dickens's** godfather. Dickens often came here to see him. Go up Newell Street and turn **L** along Commercial Road. On the opposite side is **Prince's Lodge**, recently closed but first opened in 1924. Intended for sailors, it was commonly known as '**the stack o' bricks**'. Further along Commercial Road on the **L** is **Limehouse Library**, situated inside a **Passmore Edwards** building, and also the Catholic church of **Our Lady Immaculate** whose red-coloured statue of Christ high up at the rear has been watching

us on the first part of this walk.

Keep along Commercial Road and to the **L**, on the other side of the Light Railway, is **Limehouse Basin**. Until recently this was best reached by going down **Mill Place**. This entrance may now be closed, but further on there is a tiny pathway. The area is due for redevelopment. On a gloomy evening this is one of the most 'Dickensian' parts of London. If you do manage to reach the Basin, Limehouse Cut goes off to the **E**, the **Regent's Canal** (or, officially, **Grand Union Canal**) to the **N**. Looking out over the Basin is what remains of the octagonal **hydraulic accumulator tower** of 1852. Return to Commercial Road and walk **L** towards the station.

Poplar and the Isle of Dogs

Start: West India Quay (Docklands Light Railway)
Finish: West India Quay (Docklands Light Railway)

At times on this walk pedestrians will feel as if they are exploring the moon, craters and all. Do persevere: Poplar and the Isle of Dogs are full of history. On coming down from the **West India Quay station**, go ten yards to the **S** and stand by the edge of the water. This is the **Import Dock** of the West India Dock, the first enclosed 'wet' dock in London, built in 1802. To the **S** is the **Canary Wharf** project and to the **SW** can be seen **Cascades** – sometimes known as 'Yuppie Heights' – and on this side of the Import Dock are three old cranes. Once the horizon would have been blotted out by a mass of these cranes. Walk to the **N** and turn **L** down one of the new roads. You will be walking past the **North Quay warehouses**, also of 1802, which until German bombing stretched the whole length of the Import Dock. Built to store sugar, you can see the spiked bars over the windows to discourage pilfering.

At the small roundabout turn **R** up **West India Dock Road**. Opposite is the **Dock Master's House** of 1807. At **Ming Street** turn **R**. This leads into **Poplar High Street**. On the other side of the road is the **White Horse** pub, complete with carved wooden horse. Go past it and turn **L** up **Hale Street** towards the noisy **East India Dock Road**. This busy highway was installed by the dock companies in the early nineteenth century in order to bypass the narrow Poplar High Street. Look across the road and at **133 East India Dock Road** is the fine-looking building of 1840 which was erected for seamen and now contains private flats. Also on the other side of the road is the Sixth Form Centre housed in a Gothic building with a fine clock over the street. The energetic will cross the road and venture inside; the room to the **L** is laid out as

a stateroom of one of the impressive ships built in the nineteenth century by **George Green**, a Poplar shipbuilder. A plaque on **203 East India Dock Road** commemorates the Poplar councillors, led by **George Lansbury**, who marched along here in July 1921 on their way to the High Court. Less than five years later armoured cars sped up and down protecting food-supplies during the General Strike of May 1926.

Walk into the well-kept **Recreation Ground** to the **S** of East India Dock Road. There is a sad memorial to the eighteen local children killed in 1917 during a German air-raid. In the distance to the **S**, through the trees, is **St Matthias**, originally a chapel built in 1656 for the East India company. It was largely rebuilt in later centuries. It is now empty. The hardy will venture as close as possible. Inside are the wooden columns which were once the masts of old East Indiamen. The coat of arms of the East India Company is on the ceiling. The attractive early nineteenth-century **Woodstock Terrace** is on the **E** side of the Recreation Ground. Walk along East India Dock Road to the **E**, that is, a right turn on leaving the garden. On the other side of the road is the **Lansbury Estate** built in 1951 for the Festival of Britain and called after the much-loved Labour politician George Lansbury. Outside **Poplar Baths** is a statue of **Richard Green**, also a Poplar shipbuilder like his father George. I particularly like this statue because of the portrayal of his dog. At the base are two of Green's vessels.

Keep along East India Dock Road and turn **R** down **Newby Place**. On the **L** is the imposing church of **All Saints, Poplar**. Completed in 1823, its steeple is a local landmark. Facing it on the other side of Newby Place is the **vicarage**. If you are lucky, you will glimpse the peacock resident in the garden. Cut through the garden to the **S** of All Saints. **Mountague Place** has some nice houses. Turn **R** down **Bazely Street** past the **Greenwich Pensioner** pub, whose signpost shows a pensioner and Wren's Hospital in the background. At **Poplar High Street** turn **L** and go down to the **Robin Hood Gardens** estate, a huge council development of the 1960s. Its creation involved the demolition of the **Queen's Theatre**, Poplar's much remembered local theatre. You will be able to hear and see the approach road to the **Blackwall Tunnel**. The tunnel was built in the 1890s. On the other side of it, once, was the impressive entrance to the East India Docks, but this was demolished in the 1950s. However, the original inscription was saved and is on the **S** side of East India Dock Road.

Dominating the skyline is the **Brunswick Wharf Power Station**, built in the 1950s on the filled-in Export dock of the East India Docks. The in-fill came from the South Bank development taking place at the same time. You can also see the **Steamship** pub, a reminder of the London-Blackwall railway line — now in part the Docklands Light Railway — which deposited passengers here who then took a steamship to Southend. Walk **S** down **Preston's Road**. Just by the first bridge, which is now being widened, is the **Bridge House** of 1819, built for the Dock Superintendent. Today it contains expensive flats. Cross the bridge and then go **L** down **Managers Street**. At the end to the **L** are some early nineteenth-century houses which enjoy fine views over the Thames. **Number 3** is called '**Nelson's House**' in honour of the Admiral, who is thought to have stayed there. Walk **R** down **Coldharbour**. A patch of derelict land allows the pedestrian to look out over the river. At the end of the street, on the **L**, is the **Gun** pub – well worth a visit.

Return to Preston's Road and turn **L** down to the **Blue Bridge** of 1969. If you stand here, there is the Thames on one side and the West India Dock on the other. From here the tireless walker can continue **S** down **Manchester Road** to **Island Gardens** (see the walk 'Isle of Dogs and Greenwich'). To return to **West India Quay** retrace your steps up Preston's Road but turn **L** and go past **Billingsgate Fish Market**, a resident of the Isle of Dogs since 1982. You will see the station in the distance.

Shadwell and Cable Street

Start: Shadwell station on the Underground or Shadwell station on the Docklands Light Railway
Finish: Shadwell station on the Underground or Shadwell station on the Docklands Light Railway

Both stations are new and gleaming. Yet in the nineteenth century this was a notorious slum neighbourhood, home of the infamous **Bluegate Fields**. **Watney Street** is where **Oswald Mosley** recruited many of his 'Blackshirts'. This district was badly bombed, and nothing remains of Father John Groser's **Christ Church**, the many pubs or the old **Watney Street Market**. At the **N** end of Watney Street is a new concrete shopping-

134

centre. However, there is an **'Old Pie and Mash' shop** facing the Tube station.

Turn **R** into Cable Street, once a Roman burial-ground and later with maritime associations. Past the impressive old **St George's Town Hall**, by the approach to the library, is a dazzling mural commemorating the '**Battle of Cable Street**' which took place on 4 October 1936. You can make out Mosley, the barricades, the flags and so on. Keep down Cable Street and pass on the **L numbers 194–214**, the only remaining Georgian houses in this street. Behind them is the new '**Hawksmoor Mews**'. Stop at the junction with **Cannon Street** – there was a fort here during the Civil War in the 1640s – and look **N** towards **Commercial Road**. At the junction there **John Williams**, suspected of carrying out the **Ratcliff Highway Murders** of 1811, was buried with a stake through his heart.

Keep walking down Cable Street. On the **L** side are tower-blocks, on the **R** the forty railway arches built by **Robert Stephenson**, son of George, and now used by the **Docklands Light Railway**. Turn down **Fletcher Street** into what remains of **Wellclose Square**. A new Asian school stands in the middle. You will see two ship weathervanes on the horizon. That on the **L** belongs to a school, that on the **R** to **St Paul's, Dock Street**. Grimly hanging on is **Wilton's Music-Hall** on the **N** side of the square. Return to Cable Street and walk to the **L**. You are now walking around the back of Wilton's. This neighbourhood was a terrible spot after the Second World War, but almost all the slum properties have since been pulled down. Turn **L** down **Dock Street**. According to W. O. E. Oesterley (*Walks in Jewry*, 1901, p. 49), it was a common sight a hundred years ago to see newly arrived Jewish immigrants wending their way up Dock Street. Go down Dock Street. **Beacon House** on the **L** has railings which depict ropes. St Paul's is now closed and due to be sold off. Built in 1847 as 'the

seaman's church', **Prince Albert** laid the foundation stone. **'Father Joe' Williamson** was the vicar of St Paul's in the 1950s and 1960s.

At the bottom of Dock Street you can see Rupert Murdoch's **News International** headquarters. Turn **L** along the **Highway**. Broad and straight, it was once a Roman road but became notorious later as the **Ratcliff Highway**, haunt of onshore sailors. Most evident today is the thundering traffic which explains its local name as 'the Racetrack'. A little way along on the **L** are **Swedenborg Gardens**, recently auctioned off. Keep along the Highway and Hawksmoor's wonderful **St George's in the East** looms into view with its 160-feet tower and four pepper-pot turrets. A modern building is tucked inside Hawksmoor's original exterior. The burial-ground has been turned into a pleasant garden (at least it was before the storm of October 1987).

Return to the Highway. On the other side of the road is the **Tobacco Dock** project. Cross the Highway and walk **L** again. On the **R** is **St Paul's, Shadwell**, 'the Church of Sea Captains'. Rebuilt in 1820, the church before this was where **Captain Cook** often worshipped. Further along on the **R** is the lovely and spacious **Edward VII Memorial** or **Shadwell Park**, on the site of a former fish-market. It offers excellent views over the Thames as well as a stone commemorating several Tudor explorers such as **Sir Martin Frobisher**. Behind this memorial is the ventilation-shaft of the **Rotherhithe Tunnel**. To the **E** is the huge **Free Trade Wharf** development. Cross the Highway again and walk through to Cable Street via **Brodlove Lane**. **Barnardo Street** is to the **N**, a reminder of the doctor who founded his first 'home' in the vicinity in 1870. Walk down Cable Street to the **L**, back to the stations. You will pass yet another church, the Anglo-Catholic **St Mary's**. It has a well-kept interior and has just been reprieved from closure.

Spitalfields Market, granted its charter by Charles II in 1682.

Spitalfields

Start: Liverpool Street station
Finish: Liverpool Street station

Leave Liverpool Street station, whether British Rail or Tube, by an **E** exit into **Bishopsgate**. The gate itself was down to the **R** by **Camomile Street** and **Wormwood Street**; it is marked by the bishop's mitre high up on the nearby modern building. Cross over Bishopsgate and walk **N**. Immediately on the

R is **Middlesex Street**, better-known as 'Petticoat Lane'. On a Sunday the market is packed with people. Keep up Bishopsgate, passing the **Bishopsgate Institute** of 1894 with its fine collection of books on the history of London. Turn **R** down **Brushfield Street. Christ Church**, built by Nicholas Hawksmoor, stands majestically in the distance. On the **L** is **Spitalfields Market**, granted a charter by Charles II in 1682 but soon to be banished elsewhere.

Walk down **Gun Street** on the **R** which leads into **Artillery Lane**. Both names recall that the militia from the **Tower of London** once practised their gunnery here when Spitalfields was farms and fields. **Number 56 Artillery Lane** has a handsome **Georgian shopfront** dating from 1757. On the **R** is **Widegate Street**, which is anything but. Cross over **Bell Lane** into **White's Row** where the criminal **Jack Sheppard** was born in 1702. Turn **R** down **Tenter Ground** where the cloth was once stretched out on hooks — hence our expression 'to be on tenterhooks'. Turn **L** into **Brune Street**; here is the 1902 institution '**Soup Kitchen for the Jewish Poor**', a reminder that not all Jewish immigrants prospered. At the end of Brune Street turn **L** into **Commercial Street**, a thoroughfare built in the Victorian period to join up Commercial Road with routes to the **N** as well as to clear away many slums.

Opposite is **Fashion Street**. Walk down it a little way and on the **R** is the 1905 Byzantine shopping arcade which failed to replace Petticoat Lane. Return to Commercial Street and turn **L**, walking past **Flower and Dean Street**; its name is all that survives of this notorious Victorian 'rookery'. Keep **S** and cross **Wentworth Street** — the Wentworth family owned the **Manor of Stepney** after the Reformation. On the **L** is **Toynbee Hall**. Commercial Street continues **S** into **Whitechapel High Street**. Walk back to Wentworth Street, where a market is held every day. The stalls are to the **L**.

Turn **R** and walk to **Brick Lane**, once a Jewish quarter but whose shops now testify to the Asian presence. Walk **N** up Brick Lane, passing Fashion Street on the **L**. Next **L** is **Fournier Street**. On the corner is a mosque in need of repair; this building of 1743 has also been a French Protestant church, a Methodist chapel and a synagogue. Walk down Fournier Street and notice how these superb **eighteenth-century houses**, built for wealthy Huguenots, are now being renovated. At the end is the great bulk of **Christ Church**, an East End masterpiece. The surrounding gardens are '**Itchy Park**'. Turn **R** up Commercial Street, past the grim **Jack the Ripper** pub and then go **R** through **Puma Court** past the newly renovated **Norton Folgate almshouses**. At the end is **Wilkes Street**. Turn **L** and then **R** into **Princelet Street**. On the **R** was **Jacob Adler's Yiddish theatre**. **Ben Truman** the brewer once lived at **number 4**, while a small **Jewish synagogue** occupied **number 19** until the 1960s. This building is now being turned into a local community centre.

Turn **L** up Brick Lane. Leading off on both sides is **Hanbury Street**, named after one of the brewing partners in **Truman's**, which itself stands further up Brick Lane. A brewery has stood here since the 1660s. Its buildings range from the eighteenth century to the twentieth-century extension in which pedestrians can see themselves. Turn **L** down **Quaker Street**, yet another religious grouping once prominent in the East End. To the **R** is **Shoreditch Underground station**, one of the least used in London. At the end of Quaker Street is **Commercial Street**. Cross it and walk down the attractive **Elder Street** into **Folgate Street**. Look **L** to the first **Peabody Buildings**, opened in 1864 but now private flats. Pass to the **R** along Folgate Street, going past more eighteenth-century houses. At **Norton Folgate** turn **L** and **L** again into what remains of **Spital Square**. On the **N** or **L** side a small plaque shows that we are on part of the **Priory of St Mary Spital**, founded in 1197. Pick your way through the squashy remains of the market's fare into **Brushfield Street**. Turn **R** into Bishopsgate and then **L** back to Liverpool Street station.

St Dunstan's, Stepney, one of London's finest churches.

Stepney

Start: Stepney Green station (Underground)
Finish: Stepney Green station (Underground) or Mile End station (Underground)

Turn **R** out of Stepney station and walk along **Mild End Road**. As its width and straightness suggest, this was once a Roman road. Keep along this **N** side, passing **Charrington's** the brewers who have been here since 1743 and also the famous department store with **Spiegelhalter's** embedded in the structure. Further along are the lovely **Trinity Alms-houses** on the **R**. A chapel is at the end of the two strips of houses. Built by **Sir Christopher Wren** and since restored after damage during the Second World War, an inscription high up on the outside walls records that it was a **Captain Henry Mudd** who gave the funds for their erection in 1695. Note, too, the ships on the gables.

Directly in front of you is **Mile End Waste** where there are busts of **Edward VII** and **William Booth** of the Salvation Army. This was one of his favourite spots for haranguing passers-by. The **Bryant & May matchgirls** often gathered here during their strike of 1888. Cross the road to **88 Mile End Road** where a large plaque reveals that **Captain Cook** lived on this site in the 1760s and 1770s. A hundred yards further along, turn **R** down towards **Stepney Green Gardens**. This small strip is all that remains of Stepney Green where the peasants met Richard II in 1381. The houses on the **L** are charming, particularly **number 37** which was built in 1692 with fine wrought-iron railings. It is now an ILEA careers office.

Keep on walking **S**, past the two memorials in the island which commemorate local worthies. The large open space on the **R** was, until German bombing, covered with housing. On the **R** by **Ben Jonson Road**, is the four-acre **Stepping Stones Farm** which was opened in 1979. Its farm animals are much visited by the city children of Stepney. The farm is open to visitors. On the other side of

Stepney High Street is the parish church of **St Dunstan's**. For a full history of this building, please turn to the main body of this book. Walk through the Churchyard to **Dame Jane Mico's almshouses** on the **S** side. Keep down **White Horse Lane**, passing the intimate **Colet Arms** pub on the **L** and yet more gravestones. At **Wakeling Street** turn **L** into the attractive little **York Square**, built by the Mercers' Company in the early nineteenth century and with pubs on two corners. In his autobiography **Clement Attlee** recalls that it was in **Barnes Street** that he first spoke in public.

Leave York Square by **Flamborough Street** in the **NE** corner and cross **Salmon Lane** – its name was once 'Sermon Lane' and was the route taken by the riverside inhabitants on their way to St Dunstan's in the Middle Ages. Keep **N** up **Aston Street** until it meets Ben Jonson Road. Turn **L** and **L** again, and there on **58 Solent House** is a blue plaque which marks where **Barnardo** began his work in 1866. Return to Ben Jonson Road and turn **R** up White Horse Lane past the huge old rectory. Pass **Trafalgar Square** on the **R**. Take **Shandy Street** on the **L** into **Beaumont Square**, named after the man who founded the County Fire Office in 1807 and whose Institute formed a part of the People's Palace, now **Queen Mary College (QMC)**. Return to White Horse Lane which leads **N** into **Mile End Road**. Stepney Green station is opposite.

For those with surplus energy, walk **R** along **Mile End Road** on the **N** side. You will pass the attractive **Albert Stern House** as well as the tucked-away **Mile End Place. Bancroft Road** contains the excellent **Local History Library**. Further along Mile End Road is **QMC. Burdett Road** leads **S** at the road junction; it commemorates '**the Queen of the Poor**'. Further along Mile End Road on the **N** is **Tredegar Square**, a piece of the West End in the East End. Mile End station is on the **S** of Mile End Road.

Captain Cook, who lived at 88 Mile End Road for several years.

Dr Barnardo, the Dubliner who trained at the London Hospital in the late 1860s before establishing his homes for children.

Wapping and St Katharine's

Start: Wapping station (Underground)
Finish: Tower Hill station (Underground)

The section of the Underground between Wapping and Rotherhithe passes through the Brunels' **Thames Tunnel**, completed in 1843. Panels on the wall at Wapping station tell of the tunnel's construction. You emerge on to what seems like a permanent building site but is in fact the narrow **Wapping High Street**. It is perhaps the only High Street in Britain with no shops – yet. The old warehouses are being converted into smart offices, flats and artists' studios. Turn **R** and follow the High Street around the corner. On the **R** is **Wapping Wall**; its name comes from the barrier put up here in the sixteenth century to ward off the Thames. At the end on the **R** is the **Prospect of Whitby**, which first opened its doors in 1520. It has some superlative views of the river from the rear. **Pepys** and **Turner** are just two of the celebrities who have been here before you. A hundred yards past the pub on the **L** is **Shadwell Basin**, recently opened as a marina.

Retrace your steps. Just past the Underground station on the **R** is Wapping Wall. Up here are Wapping's few shops. Further up on the **R** is **St Peter's, London Docks**, one of the most splendid churches in London. It has some excellent stained glass, including views of Wapping, a charming little chapel in memory of **Father Lowder**, and is always well kept. **Wapping Lane** was once called Old Gravel Lane. Further up is the bridge, known in Victorian times as **the 'Bridge of Sighs'** – it was a regular spot for suicides. On either side is the new **Tobacco Dock** development, touted as 'the East End's Covent Garden'.

Go back down Wapping Lane. This is the last time you will retrace your steps. Turn **R** along Wapping High Street and walk to the **police station**. Inside are the headquarters of

The tower is all that remains of the eighteenth-century St John's, Wapping.

the Thames Division of the Metropolitan Police and also the **River Police Museum**. An appointment is needed to visit the Museum, which traces the history of the River Police from 1798 up to today. The garden by the side of the station is grubby and woebegone but at least it offers a good view of **Rotherhithe** on the other side of the Thames. Directly opposite is the charming **Angel** pub. On the **W** side of the garden is the bizarre-looking **maintenance-yard** of the River Police. Walk through the garden on the other side of Wapping High Street and into **Green Bank**. Turn **L** and go past the Roman Catholic church of **St Patrick**, a legacy of the Irish presence in Wapping. On the **R** is **Wapping Gardens**. The numerous gardens in Wapping are explained by the severe German bombing. Most of the craters were not built over after the war.

At the end of Green Bank, directly opposite, is a sports centre. The high walls were once part of the **London Docks** complex. On the **L** is the tower of **St John's, Wapping**, all that remains. Walk down **Scandrett Street** to-wards the High Street. On the **L** are some toilets which, if open, are usually well kept. **Oliver's Wharf** on the river side of Wapping High Street was the first such building to be converted into living-spaces, back in 1971. In a hundred years' time a plaque will commemorate this fact. Go **R** down Wapping High Street to the **Town of Ramsgate**, an attractive old pub. This is where **Judge Jeffreys** was captured and nearly lynched by the crowd. To the side of the pub a path leads to what was once **Execution Dock**. The numerous 'stairs' off Wapping High Street – although their number is decreasing all the time – were used by the Thames watermen, particularly when there was only one bridge over the river: London Bridge.

Further along Wapping High Street on the **L** is **Wapping Pierhead**, a nice development of 1811 built for the dock officials. It offers a fine view of **Tower Bridge** in the distance. You are also reminded just how close Wapping is to the City of London. Keep going **W** down the once notorious Wapping High Street, renowned for its pubs and brothels. Today

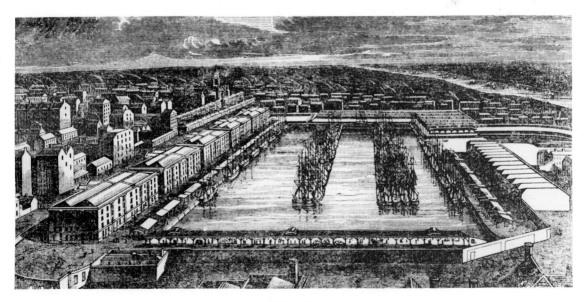

West India Dock. Some of the sugar warehouses built in 1802 still stand on the North Quay.

This shop sells Spratt's Dog Biscuits. The Spratt's factory still stands in Bow alongside the Docklands Light Railway.

much of it is empty land waiting for the developer. In the distance to the **N** can be made out Mr Murdoch's **News International** premises. The area to the **R** was once **London Docks**, now largely filled in. Continue down Wapping High Street into **St Katharine's Way**. This leads to the site of the old **St Katharine's Dock**, opened in 1828. It now contains ships, shops, the Dickens Inn in an old warehouse of the 1780s, the **Ivory Warehouse** and the modern **Tower Hotel**. Pass through St Katharine's to the **World Trade Centre** which has a pleasant little garden outside it. The path leads to the outskirts of the **Tower of London**. Follow the signs to **Tower Hill station**. Facing the

station is **Trinity Square Gardens**. This is well worth exploring. Quite apart from the memorial commemorating the site of **Tower Hill** with its list of some of the people who died here, there are the huge merchant navy memorials. Of the buildings on the **N** side of **Trinity Square**, the largest by far is the former headquarters of the **Port of London Authority**, built in 1922. To the **R** of that is **Trinity House; Samuel Pepys** drew up this body's charter. One last sight to be seen: off on the **R** of **Cooper's Row** is a substantial section of London's wall, with a helpful notice pointing out which parts are Roman, which medieval and so on. Tower Hill station is round the corner to the **L**.

Whitechapel

Start: Aldgate East station (Underground)
Finish: Whitechapel station (Underground)

Ignore the signs to **Toynbee Hall** and leave Aldgate East by the **N** exit. You emerge on to **Whitechapel High Street** where a large hay-market was held until 1928. Travellers passed along here on their way to the 'Ald Gate' which stood facing **St Botolph's, Aldgate**. On the other side of Whitechapel High Street, just around the corner, is the **Old Red Lion** pub; its predecessor was frequented by **Dick Turpin**.

Walk **L** along Whitechapel High Street, crossing **Commercial Street** and passing on the way the lovely old **Hoop and Grapes** pub, **Tubby Isaacs's** stall, the famous **Bloom's**, the recently renovated **Whitechapel Art Gallery** and the **Whitechapel Library** which bears a plaque to the poet and artist **Isaac Rosenberg** who was killed in the First World War. In the foyer of the Library are some tiles depicting the hay-market in 1788.

Cross **Whitechapel Road** and enter the gardens which were once occupied by the church of **St Mary Matfelon**, or 'the white chapel', which gave the district its name. All that remains are one fine tomb and the brick outline showing where the church once stood. Walk across the gardens into **Adler Street**, its name recalling the father and son who were both Chief Rabbi in the nineteenth century. Here is the German Roman Catholic church of **St Boniface** which at first glance, and second, looks like a fire station. Adler Street leads **S** into **Commercial Road**, the busy highway laid out by the dock companies in the early nineteenth century. Across the road is the attractive **Proof House** of the **Gunmakers' Company**. On the **L** in the modern building is the **London College of Furniture**.

Retrace your steps up Adler Street but then pass **R** along **Mulberry Street**, a reminder of the trees grown unsuccessfully by the French Huguenot weavers. Turn **L** up **Plumber's Row**, and a little way up, embedded in the wall, is an old street-sign. On the **L** is the **Whitechapel Bell Foundry**, established in 1570 and here since 1738. Admire its fine eighteenth-century frontage from Whitechapel Road. Go back a few yards and turn **L** down **Fieldgate Street**, remembering the fields which once stood so abundantly here. On the **L** is a tiny **synagogue** and then the **East London Mosque** with its colourful domes. Further on still is the gloomy **Tower House**, a block of flats catering for vagrants and the homeless – according to Bill Fishman, **Stalin** stayed here in 1907. Still on the **L** of Fieldgate Street is the charming **Queen's Head** pub and some good Indian eating-places.

Turn **L** down **New Road** into Whitechapel Road. Almost opposite on the other side of the road, although the site is now empty, was the **Pavilion theatre**. Pass up **Vallance Road** for eighty yards and on the **R** are the **Vallance Road Gardens**, where **William Booth** first pitched his tent to found the movement later known as the Salvation Army. Right at the top of Vallance Road was **number 178** where **Ronnie and Reggie Kray** lived for many years. Leave the gardens and turn **L** down **Durward Street**. Once called **Buck's Row**, its name was changed after one of **Jack the Ripper's** victims was discovered outside the now disused **Essex Wharf**. At the end of Durward Street is **Brady Street**, originally known as **Ducking Pond Road**. If you go a hundred yards to the **L**, you will find the high wall of the **Jewish cemetery**. The keepers will sometimes allow you in to look at the grave of **N. M. Rothschild**, the first of the English Rothschilds. Turn back down Brady Street. Just before you reach Whitechapel Road, on the **R** high up is a **wheatsheaf**, denoting that the building was once a baker's.

At Whitechapel Road turn **L** and walk past the **Albion Brewery** to the **Blind Beggar** pub which commemorates 'The Blind Beggar of Bethnal Green'. It is of course where **Ronnie Kray** shot **George Cornell**. Go back along Whitechapel Road to the Underground station. The **drinking-fountain** further along was put up by the Jews of East London in honour of **Edward VII**. Opposite is the **London Hospital**, here from the 1750s and which like Topsy has just 'growed and growed'. For devotees of grubby alleys, try **Wood's Buildings** past the Underground station. Still on this **N** side of Whitechapel Road are some gentlemen's urinals which were built in 1893 and smell like it.

NOTES

Unless otherwise stated, place of publication is London.

'Beyond Here Be Dragons'

1 Asa Briggs, *Victorian Cities* (1968), p. 314.
2 Jack London, *The People of the Abyss* (1978), p. 11.
3 See 'London Docklands', *Daily Telegraph*, 2 February 1987.
4 Charles Poulsen, *Victoria Park* (1976), pp. 3–4.
5 Quoted in John Gay, *The Beggar's Opera*, ed. Bryan Loughrey and T. O. Treadwell (1986), p. 13.
6 *Daily Telegraph*, 2 July 1987.

So Where Is the East End?

1 Thomas Burke, *The Real East End* (1932), p. 4.
2 Geoffrey Fletcher, *Pearly Kingdom* (1966), p. 10.
3 Ashley Smith, *The East-Enders* (1961), p. 34; Robert Sinclair, *East London* (1950), p. 32.

The East End in Myth and Legend

1 Asa Briggs, *Victorian Cities* (1968), p. 313.
2 Walter Besant, *East London* (1901), p. 127.
3 Thomas Burke, *Son of London* (1948), p. 252.
4 See the excellent introduction by D. J. Enright to Sax Rohmer, *The Mystery of Dr Fu Manchu* (1985).
5 Hugh and Pauline Massingham (eds), *The London Anthology* (1950), p. 124.
6 William J. Fishman, *The Streets of East London* (1979), pp. 103–4.
7 Horace Thorogood, *East of Aldgate* (1935), p. 187.
8 Ben Weinreb and Christopher Hibbert (eds), *The London Encyclopaedia* (1983), p. 187.
9 Elizabeth Vercoe, *Where to Live in London* (1988), p. 207.
10 *Sunday Times*, 3 January 1988.

The Thames and London's Poor Relation

1 See the concise summary in Hilaire Belloc, *The River of London* (1912).
2 James Bird, *The Geography of the Port of London* (1957), p. 22.
3 Bede, *A History of the English Church and People* trans. Leo Sherley-Price (1968), p. 104.

Monasteries and Lucky Horseshoes

1 Both stories from the church history available St Dunstan's.
2 *The Dictionary of National Biography* Vol. 16 (1888), p. 227.
3 *The Times*, 22 May 1987.

When the Queen Got a Ducking

1 H. B. Wheatley and P. Cunningham, *London Past and Present* (1891), Vol. 3, p. 326.

The Blind Beggar of Bethnal Green

1 George F. Vale, *The Legend of the Blind Beggar's Daughter of Bednal-Green* (1933).
2 A. J. Robinson and D. H. B. Chesshyre, *The Green* (1986), p. 36.

The 'White Chapel'

1 W. A. Locks (ed.), *East London Antiquities* (1902), pp. 17, 134.
2 W. Thornbury and E. Walford, *Old and New London* (n.d.), Vol. 2, p. 143.

Who Is the Gentleman?

1 H. Llewellyn Smith, *The History of East London* (1939), p. 260.
2 Charles Poulsen, *The English Rebels* (1984), pp. 1–44.

3 G. M. Trevelyan, *Illustrated English Social History* (1964), Vol. 1, p. 39.

Tower Hill

1 A. L. Rowse, *The Tower of London in the History of the Nation* (1972), p. 141.
2 P. B. Clayton and B. R. Leftwich, *The Pageant of Tower Hill* (1933), p. 70.
3 Charles Spon, *Round about Tower Hill* (1934), p. 35.
4 Clayton and Leftwich, *Pageant*, pp. 216, 229.

Ratcliff Cross Stairs and the Tudor Sea Dogs

1 H. R. Fox Bourne, *English Seamen under the Tudors* (1868), Vol. 1, p. 95.
2 William McFee, *Sir Martin Frobisher* (1928), pp. 68, 72.
3 J. E. Wrench, *Transatlantic London* (1949), p. 27.

The Port of London

1 W. A. Locks (ed.), *East London Antiquities* (1902), p. 187.
2 Sir William Foster, *East London* (1939), p. 109.
3 H. Llewellyn Smith, *The History of East London* (1939), p. 109.
4 Figures from ibid., pp. 175, 177.
5 H. M. Tomlinson, 'Down in Dockland', in A. St John Adcock (ed.), *Wonderful London* (1926), p. 148.
6 James Bird, *The Geography of the Port of London* (1957), p. 42.

The Rise and Fall of Bishop Bonner and the Manor of Stepney

1 *The Dictionary of National Biography* Vol. 5 (1886), pp. 358–60.
2 'East London Housing in the Seventeenth Century', in Peter Clark and Paul Slack (eds), *Crisis and Order in English Towns, 1500–1700* (1972), p. 246.

The Theatre and the Curtain

1 Peter Burke, *Popular Culture in Early Modern Europe* (1978), p. 99.

2 Christopher Edwards, *The London Theatre Guide, 1576–1642* (1979), pp. 16–18.
3 John Dover Wilson (ed.), *Life in Shakespeare's England* (1944), p. 231.
4 M. C. Bradbrook, *Shakespeare the Craftsman* (Cambridge, 1979), pp. 38–9.

Jolly Jack Tar in the East End

1 W. G. Bell, *Unknown London* (1951), p. 80.
2 ibid., p. 83.
3 Tony Phillips, *A London Docklands Guide* (High Wycombe, 1986), p. 13.

'Till Three Tides Had Overflowed Them'

1 Lord Macaulay, *The History of England* (1858), Vol. 5, pp. 247–9.

Truman's and the East End Breweries

1 John Stow, *The Survey of London*, ed. Valerie Pearl (1987), p. 501.
2 C. Anne Wilson, *Food and Drink in Britain* (1984), p. 336.
3 W. A. Locks (ed.), *East London Antiquities* (1902), p. 162.
4 *Trumans the Brewers, 1666–1966* (1966), pp. 16, 48, 52–3.

Big Ben and Bow Bells

1 *Whitechapel Bell Foundry* (1985), pp. 1–2.
2 *Observer*, 4 November 1984.

Judge Jeffreys and the Red Cow

1 Lord Macaulay, *The History of England* (1858), Vol. 1, pp. 644–51; Vol. 2, pp. 563–5; Vol. 3, pp. 399–403.

The Huguenots

1 Robin D. Gwynn, *Huguenot Heritage* (1985), pp. 24, 35.
2 Andrew Davies, *The Map of London* (1987), pp. 28–9, 72–3.
3 *Country Life*, 14 November 1985.
4 Gwynn, *Huguenot Heritage*, p. 155.

5   Gareth Stedman Jones, *Outcast London* (1984), pp. 101–2.
6   John Carey, 'Legacy of the Huguenots', *The Times*, 11 May 1985.

Almshouses in the East End

1   Neil Burton, *The Geffrye Almshouses* (1979).
2   W. A. Locks (ed.), *East London Antiquities* (1902), p. 171.

Three East End Masterpieces

1   *The Survey of London*, Vol. 27, *Spitalfields and Mile End New Town* (1957), p. 150.
2   Alastair Service, *The Architects of London* (1979), p. 35.
3   Some examples of Mr Ackroyd's errors – see *Spectator*, 29 March 1986, p. 40: St George's in the East is not in Wapping; the pyramid is in the churchyard of St Anne's, Limehouse.
4   *Survey of London*, Vol. 27, p. 157.
5   Jack London, *The People of the Abyss* (1978), p. 32.
6   Rev. Christopher Idle, *Some Dates and Events from the Story of Limehouse Parish Church* (1987), no pagination.
7   Elizabeth and Wayland Young, *London's Churches* (1986), p. 64.

Dick Turpin and Jack Sheppard

1   Christopher Hibbert, *The Roots of Evil* (1966), p. 28.
2   *Sunday Times*, 18 March 1985.
3   Georgina Green, *Epping Forest through the Ages* (1982), p. 38.

'The London'

1   Robert Barltrop and Jim Wolveridge, *The Muvver Tongue* (1980), p. 86.
2   Michael Harrison, *London beneath the Pavement* (1961), p. 37.
3   Walter Besant, *An East End Chapter* (1883), p. 21.
4   Mark Girouard, *Victorian Pubs* (1984), p. 205.
5   *The Dictionary of National Biography, 1901–1911* (Oxford, 1920), p. 100.
6   See his autobiography, *In Black and White* (1926).

David Garrick in the East End

1   Watson Nicholson, *The Struggle for a Free Stage in London* (1906), p. 73.
2   *The Dictionary of National Biography*, Vol. 21 (1890), p. 17.
3   W. A. Locks (ed.), *East London Antiquities* (1902), p. 80.

More Newcomers to the East End

1   Millicent Rose, *The East End of London* (1973), p. 21.
2   Kenneth Fenwick (ed.), *The London Spy* (1955), p. 257.
3   Thomas Burke, *The Real East End* (1932), p. 43.
4   Letter to *Sunday Times*, 19 July 1987.
5   Tony Coombs, *'Tis a Mad World at Hogsdon* (n.d.), p. 33.
6   M. D. George, *London Life in the Eighteenth Century* (1966), p. 125.
7   ibid., p. 129.
8   Louis Heren, *Growing Up Poor in London* (1973), p. 11; and *Tower Hamlets in Photographs, 1914–1939* (1980), p. 23.
9   Walter Besant, *East London* (1901), p. 204; J. G. Birch, *Limehouse through Five Centuries* (1930), p. 144.
10 *Evening Standard*, 5 June 1987.

'The First Godfather'

1   John Oldland, *A History of the Parish and Church of St Matthew . . .* (1984), p. 4.
2   George F. Vale, *Old Bethnal Green* (1934), pp. 31–4; and H. Llewellyn Smith, *The History of East London* (1939), p. 119.

An East End Boxing Champion

1   Thomas Burke, *The Real East End* (1932), p. 33.
2   See *The Memoirs of the Life of Daniel Mendoza*, ed. Paul Magriel (1951).
3   Robert Sinclair, *East London* (1950), p. 228.
4   Ralph L. Finn, *Grief Forgotten* (1985), p. 121.

Nathan Mayer Rothschild

1   *The Dictionary of National Biography*, Vol. XLIX (1897), p. 307.

2 Gerald Croner (ed.), *England: The History of the Anglo-Jewish Community* (Jerusalem, 1978), pp. 14–16.
3 Elizabeth and Wayland Young, *London's Churches* (1986), p. 40.

John Harriott and the River Police

1 Tom Fallon, *The River Police* (1956), pp. 40–4.
2 John Harriott, *Struggles through Life*, 3 vols (1818).

The Building of London's Docks

1 John Pudney, *London's Docks* (1975), p. 22.
2 John Weale, *The Pictorial Handbook of London* (1854), p. 347.
3 Olwen Hedley, *The Royal Foundation of Saint Katharine* (n.d.), p. 7.
4 Arthur Bryant, *Liquid History* (1960), p. 77.
5 Millicent Rose, *The East End of London* (1973), p. 186.
6 Bryant, *Liquid History*, p. 29.

Murder Most Foul

1 Tony Coombs, *'Tis a Mad World at Hogsdon* (n.d.), p. 43.
2 P. D. James and T. A. Critchley, *The Maul and the Pear Tree* (1987), p. 160.
3 Michael Harrison, *London beneath the Pavement* (1961), p. 111.
4 *Guardian*, 7 December 1987.
5 Daniel Farson, *Jack the Ripper* (1972), p. 100.

'The World on Wheels'

1 W. A. Locks (ed.), *East London Antiquities* (1902), p. 31.
2 Hugh Cunningham, 'The Metropolitan Fairs', in A. P. Donajgrodzki (ed.), *Social Control in Nineteenth-Century Britain* (1977), pp. 165, 168–70.

Petticoats and Bull Hanks

1 John Stow, *The Survey of London*, ed. Valerie Pearl (1987), p. 116.
2 H. B. Wheatley and P. Cunningham, *London Past and Present* (1891), Vol. 3, p. 78.

3 ibid., pp. 500–1.
4 William J. Fishman, *The Streets of East London* (1979), p. 16.
5 Jerry White, *Rothschild Buildings* (1980), p. 245.

The East End's Park

1 J. G. Birch, *Limehouse through Five Centuries* (1930), p. 89.
2 Charles Poulsen, *Victoria Park* (1976), pp. 17–20.
3 Millicent Rose, *The East End of London* (1973), p. 248.
4 Michael Davie, 'The Boys from King Cole's Oz', *Observer*, 17 April 1988.
5 Edgar Lansbury, *George Lansbury, My Father* (1934), p. 92.

The Thames Tunnel and 'Great Eastern'

1 D. J. Carron, *A Brief History of the Thames Tunnel* (1984), p. 2.
2 F. L. Stevens, *Under London* (1939), p. 107.
3 John Pudney, *Brunel and His World* (1974), pp. 98–102.
4 Colm Kerrigan, *A History of Tower Hamlets* (1982), pp. 26–7.

'The Queen of the Poor'

1 George F. Vale, *Old Bethnal Green* (1934), p. 29.
2 Charles Poulsen, *Victoria Park* (1976), p. 56.
3 Diana Orton, *Made of Gold* (1980), p. 155.
4 J. E. Connor and B. J. Critchley, *Palaces for the Poor* (Colchester, 1984), p. 10.
5 Poulsen, *Victoria Park*, p. 57.

'Model Dwellings'

1 *The Survey of London*, Vol. 27, *Spitalfields and Mile End New Town* (1957), p. 262.
2 Millicent Rose, *The East End of London* (1973), p. 267.

Minors and Gaffs

1 Watson Nicholson, *The Struggle for a Free Stage in London* (1906), p. 126.
2 A. S. Jasper, *A Hoxton Childhood* (1969), pp. 46–7.

3   See various articles in *Theatre Quarterly*, vol. 1, no. 4 (October-December 1971).
4   A. E. Wilson, *East End Entertainment* (1954), p. 189.
5   Millicent Rose, *The East End of London* (1973), p. 225.
6   J. Wesley Bready, *Doctor Barnardo* (1935), pp. 63–5.
7   Henry Mayhew, *London Labour and the London Poor* (1861), Vol. 1, pp. 40–2.
8   Daniel Farson, *Marie Lloyd and Music Hall* (1972), p. 14.

NB. I have spent the last ten years putting together material on the East End gaffs and minors; for further references and information, please contact me c/o Macmillan London Ltd, 4 Little Essex Street, London WC2R 3LF.

'The Handsomest Room in London'

1   Diana Howard, *London's Theatres and Music Halls, 1850–1950* (1970).
2   Iain Mackintosh and Micheal Sell (eds), *Curtains!!!* (1982), p. 146.
3   Jacqueline S. Bratton, *Wilton's Music Hall* (Cambridge, 1980), p. 12.
4   Mackintosh and Sell, *Curtains!!!*, pp. 143–4; and also *The Independent*, 22 February 1988.

Some Turbulent Priests

1   Maria Trench, *Charles Lowder* (1881), p. 180.
2   Basil F. Clarke, *Parish Churches of London* (1960), p. 5.
3   F. G. Bettany, *Stewart Headlam* (1926), p. 217.
4   L. E. Ellsworth, *Charles Lowder and the Ritualist Movement* (1982), p. 27.
5   Trench, *Lowder* p. 171.
6   C. F. Lowder, *Twenty-One Years in S. George's Mission* (1877), p. 165.
7   Bettany, *Headlam*, p. 83.
8   Hesketh Pearson, *The Life of Oscar Wilde* (1960), pp. 299–300, 314.
9   Sir Percy Harris, *Forty Years in and out of Parliament* (1947), p. 89.

The Museum of Childhood, Bethnal Green

1   A. J. Robinson and D. H. B. Chesshyre, *The Green* (1986), p. 16.
2   Colm Kerrigan, *A History of Tower Hamlets* (1982), p. 66.

The Jewish Community in the East End

1   See the excellent account in William J. Fishman, *East End Jewish Radicals, 1875–1914* (1975), and first chapter, 'In Bondage'.
2   Henry Walker, *East London* (1896), p. 11.
3   See endpaper in Lloyd P. Gartner, *The Jewish Immigrant in England, 1870–1914* (1973).
4   Jerry White, *Rothschild Buildings* (1980), p. 62.
5   W. O. E. Oesterley, *Walks in Jewry* (1901), pp. 68–9.
6   See A. B. Levy, 'The Jewish Theatre', in *East London Papers*, vol. 6, no. 1 (July 1963), pp. 24–6; and Andrew Davies, *Other Theatres* (1987), pp. 62–3.
7   David Mazower, *Yiddish Theatre in London* (1987), p. 68.
8   Harry Blacker, *Just Like It Was* (1974), p. 173.
9   White, *Rothschild Buildings*, p. 87.
10 P. G. Hall, *The Industries of London since 1861* (1962), p. 59.

The 'People's Palace' and Toynbee Hall

1   Christopher Hibbert (ed.), *Queen Victoria in Her Letters and Journals* (1985), p. 303.
2   Gordon Barnes, *Stepney Churches* (1967), p. 92.

Some East End Benefactors

1   Richard Collier, *The General Next To God* (1965), p. 70.
2   See his autobiography, *A Few Footprints* (1905).
3   See the enthusiastic article by Raphael Samuel in *History Workshop Journal*, no. 5 (1978), pp. 163–71.

Matchgirls and Dockers

1   Hector Gavin, *Sanitary Ramblings* (1971), pp. 11, 19.
2   Jack London, *The People of the Abyss* (1978), pp. 121–2.

3   Reg Beer, *Matchgirls Strike 1888* (n.d.), p. 22.
4   G. D. H. Cole and Raymond Postgate, *The Common People 1746–1946* (1961), p. 428.
5   John Pudney, *London's Docks* (1985), pp. 121–2.
6   Ann Stafford, *A Match to Fire the Thames* (1961), p. 119.

'The Sheer Joy of Living'

1   Naomi Jacob, *Our Marie* (1936), p. 55.
2   W. MacQueen-Pope, *Marie Lloyd* (1957), p. 148.
3   Frank Kemode, *Selected Prose of T. S. Eliot* (1975), p. 172.
4   Daniel Farson, *Marie Lloyd and Music Hall* (1972), p. 58.

Troxies and ABCs

1   E. Litvinoff, *Journey through a Small Planet* (1972), p. 76.
2   David Jones and Kevin Wheelan, *ABC Mile End – the First 150 Years* (Birmingham, n.d.).
3   David Jones, *Troxy: Where East Is Best* (Birmingham, n.d.), pp. 3, 4.

The East End Furniture Trade

1   Pat Kirkham, Rodney Mace and Julia Porter, *Furnishing the World* (1987), p. 3.
2   For a suggested route, see *Workshops and Warehouses* (Geffrye Museum, n.d.).
3   Kirkham *et al.*, *Furnishing the World*, p. 11.
4   P. G. Hall, *The Industries of London since 1861* (1962), p. 81.

'May the Imperial Port Prosper'

1   James Bird, *The Geography of the Port of London* (1957), p. 187.
2   Ben Weinreb and Christopher Hibbert (eds), *The London Encyclopaedia* (1983), p. 615.
3   Arthur Bryant, *Liquid History* (1960), pp. 49, 57.
4   Steve Humphries and John Taylor, *The Making of Modern London, 1945–1985* (1986), pp. 5, 14–15.
5   John Pudney, *London's Docks* (1975), p. 175.

The Siege of Sidney Street

1   William J. Fishman, *The Streets of East London* (1979), p. 124.

2   *The Times*, 4 January 1911.
3   Colin Rogers, *The Battle of Stepney* (1981), p. 109.
4   Donald Rumbelow, *The Houndsditch Murders* (1973), p. 117.
5   Edgar Wallace, *A Short Autobiography* (1929), p. 247; C. R. Attlee, *As It Happened* (1954), p. 31.

'The John Bull of Poplar'

1   *The Dictionary of National Biography, 1931–1940* (Oxford, 1949), p. 525.
2   Raymond Postgate, *The Life of George Lansbury* (1951), p. 63.
3   St John B. Groser, *Politics and Persons* (1949), p: 25.
4   Noreen Branson, *Poplarism, 1919–1925* (1979), pp. 18–19, 46.

Sir Percy Harris and Dr Alfred Salter

1   Sir Percy Harris, *Forty Years in and out of Parliament* (1947), p. 95.
2   Mary Boast, *The Story of Bermondsey* (1984), p. 23; see also Fenner Brockway, *Bermondsey Story* (1949), p. 163.

'The North-West Passage'

1   L. L. Loewe, *Basil Henriques* (1976).
2   Ralph L. Finn, *Grief Forgotten* (1985), pp. 42, 152.

The Battle of Cable Street

1   Millicent Rose, *The East End of London* (1973), p. 68.
2   Michael Banton, *The Coloured Quarter* (1955), p. 81.
3   Joe Jacobs, *Out of the Ghetto* (1978), p. 257.
4   Noreen Branson and Margot Heinemann, *Britain in the Nineteen Thirties* (St Albans, 1973), p. 318.

The Blitz

1   Angus Calder, *The People's War* (1971), p. 211.
2   George F. Vale, *Bethnal Green's Ordeal, 1939–45* (1945), p. 7.

Father John Groser and the Church in the East End in the Twentieth Century

1   Phil Piratin, *Our Flag Stays Red* (1978), p. 48.
2   St John B. Groser, *Politics and Persons* (1949), p. 73.
3   Walter Besant, *East London* (1901), p. 87.
4   Joseph Williamson, *Father Joe* (1965), p. 121.
5   Gavin Stamp, 'The Vanishing Church of Bishop Jim', *Spectator* 8 March 1986, pp. 9–12.

'Mean Streets' and Tower-Blocks

1   Simon Jenkins, *Landlords to London* (1975), p. 93.
2   Andrew Byrne and Isobel Watson, 'Speculative Symmetry', *Country Life*, 12 November 1987, pp. 192–4.
3   Virginia Woolf, *A Room of One's Own* (1928), p. 79.
4   St John B. Groser, *Politics and Persons* (1949), p. 69.
5   D. L. Munby, *Industry and Planning in Stepney* (1951), p. 76.
6   ibid., pp. 100–1.
7   Michael Young and Peter Willmott, *Family and Kinship in East London* (1986), pp. xviii, xix.

The Kray Twins and East End Crime

1   *Daily Telegraph*, 14 November 1986, 28 November 1986, 1 January 1988.
2   Raphael Samuel, *East End Underworld* (1981), p. 116; against knives, p. 156; and policemen, p. 192.
3   *Evening Standard*, 6 January 1986.
4   Norman Lucas, *Britain's Gangland* (1969), p. 17.
5   John Pearson, *The Profession of Violence* (1985), p. 28.
6   John Ball, Lewis Chester and Roy Perrott, *Cops and Robbers* (1979), p. 53.

Yet More Newcomers

1   William J. Fishman, *The Streets of East London* (1979), p. 82.

The East End in the 1980s and 1990s

1   Rupert Nabarro and David Richards, *Wasteland* (1980), p. 17.
2   Greater London Council, *East London File* (1982), pp. 11, 13.
3   Nabarro and Richards, *Wasteland*, pp. 13–14.
4   Olwen Hedley, *The Royal Foundation of Saint Katharine* (n.d), pp. 8–9.
5   London Docklands Development Corporation, *The Exceptional Place* (1986), no pagination.
6   Stephen Gardiner, 'Disaster of Docklands', *Observer*, 20 April 1987.
7   See the case of Les Gable in *Sunday Times*, 3 April 1987. This issue was brought up on two television programmes on the LDDC: 'World in Action', 30 November 1987; 'Forty Minutes', 3 December 1987.
8   *Daily Telegraph*, 5 December 1986.
9   John Mills in *The Times*, 5 August 1987.
10 Stephen Jolly and Bob Bayman, *Docklands Light Railway* (1986).
11 *The Times*, 28 December 1987.
12 *The Independent*, 3 May 1988.
13 See LDDC, *The Exceptional Place*.
14 *Guardian*, 19 November 1987.
15 H. G. Wells, *The Shape of Things to Come* (1933), p. 49.
16 *Guardian*, 18 January 1988.
17 Introduction to A. St John Adcock, *East End Idylls* (1897), p. 3.

J. Seager catered for the East End's nautical needs.

FURTHER READING

Place of publication London unless otherwise stated. The Notes contain the details of several books and articles which were useful for particular points or events. Several sections overlap.

General

The best introduction to the history of the East End, although now difficult to obtain, is Millicent Rose, *The East End of London* (1951; new preface to 1973 edition). Also useful are the more recent Colm Kerrigan, *A History of Tower Hamlets* (1982), which replaces Vera Leff and G. H. Blunden, *The Story of Tower Hamlets* (1967), and *The Streets of East London* (1979) by William J. Fishman, with photographs by Nicholas Breach.

Dated but still valuable are Walter Besant, *East London* (1901); Walter Besant (ed.), *Shoreditch and the East End* (1908); and H. Llewellyn Smith, *The History of East London* (1939). Sir William Foster's *East London* (1935) is a concise introduction. Robert Sinclair, *East London* (1950), is for me spoiled by its carping and sour tone.

Three volumes of *The Survey of London* cover parts of the East End: Vol. 1, *Bromley-by-Bow* (1900); Vol. 8, *The Parish of St Leonard, Shoreditch* (1922); and Vol. 27, *Spitalfields and Mile End New Town* (1957). Similarly detailed and with illustrations was the Royal Commission on Historical Manuscripts, *East London* (1930). Three more books that illustrate their author's likes and dislikes but which are often perceptive are Thomas Burke, *The Real East End* (1932), with lithographs by Pearl Binder; Ashley Smith, *The East-Enders* (1961); and Geoffrey Fletcher, *Pearly Kingdom* (1966). There is a fund of good stories in W. A. Locks (ed.), *East London Antiquities* (1902). The now defunct *East London Papers* often published stimulating articles, as does the continuing *East London Record*. For a thorough East End bibliography, consult Peter Marcan, *An East End Directory* (High Wycombe, 1979).

For general material on London and the East End, see: W. Thornbury and E. Walford, *Old and New London*, 6 vols (n.d.); H. B. Wheatley and P. Cunningham, *London Past and Present, 3 vols* (1891); and the excellent Ben Weinreb and Christopher Hibbert (eds), *The London Encyclopaedia*

(1983), recently issued in paperback. A good concise survey of modern London is Steve Humphries and John Taylor, *The Making of Modern London, 1945–1985* (1986).

Cockneys and their Language

Julian Franklyn, *The Cockney* (1953), is overlong and badly organised. Much better is Robert Barltrop and Jim Wolveridge, *The Muvver Tongue* (1980).

Maps of the East End

In 1746, John Rocque issued a detailed map of London as it then was, including several East End sections. They have been reprinted, alongside the equivalent *A-Z* sections of today, in Andrew Davies, *The Map of London* (1987).

The Thames and the Docks

Of the many books on the Thames, perhaps the best is Eric de Maré, *London's Riverside* (1958), which should still be in print. John Pudney, *London's Docks* (1975), is excellent, but through no fault of the author is now out of date. Sir Arthur Bryant, *Liquid History* (1960), reads well. For the River Police, see Anthony Richardson, *Nick of the River* (1955), and Tom Fallon, *The River Police* (1956). Recent guides to Docklands are Tony Phillips, *A London Docklands Guide* (High Wycombe, 1986), and Eve Hostettler, *Travelling Light* (1987). For histories of Docklands, see the volume issued by the North East London Polytechnic, *Docklands* (1986), and by the London Docklands Development Corporation, *Dockland's Heritage* (1987).

Areas

Bethnal Green: George F. Vale, *Old Bethnal Green* (1934); A. J. Robinson and D. H. B. Chesshyre, *The Green* (1986). Hoxton: Tony Coombs, *'Tis a Mad*

World at Hogsdon (n.d.). Limehouse: J. G. Birch, *Limehouse through Five Centuries* (1930). Poplar: Geoff Richman, *Fly a Flag for Poplar* (n.d). Tower Hill: P. B. Clayton and B. R. Leftwich, *The Pageant of Tower Hill* (1933).

In the past Official Guides were published of, for example, Bethnal Green, Shoreditch and Stepney. Now see those issued by Tower Hamlets. Michael Young and Peter Willmott, *Family and Kinship in East London* (1957; new introduction 1986), is in part a study of Bethnal Green but is of much wider importance. Rupert Nabarro and David Richards, *Wasteland* (1980), looks at the problem of derelict land in Tower Hamlets. For a vivid history of Tower Hamlets in photographs, see *Tower Hamlets in Photographs, 1914–1939* (1980). The Tower Hamlets Environment Trust has issued various publications such as *A Walk through Spitalfields* and *The Whitechapel Walk* (neither is dated).

Newcomers

The Huguenots: Robin D. Gwynn, *Huguenot Heritage* (1985). The Jews: Chaim Bermant, *Point of Arrival* (1975), and A. B. Levy, *East End Story* (1951). William J. Fishman, *East End Jewish Radicals, 1875–1914* (1975), is of much wider interest than its title might suggest. There are some useful essays in Aubrey Newman (ed.), *The Jewish East End, 18401–1939* (1981). Jerry White, *Rothschild Buildings* (1980), studies in close-up one largely Jewish community. For other groups, see Michael Banton's rather overheated *The Coloured Quarter* (1955) and the standard history: Peter Fryer, *Staying Power* (1984).

Crime

Joseph Merceron deserves, but lacks, a full-length study. P. D. James and T. A. Critchley, *The Maul and the Pear Tree* (1987 edition), provides a thorough account of the Ratcliff Highway Murders. There are already far too many books on Jack the Ripper; if you want to read about him, you can find your own material. Lengthy interviews with Arthur Harding were turned into Raphael Samuel, *East End Underworld* (1981). The Siege of Sidney Street is covered in Donald Rumbelow, *The Houndsditch Murders* (1973), and Colin Rogers, *The Battle of Stepney* (1981). There are several books about the Krays; probably the best is John Pearson, *The Profession of Violence* (1985).

Politics

'Poplarism' is surveyed by Noreen Branson, *Poplarism, 1919–1925* (1979). Two vivid accounts of left-wing politics in the East End are Joe Jacobs *Out of the Ghetto* (1978), and Phil Piratin, *Our Flag Stays Red* (1978 edition). Sir Percy Harris, *Forty Years in and out of Parliament* (1947), is much more lively than C. R. Attlee, *As It Happened* (1954).

Individuals

Please see under the appropriate entries in the Notes.

Churches

Several excellent, usually brief, church histories are available at a number of East End churches; for example, *St Leonard's, Shoreditch* (n.d.); John Oldland, *A History of the Parish and Church of St Matthew* (1984); Rev. Christopher Idle, *Some Dates and Events from the Story of Limehouse Parish Church* (1987); A. J. Robinson, *St John on Bethnal Green* (1978); *The Parish Church of St Dunstans and All Saints Stepney* (n.d.). For Hawksmoor, the standard account is Kerry Downes, *Hawksmoor* (1979). For C. F. Lowder, see L. E. Ellsworth, *Charles Lowder and the Ritualist Movement* (1982); for Headlam, see F. G. Bettany, *Stewart Headlam* (1926); for Father John Groser, see his *Politics and Persons* (1949) and also K. Brill (ed.), *John Groser* (1971); for Father Joe Williamson, see his autobiographies *Father Joe* (1965) and *Friends of Father Joe* (1965). On Stepney churches, see Gordon Barnes, *Stepney Churches* (1967). Also see the relevant entries in Basil Clarke, *Parish Churches of London* (1966); Mervyn Blatch, *A Guide to London's Churches* (1978); and the excellent Elizabeth and Wayland Young, *London's Churches* (1986 edition).

Work

Generally, see Gareth Stedman Jones, *Outcast London* (1984 edition), and the wealth of information in D. L. Munby, *Industry and Planning in Stepney* (Oxford 1951). Also valuable is P. G. Hall, *The Industries of London since 1861* (1962). On various aspects, see: Reg Beer, *Matchgirls Strike 1888* (n.d.); Ann Stafford, *A Match to Fire the Thames* (1961); and Pat Kirkham, Rodney Mace and Julia Porter, *Furnishing the World* (1987).

Entertainment

For an introduction to the subject, see A. E. Wilson, *East End Entertainment* (1954). For extracts from writings on the gaffs, see Paul Sheridan, *Penny Theatres of Victorian London* (1981). Charles Poulsen, *Victoria Park* (1976), is comprehensive. On individual theatres and music-halls: Jacqueline S. Bratton, *Wilton's Music Hall* (Cambridge, 1980), which accompanies a set of forty-two slides; May Scott (ed.), *Hoxton Britannia* (1981), and two academic, rather dull studies by Clive Barker in *Theatre Quarterly*, October–December 1971 and Summer 1979; David Mazower *Yiddish Theatre in London* (1987); A. S. Jackson, *The Standard Theatre of Victorian England* (New York 1985; Mr Jackson kindly sent me a copy); for Mendoza, see Paul Magriel (ed.), *The Memoirs of the Life of Daniel Mendoza* (1951).

Some East End Institutions

A. E. Clark-Kennedy, *London Pride* (1979), on the London Hospital; Asa Briggs and Anne Macartney, *Toynbee Hall* (1984); Neil Burton, *The Geffrye Almshouses* (1979); Denis Keeling, 'The City of London and Tower Hamlets Cemetery', in *East London Papers*, vol. 12, no. 2 (Winter 1969–70).

Autobiographies

The last fifteen years have seen a boom in the publishing of autobiographies and memoirs, and the East End is no exception. The following all contain much of interest and often are more revealing of the history of the East End than many academic tomes: A. S. Jasper, *A Hoxton Childhood* (1973); John Blake, *Memories of Old Poplar* (1977); Annie Barnes, *Tough Annie* (1980); Louis Heren, *Growing Up Poor in London* (1973); John Passmore Edwards, *A Few Footprints* (1905); Mary Barritt, *The Barritts of Wapping High Street* (n.d.); Anita Dobson, *My East End* (1987); Terence Stamp, *Stamp Album* (1987); Jim Wolveridge, *Ain't It Grand* (1981); Ralph L. Finn, *Grief Forgotten* (1985); and Emanuel Litvinoff, *Journey through a Small Planet* (1972). In a slightly different category are the outstanding Jack London, *The People of the Abyss* (1978 edition), and Henry Mayhew, *London Labour and the London Poor*, 4 vols (1861). The above is only a brief selection from the many autobiographies which have been published. The Local History Library at Tower Hamlets can supply further references.

Novels and Plays

Two writers in particular stand out: Arthur Morrison's *Tales of Mean Streets, A Child of the Jago* and *The Hole in the Wall* are all in print and all worth reading. The novels of Israel Zangwill are much harder to find; they deserve greater attention. Similarly the often Thames-related works of W. W. Jacobs and H. M. Tomlinson should be more widely known. Charles Dickens's *Our Mutual Friend* has much on Limehouse and the Thames. Very popular today are the novels of Lena Kennedy, which mine a rich vein of nostalgia and sentimentality about the 'old' East End. As for plays, essential are Arnold Wesker, *Chicken Soup with Barley* (1958), and Bernard Kops, *The Hamlet of Stepney Green* (19588).

The above is just a selection of material which has been published. For anyone interested in carrying out further research into any aspect of the East End, the best plan is to visit either the Local History Library in Bancroft Road or the library at the Bishopsgate Institute (see p. 157).

Generally authors despatch their books into a void and do not often get much 'feedback' other than from reviewers. If anyone, after reading this book, has any comments, suggestions or criticisms, do please write to me c/o Macmillan London Ltd, 4 Little Essex Street, London WC2R 3LF.

SOME USEFUL ADDRESSES
AND OPENING HOURS

Please check for public holidays.

Bethnal Green Museum of Childhood, Cambridge Heath Road, London E2 (01–980 2415).
Monday–Thursday and Saturday: 10–5.50; Sunday: 2.30–5.50.

Bishopsgate Institute, 230 Bishopsgate, London EC2 (01–247 6844).
Monday–Friday: 9.30–5.30.

Geffrye Museum, Kingsland Road, London E2 (01–739 8368).
Tuesday–Saturday: 10–5; Sunday: 2–5.

Hackney Empire, Mare Street, London E8 (01–985 2424).

Half Moon Theatre, 213 Mile End Road, London E1 (01–790 4000).

Hoxton Hall, 130 Hoxton Street, London N1 (01–739 5431).
Monday–Friday: 10–5.30.

Local History Library, Tower Hamlets Central Library, Bancroft Road, London E1 (01–980 433366).
Monday, Tuesday, Thursday, Friday: 9–8; Wednesday, Saturday: 9–5.

Museum of the Jewish East End and Resource Centre, The Manor House, 80 East End Road, Finchley, London N3 (01–346 2288).
Monday–Thursday: 9–5.30; Friday: 9–4.

Royal Foundation of St Katharine, Butcher Row, London E14 (01–790 3540).
Visits by prior arrangement only.

Thames River Police (officially the Thames Division of the Metropolitan Police), 98 Wapping High Street, London E1 (01–488 5212).
Visits to the Museum by prior arrangement only.

Tourist Information Centre, 88 Roman Road, London E2 (01–980 3749).
Monday–Friday: 9–5.30.

Tower Hamlets Arts Project Bookshop (THAP), 178 Whitechapel Road, London E1 (01–247 0216).
Tuesday–Saturday: 10–5.30.

Toynbee Hall, 29 Commercial Street, London E1 (01–247 3633).

Whitechapel Art Gallery, Whitechapel High Street, London E1 (01–377 5015).
Tuesday–Saturday: 11–5; Wednesday: 11–8.

Index

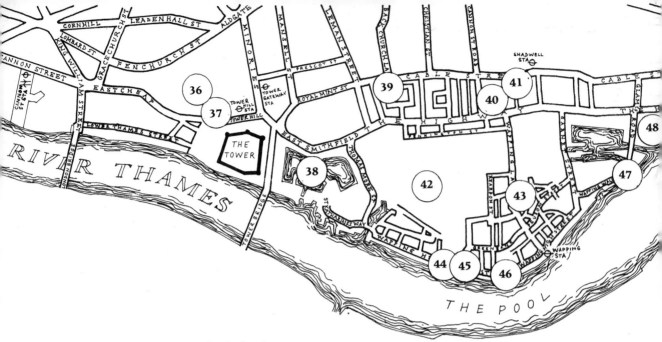